CALLED TO LEAD

*Understanding and Fulfilling Your Role
as an Educational Leader*

CALLED TO LEAD

Understanding and Fulfilling Your Role as an Educational Leader

Kenneth O. Gangel, Editor

purposeful design
p u b l i c a t i o n s
Colorado Springs, Colorado

**Books, Textbooks, and Educational Resources
for Christian Educators and Schools Worldwide**

Purposeful Design Publications is the publishing group of the Association of Christian Schools International. ACSI is committed to the ministry of Christian school education, to enable Christian educators and schools worldwide to effectively prepare students for life. As the publisher of books, textbooks, and other educational resources within ACSI, Purposeful Design Publications strives to produce biblically sound materials that reflect Christian scholarship and stewardship, and address the identified needs of Christian schools around the world.

For additional information, write Purposeful Design Publications
PO Box 35097, Colorado Springs, CO 80935-3509.

Printed in the United States of America

Called to Lead: Understanding and Fulfilling Your Role as an Educational Leader
ISBN 1-58331-025-8 Catalog # 6310

Purposeful Design Publications
A Division of the Association of Christian Schools International
PO Box 35097 • Colorado Springs, CO • 80935-3509
Customer Service Department: 800/367-0798 • Website: www.acsi.org

Most people in leadership see the future through the eye of the present.
Visionary leaders see the present through the eye of the future.

This book is dedicated to the visionary leaders of ACSI.

Founding Executive Board

William R. McKinley, Chairman
Claude E. Schindler, Vice Chairman
Earl Schamehorn, Secretary
Melvin R. Carter, Assistant Secretary
J. Wayne Temple, Treasurer
John Bennett
Eugene Birdsall
Wally Bourgeois
J. Lester Brubaker
James Burdick
Robert Eicher
A. C. Fortosis
Gene Garrick

Bill Kelly
Ronald J. Krestan
Bruce Long
Robert McBirnie
E. William Male
Marlin Miller
Robert M. Miller
Arthur Nazigian
Donald Shapland
James Swanson
David Wallace
Ira J. Westbrook
Doug Westfall

and the
Executive Staff
Chief Executives

Paul A. Kienel, Executive Director • Roy W. Lowrie Jr., President

Directors

James W. Braley Jr.
Eunice E. Dirks
G. William Davidson
Doug Horney
Jay B. Katz
Derek J. Keenan
Lou Koloze
Pat Murphy
John Schimmer
Joseph H. Smith
Jack Thiessen

Table of Contents

Section III – Strategic Functions in Administration

Foreword

The Scriptures clearly indicate that the Holy Spirit endows members of the Body of Christ with various spiritual gifts. The apostle Paul lists these in Romans 12, 1 Corinthians 12, Ephesians 4, and elsewhere. Among these vital gifts of the Spirit is administration/leadership, which, I believe, can be equated with other gifts such as preaching, teaching, evangelism, hospitality, and healing.

In 1 Timothy, the apostle Paul writes that to desire leadership is a noble ambition. The instruction and guidance offered in the following pages will aid Christian school leaders immeasurably. These chapters are crafted particularly for administrators and trustees in member schools of the Association of Christian Schools International.

In this landmark book, Kenn Gangel has enlisted the skills, experience, and knowledge of key Christian school leaders who carefully and scripturally present material related to the key aspects of this important gift. I have long since been keenly interested in this subject and am deeply impressed with the quality of information, guidance, and direction supplied in the following chapters—all from practitioners in the field. At the same time, Dr. Gangel has cut a wide swath in the selection of contributors from various disciplines and backgrounds.

There is an obvious need for spiritually and professionally competent leaders to direct Christian schools, which have a significant role in the twenty-first century. In addition, these leaders need to be challenged to step forward in their key responsibilities.

In his introduction to my book *Your Gift of Administration*, my friend and colleague Gordon MacDonald wrote, "As a pastor of more than twenty years, I have learned the hard way that directing the efforts of people in trying to bring out the best the individual can offer takes more than smooth words and slick ideas." With this comment I fully agree.

Because there has been some reluctance to affirm the fact that administrative and organizational leadership is a revealed and bestowed gift of the Holy Spirit, many well-meaning people have shunned an in-depth study of this subject. Yet Scripture contains many thrilling case studies of management and administration. Moses, Joshua, Ezra, and Nehemiah were administrative giants, and we dare not forget Joseph of Egypt. When it comes to administrative leadership, these men rank among history's very best. Leaders would do well to study and emulate their leadership skills.

Our thanks to Dr. Kenn Gangel and his contributors for their significant and meaningful presentations, through which we have the opportunity to examine the important role of the administrator in a Christian context. The book addresses vitally important themes such as how our present-day culture impacts Christian schools, how boards and administrators can work together, how leaders build effective teams, and how leaders can make wise decisions.

This publication should be in the hands of all Christian school administrators and board members, whose important roles will be enhanced by applying its principles. As a manual for God-honoring leadership, it is worthy of a spot on every Christian school administrator's desk.

Ted W. Engstrom
President Emeritus
World Vision

Editor's Preface

Writing in the September 2001 issue of *The Atlantic Monthly*, James Fallows observes that "Today's professional-class madness about college involves the linked ideas that colleges are desirable to the extent that they are hard to get into; that high schools are valuable to the extent that they get students into those desirable colleges; and that being accepted or rejected from a 'good' college is the most consequential fact about one's education.... Every part of this outlook is twisted."

This book has been prepared to straighten out twisted ideas about Christian education, its goals, and its processes. It encourages veteran administrators to rethink, and it helps rookies to "get it right" from the start. Central to the proper functioning of all Christian schools is competent and spiritual leadership, a cadre of administrators, headmasters, and principals who are *called to lead*.

For this task we have recruited a team of writers who also serve as models—men and women who have intentionally prepared for educational leadership (most have earned doctorates in the field) and have experienced frontline duty in the trenches for decades. Indeed, this work represents more than 500 collective years of experience in educational leadership at all levels.

Our goal has been to blend sound theory with practical application, both wrapped in a package of biblical understandings of leadership. In our view, the adjective in "Christian education" is more important than the noun. Leadership in Christian schools begins, proceeds, and culminates in the distinctive awareness that these are God's schools where we as administrators and board members serve as stewards. Such is our task; such is our calling.

Kenneth O. Gangel, Ph.D.

Preface

In the early 1960s when I served God as the administrator of Westminster Christian School in Orange County, California, there were no published books, manuals, or even a simple guide on how to administer an evangelical Christian school. Then administrative manuals began to appear as the regional associations flourished and matured. In 1978 when ACSI was formed, one of our early assignments was to produce an updated manual of administration for new and young schools as well as one for established schools. Both works had a stabilizing influence upon our growing constituency. Now, once again, it is time to update and to provide a new volume that will reflect administrative patterns and procedures appropriate for Christian school administration in the twenty-first century.

To keep things in perspective, it is helpful to know that our generation is not the first to publish books on Christian school administration. The first known books on the subject were written in 1523 and 1524 by Ulrich Zwingli, one of the great Protestant Reformation leaders from Zurich, Switzerland. He entitled his two volumes *The Christian Education of Boys* and *How to Educate the Young in Good Manners and Christian Discipline.* The latter title might serve us well even today, and the first, I am sure, would be interesting.

The second known writer on Christian school administration was Martin Bucer of Strassburg, Germany (now Strasbourg, France), in 1524. In the spirit of the Great Reformation, Bucer wrote a Christian school administration plan approved by the city fathers of Strassburg. It provided that "all children of Christian parents, both boys and girls, including the poorest, learn to read and write, in order that Christ might reign more fully over the republic" (Nottingham, 1962). Similar citywide plans of Christian school administration were subsequently written by Johann Sturm, also of Strassburg, whose patterns of Christian school administration at the secondary level influenced John Calvin, and by Johann Bugenhagen, Martin Luther's champion of Christian elementary education. In 1528 Bugenhagen wrote the "Brunswick school ordinance," a complete plan of Christian school administration that quickly spread to numerous other cities in Northern Germany and to the Kingdom of Denmark.

Foremost among these early pioneer writers on Christian school administration was Philip Melanchthon of Wittenberg, Germany, Luther's "right-hand man," who became known as the "preceptor (teacher) of Germany." Melanchthon was Luther's specialist on secondary education. His ideas, embodied in his *Saxony School Plan*, written in 1528, spread throughout Germany and other western countries including the fast-growing

American colonies.

Perhaps the administrative writings and procedures that would be most relevant today, in a broad sense, come to us from two Christian school leaders in eastern Europe, John Amos Comenius (1592–1670) from Moravia and August Hermann Franke (1663–1727) from northern Germany. Comenius, the best known of the two, wrote what he called *The Great Didactic*, a comprehensive guide for Christian school administration at all levels. He was also a prolific writer and publisher of textbooks. We know him as the first Christian school missionary because he traveled widely sharing his views on Christian school administration. Franke, on the other hand, emerged as the leading Christian school educator from Germany's Reformation of the reformation period known as the Pietistic Movement— the movement that spawned America's Great Awakening in the first half of the eighteenth century. Franke's system of Christian school administration spread through all of northern Germany (an area later known as Prussia) and was studied by America's early educators.

Permit me to include two more Christian school champions whose writings on administration impacted thousands of schools including America's early schools, all of which were Christian. I refer, of course, to John Calvin of Geneva, Switzerland, and John Knox of Edinburgh, Scotland. The centerpiece of John Calvin's ministry was his system of schools called Geneva Academy, elementary through seminary in six locations in Geneva. In great detail, Calvin describes the curriculum at each of seven levels of learning, the spiritual and professional requirements of the school administrator and faculty, and the school's rigorous requirements for academic advancement. Fifteen hundred students attended Calvin's school.

Fortunately for Scotland, John Knox studied under Calvin at Geneva. When Knox returned to Edinburgh in 1559, he wrote his *First Book of Discipline*, in which he describes a complete plan for a national system of Christian schools for his homeland. His system of Christian schools, elementary through university, transformed Scotland "and caused the Scottish peasantry to be the best educated in the world" (Renwick, 1960). There is no question that the fingerprints of Calvin and Knox were present everywhere on America's schools well into the nineteenth century.

The history of things is important. The English historian Thomas Macaulay wrote, "A people who take no pride in the noble achievements of remote ancestors will never achieve anything worthy to be remembered with pride by remote descendants." Even as Christian school administrative guides were essential to our forefathers in the past, they continue to be essential to us today. My highly respected friend, Dr. Kenn Gangel, the general editor of this work, has assembled an impressive group of writers for this project. As a team of modern-day, seasoned Christian school educators, they have hammered out a noteworthy guide that perpetuates the long tradition of helping one another in this ministry. Adjectives lose their descriptive adequacy to fully express my admiration and appreciation for the good work they have done.

Dr. Paul A. Kienel
Founder and President Emeritus
Association of Christian Schools International

Bibliography

Nottingham, W. J. (1962). *The Social Ethics of Martin Bucer*. Unpublished doctoral dissertation, Columbia University, New York.

Renwick, A. M. (1960). *The Story of the Scottish Reformation*. London: InterVarsity Fellowship.

Protecting Your Quiddity
Emphasizing Christian School Uniqueness

Janet Lowrie Nason, Ed.D.

Chapter Summary

How do you describe your school to others? What characteristics do you identify first? What you say defines for others the most important aspects of your school. But what makes your school different from the government school down the street? Are Bible classes the only mark of your quiddity?

Dr. Janet Nason articulates the qualities that distinguish (or ought to distinguish) Christian schools. She identifies numerous ways in which you can specifically incorporate these qualities into the life of your school. Your school's uniqueness ought to be discernible throughout your entire program, from academics to athletics, from your mission to your management of people, and from expectations to emphases.

About the author
Janet Lowrie Nason, Ed.D.
Chair, Graduate Education Programs, Philadelphia Biblical University
Langhorne, PA
26 years of educational leadership experience

Chapter 1

Protecting Your Quiddity
Emphasizing Christian School Uniqueness

Janet Lowrie Nason, Ed.D.

"The Quiddity of the University of Pittsburgh*" appeared odd on the cover of the university's view book. I'd never seen a school's marketing piece use an unknown vocabulary word on the front, but there it was, standing out from similar brochures of competing schools. Clearly responding to their intent, I reached down, picked it up, and followed the asterisk to the definition inside. I read, "Quiddity: that which makes one unique or different."

What text would you include in your school's brochure entitled the same way? How would your teachers define the quiddity of your school? Can your students and parents articulate distinctives? How does your school differ from other public and private schools in your area?

As a Christian school principal, I was responsible for prospective students who visited our school. One spring, I received a phone call from a parent whose daughter had visited third grade the day before. "I want to enroll my child in your school right away," the mother insisted. "Christina came home and said, 'Mommy, I want to go to the Christian school I visted because God lives there.'" Christina had identified the difference between the strong private school she attended and the Christian school she visited.

Perceptible differences make our Christian schools unique. They begin with our view of God. He is either welcome inside or kept outside. Students throughout the world walk into school buildings and are aware of His position. Another mother in Wisconsin decided to enroll her son in a Christian school because of his comment one morning about his public school: "Mom, when I walk through the door of my junior high, God is on the outside."

Discerning and articulating the uniqueness of a Christian school is important for everyone connected to the institution. It defines the mission and brings cohesion to parents, teachers, and students. Integrity of purpose stands at the heart of institutional identity and permeates every facet of the school's life.

Uniqueness in Theology

View of God

Christian educators believe that God exists and can be known personally. "[T]he Lord is God in heaven above and on the earth below" (Deuteronomy 4:39). Teachers talk about Him in the classroom as the cornerstone on which to build lives and view the world. Headmasters and principals affirm the supernatural as real by placing God and His Word at the center of the curriculum. Board members seek His wisdom and direction as they strategically plan for the future.

"The fear of the Lord is the beginning of knowledge" (Proverbs 1:7) clearly means that as learners revere God, they begin to understand life and God's creation. Fearing the Lord is also the beginning of wisdom (Psalm 111:10). Raising wise, discerning children requires that education begin with the knowledge of God.

View of Jesus

The existence of God provides a defining underpinning; further explanation makes us more distinct. God the Father sent His Son to live with us, die for us, and rise from the dead. He then called Jesus back to heaven, where He now intercedes as a mediator between us and the Father who judges sin (1 Timothy 2:5). The third person of the Godhead, the Holy Spirit, lives in the hearts of believers to give spiritual discernment, comfort, and encouragement.

Christian educators believe that Jesus created and sustains the earth. The passage in Colossians 1:16 and 17 says, "For by him all things were created: things in heaven and on earth.... He is before all things, and in him all things hold together." John 1:3 reveals, "Through him all things were made; without him nothing was made that has been made."

Dr. Roy W. Lowrie, one of the founders of ACSI, wrote, "No subject can be taught in the totality of its truth if the Creator is ignored or denied." A secular astronomer with three earned doctorates can study the heavens and determine truth about solar systems, black holes, and red dwarfs, yet not know the reality of their origin. On the other hand, a second-grader attending a Christian school can know more truth about the origin of the universe than the esteemed scientist. This truth is what David espoused in Psalm

119:99 when he wrote, "I have more insight than all my teachers, for I meditate on your statutes."

"All the treasures of wisdom and knowledge" are hidden in Jesus Christ (Colossians 2:3). Christian education acknowledges His paramount position.

View of the Holy Spirit

At a recent Christian school conference in Rheinfelden, Germany, a European delegate asked, "What is Christian education?" I answered by saying, "It is the Holy Spirit directing a born-again teacher to meet the needs of a learner." When that learner is also a believer, the Holy Spirit in the life of the learner works in dynamic interaction to apply and relate truth. We maximize Christian education when teacher and learner are both believers, clean channels for the Holy Spirit and dependent on Him for direction. The exciting reality in Christian education recognizes that the teaching and learning process works in reverse! The Holy Spirit may direct a student to make a comment or a point that meets the need of the teacher. Christian education takes place when the Holy Spirit activates the teaching and learning process, regardless of the subject.

Jesus Christ spoke regarding the role of the Holy Spirit within the teaching and learning dynamic in John 16. He taught that "when he, the Spirit of truth, comes, he will guide you into all truth" (John 16:13). Indeed the Holy Spirit is the teacher and revealer of truth to all students and teachers (John 16:14).

The Holy Spirit's role in ministry is also evident in the Christian school as He facilitates Christians working together "through the bond of peace" (Ephesians 4:3). Teachers, students, and parents practicing the fruits of the Spirit are characterized by their unity and love for one another (Galatians 5:22). We can minimize or quench the Spirit's role. For this reason, Paul exhorts believers in 1 Thessalonians 5:19, "Do not put out the Spirit's fire." Unity is to be treasured and is an evidence of the healthy Body of Christ (Psalm 133:1).

View of the Bible

Christian educators acknowledge that God has revealed Himself through the Bible and creation. Unlike secular schools, Christian schools give the Bible a central position in every dimension of curricular and cocurricular activities. As truth, the God-breathed Word of God defines our worldview and lifestyle. It provides the vantage point from which to develop character, ethics, attitudes, and values that please God.

If we were to picture the school as an archery target with concentric circles moving out from the bull's-eye, the bull's-eye would be biblical truth. Jesus Christ is the source of all truth, and we know His specific truth as revealed in Scripture.

A Christian mother in upstate Pennsylvania once commented regarding the position of the Bible in her son's public school: "We have two Bibles at our high school, one Protestant and one Catholic, and they're kept in the library." I wonder what their circulation statistics are. In secular schools of America, the God-breathed truth "useful for teaching, rebuking, correcting and training in righteousness" (2 Timothy 3:16) has been removed from the classroom and relegated to a resource shelf.

Christian schools around the world teach Bible as a priority subject in the curriculum. Grade-appropriate memory programs, homework, and tests allow teachers to measure the levels of student understanding and to correct wrong thinking. *Excellent Christian schools do not exist apart from excellent Bible teaching.*

Biblical truth integrates into all subject matter throughout the curriculum. From its perspective we teach social studies, psychology, health, and drama. Where disagreement exists between Scripture and a secular textbook, video, or software program, the Bible settles questions of truth. Christian schoolteachers make the most of opportunities to teach discernment and wisdom. With biblical wisdom, we carry out personnel decisions, financial policies, and discipline. It governs the interaction of all school populations.

The Bible is taught in Christian schools through the example of teachers, administrators, and staff. They daily model godly behavior and character traits that students pattern. Their interactions validate the direct Bible instruction that takes place on a daily basis. People learn in powerful ways by observing the models of others. The educated apostle Paul repeatedly challenged New Testament Christians to follow "my example" (Philippians 3:17, 4:9) and "imitate me" (1 Corinthians 4:16), and said, "we did this ... to make ourselves a model for you to follow" (2 Thessalonians 3:9). Every day adults in Christian schools say to students with their lives, "Model me, as I model Jesus Christ."

View of Humanity

Every Christian school teacher must articulate and teach the biblical view of humanity. Administrators find it necessary for understanding school populations of students, parents, teachers, board members, and staff. Each person is uniquely created in God's image (Genesis 1:27). Behaviors do not depend entirely on conditioned responses but reflect sin and self-centeredness, or they reflect the fruits of the Spirit. Interpersonal issues and behaviors stem from either God or self. Teachers and administrators in Christian schools use this guideline when they work with people.

As I prepared this chapter, I had the opportunity to watch Zoè, the six-month-old daughter of one of my French graduate students. She was beautiful in her white dress with her blue eyes sparkling as she kicked and laughed throughout our banquet in Kandern, Germany. Many find it hard to believe that she entered this world as a sinner. Created in God's image as much as Adam and Eve, Zoè also has a sin nature (Romans 3:23).

As she matures, her parents will tell her about her heavenly Father and the need to accept Jesus Christ as her personal Savior. Perhaps one night sitting on her father's lap before bedtime, she will invite Jesus into her heart. Christian educators believe Jesus Christ took our sin on Himself, shed His blood in our place, and paid our death penalty for sin. Through His resurrection, He conquered death so that one day we will live forever with our Father in heaven (1 Corinthians 15:54, 55).

Uniqueness in Philosophy

View of Truth

Secular educators don't understand absolute truth because they consider all truth relative. They invest entire lives, academic careers, and international treks in the quest for truth. They evaluate ancient ruins, ceremonies of tribal nomads, bizarre phenomena, and obscure religious writings in an attempt to find it. Aiming for the zenith of human knowledge, they search with an open mind and build their own truth from both religious experience and progressive culture.

Society charges educators with finding truth—or constructing it—from multiple venues in order to improve society and teach the next generation of leaders. These educators sift knowledge through the grid of collective wisdom in order to distill and categorize it. Despite protestations to the contrary, the secular perspective is closed minded, biased, and lacking in academic integrity. The messianic hope of education—that humanity is getting better and better, and will save itself and subsequent generations through education—lacks credibility. Secular humanists believe that truth emerges through the journey toward it; it doesn't exist separately from human experience. Only an intolerant, dogmatic person claims to have found it apart from intellectual reasoning.

The quiddity of Christian education centers in the axiom *all truth is God's truth*. We study how God created the heavens and the earth, how He created order in geometric equations, and how His story unfolds in history. Any educational system, whether public or private, is flawed, noninclusive, and dogmatic if we lock God out of the classroom. The most pervasive sheltering in education occurs in secular schools. Sheltered from the truth, students are kept from the very knowledge that would impart freedom, peace, self-control, and eternal life.

Origins

Scientists, philosophers, educators, and students have pondered the question, Where did human beings come from? Most classrooms around the world answer that question in pictorial form with a chart showing our evolution from lower forms of life. Charles Darwin observed animal life in the sea around the Galapagos Islands and came up with his evolutionary theory about sea life evolving into land animals. Recently, while scuba diving with my son off the island of Ko Tao in the Gulf of Thailand, I had the chance to explore underwater life for the first time. God's creativity radiates under the sea that covers over half the planet. One only has to dive to know that God originated unique shapes and fluorescent colors! As much as I studied abundant plant and animal life around the pristine coral reefs, I didn't see any remote evidence of half-fish becoming land creatures.

Education that fails to teach children the truth about origins teaches from a false perspective and inhibits student knowledge. Genesis 1:1 clearly states, "In the beginning God created the heavens and the earth." God formed man in His image and breathed into him the breath of life. Humanity is not the chance product of primordial chaos, but uniquely planned, knit together in a mother's womb, and designed to bring honor and glory to our Creator (Jeremiah 1:5).

Purpose of Life

My supervising teacher, Mrs. Rice, voiced some concern as I spent a day with her in August preparing for the opening of school. She knew that I'd spent my K–12 years in a Christian school and that student teaching marked my first exposure to the public school system in conservative, small-town Indiana during the midseventies. "Children are naturally curious," she said. "They want to know where they came from, what the purpose of life is, and what will happen when they die. I don't want you to get into trouble when you're asked these questions, so minimize them and move on to something else."

That morning in Marion, Indiana, God provided a focus. Mrs. Rice gave me career direction with her comment. From my educational studies, I knew that children were impressionable and curious, and that their probing questions provided opportunities to make an eternal difference in their lives. However, she implied that I should shield them from truth about the purpose of life in order to protect myself from separation of church and state legalities. I knew that when I was a student, my teachers had *maximized* such opportunities at the Christian school I attended.

The purpose of life is to please God, and the Bible explains in Revelation 4:11 that God created us for His pleasure. We accomplish this through receiving Jesus Christ and subsequently doing the will of God. To ignore the why questions or to teach that we don't know the meaning of life misleads children or teaches error. Those who teach falsely are ever learning but never able to come to the knowledge of the truth (2 Timothy 3:7).

Moral Standards

What governs our behavior as we interact with friends, strangers, and the environment? On what basis do we make decisions? Is it what feels right? abstract random chance? what others think? what the situation calls for? political expediency?

People make moral decisions on the basis of either biblical principles or human wisdom arising from an egocentric perspective. Moral and ethical choices that ignore or run contrary to truth come from moral relativism or situational ethics. Further defining their uniqueness, Christian schools teach that biblical standards help govern moral choices.

Uniqueness in Educational Management

Facilities

Christian school leaders have a distinct perspective on school facilities. God has provided the buildings. An old estate, a former army base, an old public school, or other property may have been converted into your Christian school.

The sign "Christian" at the front defines the school and places high value on maintaining the resources God has entrusted to you. A school that does not take good care of its facilities should not pray for additional ones. Before they give additional resources, prospective donors often request a site visit to ensure that a school is maintaining the current property in a manner that identifies it with Jesus Christ. What does your school plant say about your stewardship of facilities?

School buildings should be built or remodeled when necessary to enhance learning. Areas of distractions should be modified in order to enable teachers and students to focus on learning tasks. Attractive bulletin boards, learning centers, and hallways reflect the unique education occurring in the classrooms. School flyers announcing events are not taped all over walls and bulletin boards in a chaotic way and never removed. Orderliness and respect for property should be obvious. Although environment does not make a school Christian, references to the biblical foundation of the well-maintained school should be obvious. If teachers can simply slide their classrooms out of their Christian school and into the local public school without raising any objections, the physical environment does not reflect its quiddity.

Teachers should strive to develop attractive classrooms that stimulate learners. Chipped paint, dirty stairs, and dreary hallways offer poor testimonies for Christian institutions. Good schools remove the clutter of papers, lost books, and clothes from classrooms every day. The total school environment teaches all the time, so the question becomes, What does it teach in your school? Godly stewardship is a requirement, not an option.

Administrators are ultimately responsible for the cleanliness, safety, and attractiveness of their schools. They set maintenance standards, design systems for upkeep, and determine funds for ongoing improvement. Failure to set and meet such standards indicates surrender to mediocrity.

Christian schools depend on parents, students, teachers, and janitors for the upkeep of facilities. Often parents struggling with tuition payments, or perhaps folks serving as volunteers, function as custodians. This scenario may lower maintenance standards because principals hesitate to confront these gracious people with the challenge of quality. Yet any system that fails to set standards and require ongoing accountability will drift to lower and lower levels. Effective leaders evaluate the quality control of facility maintenance because they know that the school plant impacts school populations and reflects on the name of Jesus Christ.

Outsourcing maintenance sometimes works better. If we hold caretakers accountable, we do not tolerate smelly restrooms; we require that dirty windows and hallways be recleaned; and we insist that locker-room clutter be put away. Children and teachers must have the freedom to focus on learning without being distracted by their environment. In fact, the environment must enhance the learning process.

Board Leadership

Christian schools are primarily organized as parent-controlled schools, church-related schools, or board-controlled schools, although hybrid models abound. In most parent-controlled schools, the parents form a society that elects board members. In others, the board serves as its own nominating committee for new members. Many church-related school boards work under or in concert with a church board. Board-controlled schools usually have self-perpetuating boards whose members may or may not have term limits.

Christian school board members must practice more than just effective boardmanship. A Christian school board consists of men and women with godly qualifications for leadership. Since boards constantly seek God's wisdom for direction and decision making, a close and growing relationship with Jesus Christ is imperative. Schools that select board members exclusively on the basis of each candidate's annual fund-giving potential conform to the best private school wisdom, not God's wisdom.

Administration

Trustees and administrators determine the spiritual, social, and educational climates of their institutions. They function as the change agents who lead students, teachers, and parents. Their spiritual role cannot be underestimated because they articulate the school's mission and direct its course. Schools rarely rise above the standards of their leaders; their models reflect a superior, mediocre, or below-average level.

Effective administration germinates from men and women of prayer, godly educators guarding the academic integrity of the school. We assume they have the multitasking ability to focus on planning, fiscal responsibility, curriculum development, effective management, systemic analysis, and communication. At the same time, they have the interpersonal skills to reach out to needy individuals and subgroups within the school population.

Quality administrators must manage both the people and tasks of the school well. Gregarious leaders, gifted in talking to people and making sure everyone is happy, may neglect advance planning and confrontation of systemic problems. This negligence results in loss of credibility. On the other hand, schools may have principals who lock themselves in their offices and send out three-page emails to everyone, and lose credibility because they lack interpersonal skills. Many claim that lack of communication skills is the number one reason why principals fail.

The unique dimension of the administrator-as-spiritual-leader may be perceived differently by various school populations. To some, a spiritual leader should not confront other Christians who fail to meet standards. To others, spirituality means accepting every child without regard to admissions standards. To many, it suggests not exercising discipline procedures outlined in the student handbook. Principals are often misunderstood and usually cannot explain their decisions because of confidentiality issues.

Christian school administrators must be anchored in deep relationship to the immutable God as they face constant change and unexpected problems. They must maintain the imperative relationship with our heavenly Father, who communicates wisdom through His Word. They must balance healthy family relationships and outside activities. The God-given understanding of their position in Christ provides an anchor during the pounding of circumstances, and it enables them to persevere during overwhelming tragedy. A leader with deep spiritual roots may draw on those resources during times of drought and difficulties. Working in Satan's battleground presents a constant challenge. Spiritual warfare that demands spiritual resources becomes a weekly reality.

Christian school administrators set the tone for inclusion within the Body of Christ and demonstrate its global focus. How we educate children about God's international school system impacts the spiritual maturity of students. Teaching children to think and give beyond self to others within the Body of Christ should be a major goal of the Christian school. Schools cannot develop mission-mindedness and prepare world Christians without the strong support and model of their leader. The principal is ultimately responsible for designing curriculum that integrates missions at *all* levels throughout *all* subjects in the school. The administrator's personal enthusiasm for and understanding of missions set the tone for reaching out to international Christian schools. For example, the impact would be significant if an animated leader shared in chapel what he personally learned from God while giving to and visiting Nigerian Christian schools.

Being a Christian school administrator doesn't mean that one takes life easy with a *c'est la vie* mentality. Effective principals project programs and roster schedules years into the future, clearly communicating information to boards, parents, and students. Sometimes the lack of a centralized district office causes a school leader to fall behind with strategic and long-range planning, to the frustration of many. When this situation happens, leaders lose their credibility.

Christian school leaders must implement sound fiscal procedures for handling and utilizing money. The integrity of any school links inseparably with the way it handles finances. Its approach may take the form of extending grace to a family undergoing difficulties, or releasing a family habitually delinquent with accounts. Financial responsibility is a crucial administrative job.

Christian school administrators rely on godly discernment for systemic evaluation and improvement. God-given wisdom is critical as we hire new teachers, evaluate current faculty, analyze curriculum, assess program effectiveness, and move our institutions toward accreditation. Biblical leadership evaluates outcomes and makes decisions.

The administrator either encourages the professional development of teachers by requiring graduate degrees and Bible courses or stands to lose a crucial distinctive. Principals who hold graduate degrees themselves lead by example. Often administrators must educate board members about this budget item, which affects the school's academic integrity. It takes significant institutional commitment to fund the personal development of teachers and staff members.

The Christian school administrator at times must make difficult decisions to release teachers, staff members, parents, and students to protect the integrity of the school. These decisions seem more difficult in smaller schools, and all such issues are complicated because of the uniqueness of Christian schools. We always face political ramifications when confronting issues within the Body of Christ. But leaders can be effective if they solve problems through the power of Jesus Christ and exercise His direction.

Teachers

Christian school teachers are unique. They have been given the gift of salvation through Jesus Christ as well as the spiritual gift of teaching. Exercising these gifts daily in the classroom is spiritually invigorating despite both the physical and emotional stress. Wise teachers depend on the Holy Spirit to work in the teaching and learning process. The Spirit often leads teachers to cover material or move in an unexpected direction. This truth does not mean we ignore lesson planning or identifying outcome behaviors any more than a Christian dentist does away with X rays or drilling whenever she feels led.

Faculty recruitment is the most important decision administrators make. Teachers define the school by working either in concert with its quiddity or against it. Administrators conducting interviews must ask themselves, Will this candidate model spiritual health within the Body of Christ as he interacts with administration, board, fellow teachers, staff members, parents, and students? By virtue of their position, standing *in loco parentis* and teaching godly character, educators say daily to their students, "Follow my example as I follow Jesus Christ." We must have emotionally healthy, mature Christians teaching our children, but we don't hire only perfect, plastic Christians. Students need to see and be taught by teachers with scars who have weathered suffering and attacks, yet love and trust God one-hundred percent. It is important for children to know that life is not always easy and teachers sometimes bleed.

Teachers must possess a growing relationship with the Lord. If they just recycle Sunday sermons in class instead of sharing firsthand what God is teaching them personally, their teaching lacks an essential dynamic. Because the Bible tells us that when a student is fully trained he will be like his teacher (Luke 6:40), administrators must expect the students to imitate their teachers.

Research indicates that the most significant influence on learning is not the environment or the curriculum, but the teacher. When our heavenly Father wanted to communicate the most important spiritual truths to us, He did not just deliver Bible curriculum. He could have done that. Instead, He sent us His Son as our master teacher to teach us and model how we should live.

Teachers in Christian schools study Jesus' teaching, evaluate His methodology, look at the way He developed critical thinking, consider the way He handled the disciples' mistakes, model His patience with adults, and study His core curriculum. How would Jesus teach beginning reading, eighth-grade Bible, and European history? If teachers can't imagine the master teacher teaching in a certain way, they should not do so either.

Christian teachers teach Bible as a specific subject. Elementary teachers realize that we teach reading so that students can comprehend the Word of God for themselves and can interpret everything they hear and read from its perspective. In order for us to maintain our uniqueness, our schools must have excellent Bible teachers. Have you ever listened to students say that their Bible class is boring? Have you heard them say that their Bible teacher isn't prepared and just wastes the time? These attitudes should never be present in our schools. For students to know truth, their teachers must communicate the Word with enthusiasm. Wise administrators hire teachers who have studied the Bible, comprehend it, and are skilled at teaching its truth. Furthermore, principals and headmasters should plan great Bible lessons themselves if they assume classroom duties.

The process of leading a child to Jesus Christ should be discussed during the teacher interview process. Teachers who are uncomfortable talking about their salvation experience in an interview will be even more so in a classroom full of students. Christian school teachers look for unsaved children and identify moments when they can lead them to Jesus Christ. Teachers repeatedly say that their most exciting teaching days happen when they have led children to the Lord.

How prospective teachers view global missions and its curriculum integration is another significant area to cover in the interview process. Hiring teachers who participate in global activities in the Body of Christ and who want to involve students with international Christian schools becomes a priority if a school wants to achieve the major objective of preparing Christians who make a lifelong habit of giving time and money to missions.

Christian school teachers pray for their students on a regular basis. Some keep a class list in their Bibles; others close their eyes and picture a map of their classroom, praying for each student they see. While all good teachers pray for problem children, wise teachers pray for God's protection and wisdom for all students, even the quiet, well-behaved ones. Christian teachers recognize no substitute for the spiritual power of prayer.

Curriculum

Effective teachers design all curriculum with the end product in mind. They identify outcome behaviors, determine ways to measure achievement, and then create learning experiences that target identified objectives. They know that the curriculum is more than the textbooks; it includes all the resources used to meet learning objectives. While some teachers just design activities, effective ones tailor well-structured curriculum to objectives and try to meet the needs of all students.

Quality teachers integrate biblical principles and godly character traits throughout all subject areas. The integration of biblical truth throughout curricular and cocurricular programs is a key distinctive of the Christian school. Only teachers with an integrated life, a knowledge of the Word, and an ability to make biblical connections demonstrate proficiency at integration. Teachers who know the Word and know their subject matter will be disciplined and will teach from the bull's-eye of Scripture. They do not classify subjects as sacred or secular since *all truth is God's truth.*

We also maintain a biblical basis for and Christian approach to cocurricular activities. Music, choir, and band provide ways to praise God and offer a means of worship. Art reflects our Creator. Exercising creativity in the art room leads to creative problem solving in the classroom, headmaster's office, and boardroom. We retain a Christian perspective to athletic competition—coaching, winning, losing, playing, and competing with fellow members of God's international school system.

School Climate

Institutional climate is impacted by the host culture around the school and community. The culture of most countries grows increasingly secular and humanistic. "How do I maintain the distinctiveness of our Christian school?" the director of a Christian school in Bangkok asked me recently. All administrators must address this excellent question.

The most significant focus targets the quality of the faculty. Adhering to a high standard can be a unique challenge in international schools where in any year a third of the teachers may be on furlough raising support. Teachers must be competent in their fields with certification that assesses both biblical and professional studies. They must articulate biblical philosophy and demonstrate skill at integrating biblical truth in their subject matter. It takes a teacher about three years to develop this competency and a lifetime to master it.

Continuous change in teachers, board members, parents, and students necessitates ongoing initiatives to educate new people about the distinctiveness of Christian school education and the culture of your particular school. Training programs must teach and reteach current populations. We need ongoing orientation and mentoring programs for new teachers and board members.

Administrators must utilize parent/teacher meetings, back-to-school nights, in-service days, banquets, retreats, graduations, and other programs to articulate the unique mission and the quiddity of their schools. This responsibility is a key to preserving the school's uniqueness. Young Christian schools benefit from inviting graduates of other Christian schools to speak. Young parents need to see the products of Christian schools as they work with their own children and anticipate their development.

Exposing parents to clear Christian school distinctiveness is an ongoing and necessary administrative communication task. Don't miss any opportunities to convey the essential uniqueness of your school.

Christian schools set boundaries in order to maintain their integrity. We are characterized by our uniqueness in relationship to theology, philosophy, origins, and educational management. Leaders must constantly articulate the story of how God has led the school and will continue to do so. We strive to promote unity and to address those who threaten the school's identity. We hold in our hands a gift from God—and He holds us responsible for handling it carefully and prayerfully.

Who's in Charge Here?
Working with the Board

John Schimmer Jr., Ed.D.

Chapter Summary

Who is in charge here? Too often those asking this question are experiencing tension between the board and the administrator about who is "in control." But that question is the wrong one. The appropriate question is, Do both the board and the administration have an accurate understanding of their separate but complementary roles?

Dr. Schimmer, having studied this issue throughout his career, addresses with clarity and purpose the crucial role of the board in the Christian school and the board's relationship with the head of the school. He offers a wealth of practical suggestions for every Christian school troubled with uncertainty over how to deal with board/administrator relationships and how to turn an unfavorable situation into a blessing.

About the author

John Schimmer Jr., Ed.D.
Director, ACSI South-Central Region
Dallas, TX
38 years of educational leadership experience

Chapter 2

Who's in Charge Here?
Working with the Board

John Schimmer Jr., Ed.D.

In response to parental objections, a school board reverses an administration's suspension of two students. An administrator moves funds
from the maintenance account to salaries in order to hire another football coach. A board chairman orders the athletic director to appear before
the board to discuss parental taunting of basketball officials. An administrator calls a board member and reprimands him for caustic remarks
about a proposed plan to change the grading system.

Such examples too painfully describe the ambiguity over authority in
Christian schools. This vagueness results from the board's failure to define
clearly its own role and that of the administrator, or its lack of the discipline
required to function within prescribed limits.

The administrator contributes to this confusion when he says to the
board, "We have a problem." Such language invites the board to assume the
role of the administration in solving the problem.

Continued vagueness and commingling of roles result in a school
plagued by a malaise of friction and disunity between the chief administrator and board. Each potentially pulls the school in different directions, leaving parents in a state of bewilderment. In the words of James, "My brethren,
these things ought not to be this way" (3:10, NASB). The psalmist reminds
us, "How good and pleasant it is when brothers live together in unity!"
(Ps.133:1).

Despite the inherent difficulties of building a relationship in which a number of strong personalities and gifted leaders must learn to work together, there is an answer. It begins by acknowledging our need for one another, the interdependency that binds our hearts and minds because of a common goal. In the words of the Preacher, "A cord of three strands is not quickly torn apart" (Ecclesiastes 4:12b, NASB). The apostle Paul, in reference to the church, teaches us this principle: "For just as we have many members in one body and all the members do not have the same function, so we, who are many, are one body in Christ, and individually members one of another" (Romans 12:4, 5, NASB).

Any administrator and board team ministering to each other and behaving Christlike in thought and actions must clearly define their respective roles and clarify expectations. This chapter will help administrators understand what boards do and what they should not do. It will also recommend steps to make the board strong and secure in its governance role. Administrative retention critically links to a philosophy of governance and responsibilities that all leaders must thoroughly examine before hiring or accepting an administrative position.

Historical Context of School Boards

The idea of a group of citizens, lay people, overseeing and regulating the function of schooling can be traced back to Colonial America. The governing body of a township or village appointed a school committee to locate an appropriate site for the school, interview and hire a teacher, and approve the course of study. The committee established rules of conduct for the teacher and students, selected teaching materials, and visited the school to listen to recitations. Some New England towns still use the title "school committee."

This model has been passed down through the years with relatively little change. School committees evolved into local school boards, which eventually came under the purview of state boards of education. In John Carver's (personal communication, 2001) opinion, "Governance, as we have inherited it, is significantly flawed."

The following passage, written in 1925 by school historian Ellwood Cubberly, might describe many school boards today:

> [O]ften their procedure is ill-advised, and commonly they are divided into groups or factions primarily interested in political or other advantages, rather than in the promotion of the best interests of the schools....

> Nearly all cases of mismanagement, caused by the overactivity of school board members, are due to a misconception as to what the members were elected to do.... Their great work is to select experts to advise them, and on their advice to determine the larger policies of the school system....

They have in no sense been elected to become a board of superintendents to supervise the detailed work of the schools.

This problem seems ageless. An article called "TEA Expert Faults Trustees' Behavior" in the *Dallas Morning News* noted, "[S]chool trustees inappropriately act like 'on-site administrators' and tell principals what to do.... Board members have directly interfered at [local] schools rather than carrying out their role as policy makers" (1999).

For generations citizens have struggled to distinguish between the authority of the board and the authority of the administration. When consulting with administrators and board members, I have found considerable consternation over authority and roles. Administrators believe that the board is either too involved in the day-to-day operations of the school or that it fails to give sufficient leadership, especially in policy development, fund-raising, and planning. Board members express frustration over lengthy board meetings and the lack of appropriate information and administrative responsiveness to parental concerns.

John Carver contends that the problem is not with people but with the process. By tradition, boards have assumed the wrong job (Carver, 1997).

The Role of the Board

Roy Lowrie, cofounder of ACSI, stated, "Failure to comprehend the board's responsibilities will result in confusion, awkward situations, poor decisions, and oversights. The board should define in writing its own major responsibilities" (Lowrie, 1998). Board literature abounds with lists of board responsibilities. David Hubbard, president of Fuller Seminary, suggests that boards function as governors, sponsors, ambassadors, and consultants (Drucker, 1990).

The board governs the organization when the trustees assemble in a legally constituted board meeting to debate issues, vote on motions, draft policies, determine goals, and plan for the future. When governing the organization, the board speaks with *one voice*, the only governance voice heard outside the boardroom.

The board acts as sponsors collectively and individually. Each board member should contribute to the school and solicit financial support for the school. Corporately the board establishes and oversees fiscal programs designed to meet the current and future needs of the school.

Board members become ambassadors when they publicly support the school. They invest time interpreting the school's mission, celebrating God's faithfulness, representing the school at civic functions, expounding the virtues of the school, and defending it when under attack. Trustees serve as consultants by bringing to the board table their gifts and talents, professional expertise, and most importantly, their dreams and vision for the school.

Hughes, Lakey, and Bobowick list the board's main duties as setting the direction, ensuring resources, and providing oversight (2000). Daniel Vander Ark, the executive director of Christian Schools International, states that the board has two major responsibilities: to govern and to sell. Within this context, he describes the board's job as "preserving the heritage, auditing the present, and planning the future" (1995). I especially like this description.

In a meeting with the executive staff of ACSI, Robert Andringa, president of the Council for Christian Colleges and Universities, presented fourteen responsibilities of school boards (see table 1). Item two on the Andringa list indicates that boards write policies on how they will govern rather than on how the board wants the administration to direct the school. Governance policies appear in the board policy manual. Administrative procedures or regulations, developed by the administration, constitute the school procedures manual.

Table 1
Basic Responsibilities of School Boards

1. Determine mission and basic values
2. Maintain board standing policies on all aspects of governance
3. Select a chief executive and hold accountable to policies
4. Support the chief executive and assess his or her performance
5. Ensure effective organizational planning
6. Approve the major goals/desired results—strategic plan
7. Ensure financial solvency and integrity
8. Approve, monitor, and strengthen the school's programs and services
9. Help represent the school externally
10. Ensure legal and ethical integrity and maintain accountability
11. Encourage/nurture chief executive and staff
12. Serve as "final court of appeals" for unresolved internal disputes
13. Recruit and orient new board members
14. Evaluate and improve itself and the governing board

Note: Robert C. Andringa for ACSI staff training in December 1998. Reprinted with permission.

The above list of board responsibilities shows that board literature places the emphasis on the board's fiduciary responsibilities. As fiduciary trustees, the board is entrusted with the property of another party in whose best interest we expect the board to act. In the case of private and Christian schools, the board must determine who owns the school. Some schools function as a ministry of a church; therefore, the church owns the school. An individual or group of individuals may own the school. The membership of a society or association owns their school. Independent schools have the greatest difficulty identifying their owners. If the school does not have *real* owners, the board acts on behalf of the *moral* owners. The board cannot be all things to all people. It must resist being pulled in all directions, but it must represent well the interests of the owners.

This discussion on the role of the board would not be complete without mentioning John Carver's Policy Governance model. According to John and Miriam Carver, the board "defines, delegates, and monitors." It does so by writing policies in four specific domains: ends policies, governance process policies, board-CEO linkage policies, and executive limitations policies (Carver & Carver, 1997). Policy governance is neither another way to organize the board nor a cafeteria of tips from which to pick and choose what looks attractive. It cannot be accomplished piecemeal as board work was in previous times. "Governance is more than management writ large" (Carver, personal communication, 2001).

Policy governance represents a conceptual shift, a new way of looking at the board's job and its relation to the staff. It is not intended as a rescue model for boards in trouble. Boards that are functioning well, yet wanting to reach a higher level of leadership, should study this model. Before a board will feel comfortable in adopting Policy Governance, it must be confident in the administrator's ability to lead the school skillfully and prudently, and to do so according to the board's written policies.

Trusteeship Is a Gift of Time

Trustees are volunteers. They give generously of their time to serve on the board because of their love for the school and their commitment to Christian education. But nonprofit boards conduct notoriously long board meetings.

> [M]ost nonprofit and church boards spend more time in meetings than boards of large corporations ... because most nonprofit boards do not distinguish between governance and operations. They burn themselves out doing administrative work while neglecting their primary function, which is to govern. (Stoesz, 2000)

Herb Perry writes:

> [I]f [potential good board members] attend a few meetings only to discover that the board has poorly prepared agendas, wastes time on petty matters, refers all major matters to the Executive Committee, rehashes decisions already made, and that the meetings are poorly chaired and thus last unnecessarily long, then these high-potential directors will leave. Often in order to spare people's feelings they will say they are too busy. (1990)

The school administrator, working in concert with the chairman, must assist the board in managing time. Generally, boards spend an inordinate amount of time deliberating the past or the present, and they rarely discuss planning the future. They should invest the greater part of their time looking outward and forward, not inward and backward. Boards must replace the time they spend solving problems with visionary thinking and planning in order to secure the school's future. They must focus on end results, leaving the means of accomplishment to the administration and staff.

The Agenda Belongs to the Board

A carefully prepared agenda offers the key to shorter meetings. The agenda belongs to the board, not to the staff. Although the board chairman prepares the agenda, he usually seeks advice from the chief administrator, who diligently keeps staff issues off the agenda. *A staff agenda invites the board to micromanage.* Aim for a two-hour board meeting. It is possible! Some boards have short meetings and only meet every other month. A few meet only quarterly. Additional meetings are scheduled as needed. Think about it. College and university boards usually meet twice a year, and their institutions operate quite well under the leadership of the president and his or her administrative team.

Board Committees

"[B]oard committees mount their steeds with enthusiasm and madly ride off in all directions" (Stoesz & Raber, 1994).

When boards focus their efforts on governing, they can jettison most traditional board committees. John Carver cautions, "Have no more committees than absolutely needed. Do not compromise the clear accountability linkage between the board and its CEO" (1997).

> When board committees are assigned tasks that make them essentially oversee, become involved in, or advise on management functions, it becomes less clear who is in charge of these activities. The CEO role deteriorates as a result of these committees' well-intended, official interference. (Carver, 1997)

How can we grade the chef if we helped prepare the entrée? Examples of board committees with administrative responsibilities include buildings and grounds, personnel, education, finance, and public relations. These are staff functions for which the board holds the staff accountable.

A Christian school in our region had constant administrative turnover every three to four years. After approximately six months on the job, each new superintendent would call to invite me to lunch. It was always the same problem. Two administrators of large public high schools, both with doctorates, served on the board's education committee. The superintendent had little control over the school's curricula.

Board committees must do board-level work, not sub-board work. Meeting before the board meets, they bring well-researched recommendations to the board. All committees speak *to* the board, not *for* the board. Board committees do not work for the staff, nor do they assign work to the staff. When specific studies require staff input, this need funnels through the administrator, who then directs the staff.

Some boards would argue that board committees should advise the administrator. This argument is suspect. When board members give advice, the administrator feels compelled to comply. Ad hoc committees often provide a more effective and nonthreatening way to study, debate, and formulate a recommendation. Since this nonboard committee gives *only* advice, the administrator may choose which advice to accept and which to reject. An ad hoc committee functions best when made up of board members (now serving as volunteers), parents, experts from the community, and when appropriate, teachers and students. The administration assigns them a specific task, gives clear guidelines and limits, and dismisses them with appreciation upon completion of the task. "Without consultation, plans are frustrated, but with many counselors they succeed" (Proverbs 15:22, NASB).

Board and Administrator Relationships: Mutual Respect and Support in Leadership

When working with boards, I try to assist them in moving away from the demeaning conventional position of directing and checking, to a more rewarding relationship of encouraging, training, empowering, and monitoring. To empower an administrator means to recognize this person as the leader, the one in whom the board has vested the authority to make decisions. She need not always come to the board for permission. She must be trusted to do what is safe, lawful, prudent, ethical, and best for the school. When defining roles and writing a job description, the board should think of the administrator as the chief educational officer (CEO), a partner with the board in leading the school.

The relationship between the administrator and the board chairman is extremely crucial in any organization and certainly in Christian schools, as evidenced by the extraordinarily high administrative turnover. Very competent administrators have been released, often because of fractured relationships or because of the lack of clearly defined roles.

A board chairman called to ask if a school needed to have a chief administrator before it could be accredited. I knew their administrator, so I inquired further. He replied, "Since we both do the same thing, the board thought we could save money by not paying an administrator's salary." If the chair and the administrator even remotely perform the same duties, something is very wrong.

Schools have two key leaders: the chairman of the board, who manages and directs the activities of the board, and the chief administrator, who directs and oversees all aspects of the school. How they perform individually and jointly sets the tone for the organization. They must be a team (Stoesz & Raber, 1994).

The chair and the administrator must develop a strong, supporting relationship. The chair confers regularly with the administrator, keeping him or her apprised of board issues, priorities, and concerns. Together they review the board meeting agenda before sending it to the board members. The chair takes every precaution to assure that the administrator is not blindsided in a board meeting. Stoesz and Raber wrote:

> The two should meet regularly, at least once between meetings of the board, to talk about issues they face in their respective assignments. They should plan together and dream together. The fact of just being together, like at a sporting event, may serve the important purpose of deepening their relationship.

> It would be highly unusual if these two strong individuals did not disagree on occasion. They can and they should. But the disagreement must be at the objective level. It cannot be allowed to disintegrate and become personal or acrimonious.

> ... the chair and the CEO must have respect for the office of the other. An effective chair does not usurp the authority which is vested in the office of CEO.... The effective CEO humbly and joyfully submits him/herself to the board to which he/she is accountable through the chair.... The atmosphere is one of mutual respect and collaboration. (1994)

Building a Strong Board

Generally, Christian school boards do not have a plan for identifying and cultivating prospective board members. At the last minute, they scurry to find people to fill vacancies. While we know the Lord can supply all our needs, I wonder if this last-minute practice demonstrates faith or just negligence. Unfortunately, last-minute tactics usually include some arm-twisting or pressure to fill in until someone else can be found. Often, a warm body and a willing heart constitute qualification to serve on the board. As someone once said, "Small fish bite on small bait."

Instead, the board should be proactive, always searching for qualified candidates. Administrators must also continuously seek to enlist the very best candidates, and then do their part in helping them find joy and fulfillment in serving as school trustees. Administrators may need to motivate and guide the board in developing a recruitment plan.

Trustee Development Committee

We can learn a lesson here from elite private schools. Their trustee development committees carry out the following responsibilities:

- Maintain a board profile—documenting the skills presently represented and determining what new skills may be needed.
- Track board member terms, noting who rotates off next.
- Identify, screen, and recruit potential board members.
- Serve as the nominating committee.
- Coordinate new-board-member orientation.
- Plan continuing education programs and board retreats.
- Develop systems for annually evaluating individual board members, the chair, and the collective board.

Together, these tasks help develop a strong board.

Identifying Potential Board Members

The committee begins by focusing on the spiritual qualifications of each candidate. Only spiritually qualified men and women should serve on a Christian school board. Just as Paul, in his letters to Timothy and Titus, describes the spiritual qualifications for church leadership, so the board should clearly state the spiritual qualifications for school trustees.

> Board members should be thinking Christianly when they come to the decisions that they have to make. Their decisions need to be as biblical as the decisions of teachers and of administrators. This is why it is critical to have spiritually qualified board members who can do that. It is better to have a smaller board of qualified people than to have a larger board with some being unqualified spiritually. (Lowrie, 1984) (For suggestions on the spiritual qualifications, see table 2.)

The committee focuses next on the personal qualities and skills necessary for effective board service. These include integrity, respect for the opinions of others, a nonjudgmental attitude, a spirit of encouragement, impeccable moral character, good listening skills, team cooperation, ability to support the majority vote, confidentiality, a biblical worldview, and vision. Each board member must show personal conviction and unequivocal support for Christian schooling.

Table 2
The Spiritual Qualities of a Christian School Trustee

1. Board members are mature Christians who daily grow in their personal relationship with Christ.
2. Board members are involved in the ministry of a local Bible-believing church.
3. Board members have a Christ-centered focus with the desire to bring honor and glory to Him through all they say and do.
4. Board members are godly role models in the performance of their board duties and decisions.

5. Board members view their service on the school board as a ministry and a calling from God.

6. Board members believe in the power of prayer and are exemplary in their commitment to pray for the school, leadership, faculty, and students.

7. Board members acknowledge the Lordship and sovereignty of Christ.

8. Board members realize that nothing can be accomplished apart from the work of the Holy Spirit.

9. Board members understand and are committed to a biblical worldview and a Christian philosophy of education.

10. Board members balance their work with their spiritual lives and home responsibilities—and have the same expectations for the staff.

John Schimmer, Ed.D., Director, ACSI South-Central Region, 1999

Searching for new board members means looking beyond the friends of present trustees. Consider having a percentage of trustees from outside the school family in order to provide greater objectivity in board deliberations.

Cultivating Prospects

No one should join the board without demonstrating a proven track record. Assigning prospective members to special committees (for example, parent advisory committee) gives the board the opportunity to observe their diligence, dependability, punctuality, energy, and contributions.

When Parents Serve on the Board

"Hey Dad, don't forget to bring up at the board meeting tonight what happened in my class and that Miss Jones didn't do anything about it."

Commonly, parents of children in the school serve on the board. In fact, most Christian schools require parent-trustees to enroll their eligible children. Some bylaws require all trustees to be school parents. A few writers have suggested that this practice may pose an inherent conflict of interest. Parent-trustees could bring to the board table issues that could directly help their own children, such as a trustee challenging guidelines for determining the valedictorian, or a particular class having too much homework. Whenever a potential conflict of interest exists, it would be prudent for the trustee to excuse himself or herself from both the debate and the vote.

When the committee considers school parents for an opening on the board, it should inform the administrator. A candidate may appear well qualified, but the staff knows if he has a history of engaging teachers about his children, or if she complains regularly about school policies. The administrator should counsel all parent candidates about the unique challenge and potential problems of being a parent-trustee.

Trustees must focus on what is best for all children, the school, and the future. They must understand and commit to applying all policies consistently and being impartial in all decisions. April Moore shares a wonderful illustration from school administrator Paul Horovitz comparing the parent-trustee to a camera:

> The parent is naturally equipped with a single, close-up lens.... The task of the head and others on the board is to provide the parent-trustee with two additional lenses—a wide angle for viewing the school as a whole and a telephoto for taking the long view of the school's future. (Moore, 2000)

The board chairman may also have children in the school. The chair serves as a model of board behavior. From the chair, new trustees learn how to respond as parent-trustees. The administrator and the chair must agree on all parent-trustee issues.

We should remind parent-trustees that their role in the school, and their relationships with other parents, will change. Parents may urge them to bring specific concerns to the board. But their trustee role centers in facilitation rather than problem solving. What they say carries more weight now because people interpret it as a board opinion.

When a parent-trustee brings a family problem to a board meeting and the chair allows it, the administrator should politely remind the board that this issue should be resolved outside the boardroom.

Having a Diverse Board

Occasionally someone will say, "We have a good board; we all think alike" or "We seldom have a disagreement." These comments may not mark a good board. A strong board welcomes, even encourages, diverse opinions. If everyone thinks the same way, the board could be reduced to two or three people. A homogeneous board is not usually the most effective board.

Diversity takes several forms. For example, the board should reflect the diversity within the school's constituency. Varied occupations and life experiences among trustees bring a breadth and depth of insight to the debate.

> Healthy organizations allow—even welcome—differing points of view.... Few ideas, it seems, fall from heaven fully developed. Ideas originate in creative minds, often in response to something which needs to be improved. They are refined in debate, and in this process they also become owned. Only ideas which can survive vigorous analysis deserve to be adopted. (Stoesz & Raber, 1994)

Roy Lowrie also addressed the issue of all trustees having freedom to express their opinions:

> To deal with serious issues affecting the school, board members must be able to speak freely in their meetings. Two things are prerequisites for openness: a nonjudgmental attitude toward one another, and a commitment to confidentiality. Board members

should not feel that they must hold back from saying what they think about a matter to avoid judgment or the risk of having their ideas passed on. When members hold back, the board does not have the advantage of its own full counsel. (1998)

Remember, debate belongs inside the boardroom; outside the boardroom, trustees speak with one voice.

Training the Board

I have never met a board member who has taken a college or graduate course about serving on a board. Probably no course exists. Boards rarely budget funds to bring in a consultant for board training, and only a few board members attend ACSI board conferences. Often new trustees begin their service without the benefit of any orientation. Indeed, joining a Christian school board is like trying to board a fast-moving train.

New Member Orientation

A month or two before their first board meeting, new trustees should meet with the board chair and administrator for training and a visit to the school. This training includes:

- The history and heritage of the school
- The Christian philosophy of education
- A discussion on core values, distinctives of the Christian school, and the culture and ethos of the school
- Tips for new board members
- The application of Matthew 18 in a school setting
- A review of the board policy manual, code of ethics, and strategic plan
- A presentation of the teacher handbook, parent/student handbook, and other pertinent school literature
- A meeting with the business manager and development director to review the financial condition of the school and strategies for raising financial support
- A visit to classes and chapel, and an opportunity to meet the staff

Continuing Education

Good boards budget monies for growing professionally and increasing their understanding of governance. One Christian school policy reads:

The board will invest in its governance capacity.... Training and retraining will be used liberally to orient new board members and candidates for board membership, as well as to maintain and increase existing member skills and understanding.... Costs will be prudently incurred.... (Graybeal, 2001)

Training should focus on board members maintaining and increasing their skills to serve effectively, examining current educational issues, and developing new and more effective means for listening to the values and viewpoints of the owners. Examples of training opportunities include attending conferences, inviting speakers to board meetings, participating in retreats, subscribing to board member periodicals, reading and discussing current educational literature, and networking with trustees from other schools.

Expectations of Boards and Administrators

The Board Expects the Administrator to:

- Provide spiritual leadership to the board, staff, students, and, where applicable, the parents of the school.
- Understand and support the role of the board, submit fully to the board's authority, and develop a collegial working relationship with the board.
- Direct the school in accordance with the board's written policies and develop administrative procedures that require the staff to function prudently, ethically, legally, and safely.
- Deal openly and honestly with the board, keeping the board well informed so they are neither embarrassed, nor forced to "save face."
- Lead the board in its understanding of educational research, trends, and successful practices.
- Keep the board informed on school accomplishments, events, potential obstacles, and threats to the school's well-being.
- Articulate a Christian (biblical) philosophy of education and implement this philosophy at all levels of the school.
- Communicate effectively and convincingly with the Christian community regarding the philosophy, distinctives, and biblical mandate for teaching our children Christian principles and values.
- Deal with parents, students, employees, and the public in a Christ-honoring way. Always follow the Matthew 18 principle and insist others do so as well.
- Love the school and the families it serves.
- Be professionally competent:
  - A good administrator.
  - An experienced teacher/educator and academic leader, able to lead the faculty.
  - A teacher of teachers.
  - A competent business manager—financially astute.
  - A good communicator—both verbal and written.
  - A working knowledge of development: student recruitment, public relations, and fund-raising.
  - A bold leader—wise, energetic, and enthusiastic.

• One who maintains proper priorities in personal life—God, family, and ministry—particularly protective of home life and quiet time with God.

The Administrator Expects the Board to:

• Be men and women of faith and spiritual maturity who daily practice biblical living.
• Be exemplary in praying for the school, staff, students, and families.
• Model biblical principles of leadership in its relationships with and treatment of the faculty and staff.
• Define in writing its major responsibilities and scope of authority, and operate accordingly.
• Develop written governance policies.
• Function only as a collective board speaking with one voice.
• Make all decisions without partiality and in the best interest of the entire school.
• Strictly require all members of the school family to practice the principle of Matthew 18 in resolving conflicts, and deal immediately with rumors, gossip, dissension, discord, or anything else that will fracture the unity of the body.
• Encourage the administrator to function as the chief education officer, and provide a job description specific enough to clarify the board's expectations but broad enough to allow the administrator liberty to function within the boundaries set by the board.
• Be committed to nurturing the administrator to use gifts and talents fully, providing annually for professional growth opportunities.
• Provide an annual evaluation of the administrator on the basis of a pre-determined instrument, procedure, and expected outcomes.
• Publicly support the administration at all times. When someone needs admonishment or correction, do it in the privacy of the boardroom.
• Recognize the administrator as an ex officio member of all committees of the board and include him or her in all meetings, executive or regular, the only exception being the duly called meeting to evaluate the administrator.
• Have reasonable expectations of the administrator's workload in order to be sure his or her home and church life do not suffer because of the school.

Who, then, is in charge of the school? This question does not challenge the legal and ultimate authority of the board. It simply asks, Who runs the school? Who makes the daily decisions about curriculum, textbooks, grading practices, conduct, discipline, and dress codes, and makes the myriad of other decisions often questioned by students and parents? Parents often seek out board members, assuming the board makes every decision, or perhaps hoping the board will reverse administrative decisions.

The answer should be clear. The school board hires a competent educator qualified by training and experience to direct the school. This director, holding the title administrator, superintendent, headmaster, or principal, is expected to function prudently, ethically, safely, and lawfully. He does not violate guidelines and boundaries set by the board in written policies. He strives to achieve what the board wants achieved and to avoid what the board wants avoided.

This scenario does not in any way imply that the administrator does not answer to the board. The board monitors all school programs and services, and annually evaluates the administrator. However, the board avoids tightly controlling or second-guessing administrative decisions. The board always has the option of writing more specific policies, but it should do so only in extreme situations.

The board sets the course for the school through its statements of mission, vision, values, and goals. These issues concern ends, not means. The administrator develops the means, the plan to achieve the objectives of the board.

Christian school administrators have been called by God to serve as spiritual and academic leaders of our schools. Several qualities mark them:

- They pursue this calling passionately.
  Whatever you do, do your work heartily, as for the Lord rather than for men (Colossians 3:23, NASB).
- They never stop teaching.
  And the things which you have heard from me … these entrust to faithful men, who will be able to teach others also (2 Timothy 2:2, NASB).
- They submit joyfully and humbly to the authority of the board.
  Obey your leaders, and submit to them; for they keep watch over your souls, as those who will give an account. Let them do this with joy and not with grief, for this would be unprofitable for you (Hebrews 13:17, NASB).
- They serve in humility and love.
  [M]ake my joy complete by being of the same mind, maintaining the same love, united in spirit, intent on one purpose. Do nothing from selfishness or empty conceit, but with humility of mind let each of you regard one another as more important than himself; do not merely look out for your own personal interests, but also for the interests of others (Philippians 2:2–4, NASB).
- They depend completely upon the Lord as their source of strength and wisdom.
  "My grace is sufficient for you, for power is perfected in weakness." Most gladly, therefore, I will rather boast about my weaknesses, that the power of Christ may dwell in me (2 Corinthians 12:9, NASB).
  And if, in the process, any of you does not know how to meet any

particular problem he has only to ask God—who gives generously to all men without making them feel foolish or guilty—and he may be quite sure that the necessary wisdom will be given him (James 1:5, Phillips).

- They do not give up.

...since God in his mercy has given us this wonderful ministry, we never give up.... We are pressed on every side by troubles, but we are not crushed and broken. We are perplexed, but we don't give up and quit. We are hunted down, but God never abandons us. We get knocked down, but we get up again and keep going (2 Corinthians 4:1, 8, 9, NLT).

For I am confident of this very thing, that He who began a good work in you will perfect it until the day of Christ Jesus (Philippians 1:6, NASB).

- They must not seek popularity—not simply do the expedient, but do what is right.

Obviously, I'm not trying to be a people pleaser! No, I am trying to please God. If I were still trying to please people, I would not be Christ's servant (Galatians 1:10, NLT).

Our purpose is to please God, not people. He is the one who examines the motives of our hearts (1 Thessalonians 2:4, NLT).

- They must lead with consistency and integrity.

"But let your statement be, 'Yes, yes' or 'No, no'; and anything beyond these is of evil" (Matthew 5:37, NASB).

They can't make up their minds. They waver back and forth in every-thing they do (James 1:8, NLT).

- They must honor and glorify the Lord passionately.

Whether, then, you eat or drink or whatever you do, do all to the glory of God (1 Corinthians 10:31, NASB).

Who Is in Charge? You Are and *He* Is!

He promises, *"Never will I leave you; never will I forsake you"* (Hebrews 13:5b). He commands, *"[A]bide in My love"* (John 15:9, NASB). We respond, *"And let us not lose heart in doing good, for in due time we shall reap if we do not grow weary"* (Galatians 6:9, NASB).

Bibliography

Andringa, R. C., & Engstrom, T. W. (1997). Nonprofit board answer book. Washington: National Center for Nonprofit Boards.

Baldwin, R. P., & Hughes, J. T. (1995). Boards at their best: A new approach toward improved board effectiveness. Danbury, CT: Connolly-Cormack.

Carver, J. (1997). Boards that make a difference: A new design for leadership in nonprofit and public organizations. San Francisco: Jossey-Bass.

Carver, J., & Mayhew Carver, M. (1997). Reinventing your board. San Francisco: Jossey-Bass.

Chait, R. P., Holland, T. P., & Taylor, B. E. (1991). The effective board of trustees. New York: Macmillan.

Cubberley, E. P. (1925). An introduction to the study of education and to teaching. Boston: Houghton Mifflin.

DeKuyper, M. H. (1998). Trustee handbook: A guide to effective governance for independent school boards. Washington: National Association of Independent Schools.

Drucker, P. F. (1990). Managing the non-profit organization. New York: HarperCollins.

Graybeal, P. (2001). There is hope for boards. Greenville: Graybeal & Associates.

Hendrix, O. (2000). Three dimensions of leadership. St. Charles, IL: ChurchSmart Resources.

Hughes, S. R., Lakey, B.M., & Bobowick, M. J. (2000). The board building cycle: Nine steps to finding, recruiting, and engaging nonprofit board members. Washington: National Center for Nonprofit Boards.

Independent School Management. (1991). How to lead your school through hard times (and other times): A primer for trustees and heads. Wilmington, DE: Independent School Management.

Independent School Management. (1992). How to put your board together in ways that make sense: The ISM trustee guidebook. Wilmington, DE: Independent School Management.

Lowrie, R. W. Jr. (Ed.). (1984). Administration of the Christian school. Colorado Springs: Association of Christian Schools International.

Lowrie, R. W. Jr. (1998). Serving God on the Christian school board. Colorado Springs: Association of Christian Schools International.

Moore, A. (2000, November). Make those parent board members the asset they can be. Inside private school management.

Perry, H. (1990). The board. Owen Sound, Ontario, Canada: Big Bay.

Rosenberger, M. K. (1997). Team leadership: School boards at work. Lancaster, PA: Technomic.

Stoesz, E. (2000). Common sense for board members. Intercourse, PA: Good Books.

Stoesz, E., & Raber, C. (1994). Doing good better! Intercourse, PA: Good Books.

TEA expert faults trustees' behavior. (1999, March 6). The Dallas Morning News.

Vander Ark, D. (speaker). (1995). Holding Christian schools in trust [film]. Grand Rapids, MI: Christian Schools International.

Subscription Newsletters

(Newsletters that deal specifically with nonprofit board issues)

Board Leadership. San Francisco, CA: Jossey-Bass. Bimonthly newsletter with John Carver serving as executive editor.

Board Member. Washington, DC: Newsletter published by the National Center for Nonprofit Boards.

Boardwise. Seattle, WA: Bimonthly newsletter published in cooperation with the Christian Stewardship Association.

Ideas & Perspectives. Wilmington, DE: Newsletter published for the membership of Independent School Management.

IFCSB BoardTalk. Colorado Springs, CO: Newsletter published by the Association of Christian Schools International for the membership of the International Fellowship of Christian School Boards.

Inside Private School Management. Frederick, MD: Newsletter published by Aspen Publishers, Inc.

To the Point: Practical Strategies for Private School Leaders. Wilmington, DE: Newsletter published for the membership of Independent School Management.

Other Resources

NCNB Governance Series (Booklets 1–10). Washington, DC: National Center for Nonprofit Boards.

1. Richard T. Ingram. *Ten Basic Responsibilities of Nonprofit Boards.* 1996.

2. Maureen Robinson. *The Chief Executive's Role in Developing the Board.* 1998.

3. Karen Simmons and Gary J. Stern. *Creating Strong Board-Staff Partnerships.* 1999.

4. Ellen Cochran Hirzy. *The Chair's Role in Leading the Nonprofit Board.* 1998.

5. Richard P. Chait. *How to Help Your Board Govern More and Manage Less.* 1994.

6. Kay Sprinkel Grace. *The Board's Role in Strategic Planning.* 1996.

7. Andrew S. Lang. *Financial Responsibilities of the Nonprofit Board.* 1998.

8. John Paul Dalsimer. *Understanding Nonprofit Financial Statements.* 1996.

9. Fisher Howe. *Fund-Raising and the Nonprofit Board Member.* 1998.

10. Peter Szanton. *Evaluation and the Nonprofit Board.* 1998.

Managing Mountains
and Molehills
Developing Executive Skills

Kenneth O. Gangel, Ph.D. and April L. Moreton, Ph.D.

Chapter Summary

Can my life get any busier? you ask. Every day, every week, the demands seem to increase without a commensurate addition of time. What can you do, as someone new to school administration or as a veteran to the field, to maximize your effectiveness as a leader? How can you make the best use of the available time, energy, and resources? The key is to develop the necessary skills and to cultivate the right practices.

Drs. Gangel and Moreton, while not offering a quick-fix formula for success, describe the characteristics of the Christian school leader and then delineate in practical terms the skills a person must develop in order to succeed in that role. In addition, they identify specific ways to endure as a leader in the face of long hours, tough decisions, and difficult people.

About the authors

Kenneth O. Gangel, Ph.D.
Distinguished Professor Emeritus, Dallas Seminary
Dallas, TX
41 years of educational leadership experience

April L. Moreton, Ph.D.
Research Director, Christian Education Leadership, Inc.
Toccoa Falls, GA
10 years of educational leadership experience

Chapter 3

Managing Mountains and Molehills
Developing Executive Skills

Kenneth O. Gangel, Ph.D. and April L. Moreton, Ph.D.

H ave you noticed lately the busyness of most people? On our morning and evening commutes through Dallas for many years, we were often amazed at the speed of others around us. Some scurry between lanes, cutting between drivers, pushing the limits of the law. What do they hope to gain? Is their goal an extra minute on their arrival time? As we ponder their actions, we wonder what drives them to rush. Maybe they have too many responsibilities packed into an eight-, nine-, or ten-hour day and can't accomplish what's expected of them. Or perhaps they do not utilize their time wisely and effectively.

Solomon reminds us that there is nothing new under the sun. We live busy lives, striving to manage our personal growth, homes, ministries, and contributions to our community. Even in our postmodern, technology-infused society, nothing seems new. We have greater capabilities to communicate with others around the world, and we have greater access to information, but do these changes help our management and administrative skills in our respective leadership callings?

In this chapter, we will examine the administrative skills necessary for effective Christian school administrators today, and discuss ways to attain those skills. First, we must define biblically the role and character of a leader.

Defining the Christian Leader

Christian leaders have a divine appointment, specified and entrusted by God, to live out their roles cautiously and graciously. Their abilities as leaders develop over time, constantly refined through spiritual growth and practical experience. Ideally, the Christian leader functions within her spiritual gifts. If her gift is mercy, she leads with mercy. If his gift is administration, he undoubtedly utilizes organizational scenarios to lead those around him.

Eugene Habecker reminds us that Christian leaders are called of God. However, this calling is not a supernatural appointment in which we have little responsibility. Rather, leaders must know for certain that their assignment comes from God, or that "God is in it" (1996). All of us can reduce much tension and conflict if we view our leadership positions from that perspective and intently evaluate before the Lord our opportunities.

Leaders are made, not born. Ultimately, Christ represents the greatest example of biblical leadership, and the New Testament offers countless examples of His leadership style. In 1 Timothy 3, Paul's instruction to Timothy includes the basics for Christian leadership:

- Above reproach and respectable
- Temperate and self-controlled
- Hospitable
- Able to teach and teachable
- Not given to much wine
- Not violent but gentle, not quarrelsome
- Effective family managers with believing children
- Not a lover of money
- Not a recent convert

In addition to the foundational qualities of biblical leadership, those called to lead should envision their school's future clearly. They should be visionaries. In *The Leader of the Future*, Alfred C. Decrane Jr. defines the role of a visionary as someone "who can spark the imagination with a compelling vision of a worthwhile end that stretches us beyond what is known today, and who can translate that to clear objectives…." (Decrane, 1996).

Having "too many chiefs and not enough Indians" plagues Christian schools as much as it does other organizations. Before we can lead effectively, we must be effective followers. Jesus and the disciples illustrate this point perfectly. The Twelve spent much time learning from and observing Jesus' leadership. Not only did they see His teaching and management style, they also observed His anger in the Temple, His compassion and grief over Lazarus, and His grace with Zacchaeus. When their appointed time arrived, the Apostles stepped forward to assume their leadership roles.

Sometimes leaders must reassume a followership role. Our submission to God the Father offers the most obvious example of followership. All Christians must assume this role, regardless of their earthly titles. In the context of team leadership, we may also find ourselves following the leadership of our teams—either by embracing their ideas or decentralizing our own responsibilities. Followership also communicates to a team that their leader does not consider himself above them in any sense, but rather a fellow servant striving for the same goals. Christ reminded the disciples of this important aspect when the group disputed who would be the greatest among them (Luke 22:24).

Godly administrators function as servant-leaders. They serve followers as well as other leaders. This characteristic in no way undermines our authority or God-given responsibility to accomplish tasks assigned to us, but it establishes the required biblical context of leadership. Authoritarian and free-rein leadership often contradict the scriptural model. The former oppresses the team, while the latter often provides too little stability. Servant leadership lies in between. It results in a person demonstrating a commitment to a New Testament approach to team leadership, working alongside team members, providing vision, and encouraging and admonishing others.

Distinguishing Between Administration and Leadership

What differences exist between administrators and leaders? Are these roles synonymous, or do they differ slightly? Again, Scripture may shed light on these questions.

Administration

Paul identifies administration as a spiritual gift in 1 Corinthians 12:28. Old Testament passages, such as Ezekiel 27:8, describe an administrator as a helmsman—one who steers a ship. Society views administrators as the paper pushers of an organization and often refers to them as managers of both tasks and people.

Leadership

Leadership, on the other hand, implies a visionary appointment—one that focuses the school's mission and motivates others to help cast the vision. A leader's role is visible, relational, motivational, and achievement orientated. He makes the decisions that propel the vision; he perseveres in order to achieve the goals. In Romans 12:8, Paul specifies that leaders should lead or govern diligently.

Relationship Between Administration and Leadership

Many argue that administrators lead, but do leaders administer? Both make decisions and have responsibilities for tasks and people. Thus, both require similar characteristics in order to function effectively. In government or industry, the differences would draw attention; ministry requires both administration and leadership.

Educational leaders must have the ability to *organize tasks and people* in an efficient manner. Without organization, your team lacks boundaries in which to perform. We utilize the tasks of administration to organize school priorities and to communicate those priorities to our team members. These skills may be as simple as keeping your calendar up-to-date, or as complex as designing a ten-year strategic plan for your school. Effective educational leadership begins with organization.

But leadership also focuses on *vision and human resources*. Without teamwork, achieving our educational goals often becomes drudgery. Good administrators use their administrative abilities to organize faculty and staff according to individual gifts. They recognize the personalities, competencies, and giftedness of those around them and strategically place each person in task areas that propel the organization toward its goal. When we handle this strategy wisely, team members feel a sense of ownership for the school and its vision—a necessary attitude. Gifford Pinchot, in *The Leader of the Future*, said it well: "If people feel part of the corporate community, if they feel safe and cared for, if they are passionate about the mission and values and believe that others are living by them, they will generally give good service to the whole" (Pinchot, 1996).

Describing Leadership Skills

Day to day, we all face a myriad of tasks. This reality often forces us to function in a crisis management mode, weaving and dodging through the traffic of obligations, barely avoiding a collision. We've already discussed a few of these obligations: organizing, developing and utilizing human resources well, and pursuing a vision. Each consists of finite and specific tasks necessary to accomplish the goals of the school. We've met administrators who doubt they can avoid crisis management by carrying out their duties in an efficient and effective manner. They struggle to match obligations with skills. We have no secret formulas to cure this pandemic disease, but the remaining portion of this chapter will focus on these specific tasks and suggest ways to develop them fully.

Developing and Following a Clear Mission Statement

A clear mission statement makes possible the achieving of goals in an organization. The mission statement functions as the standard by which all goals, tasks, and decisions proceed. Obviously, without a clear mission statement, Christian schools struggle.

Establishing a clear mission statement for an organization often begins with the leader's personal mission statement—your life purpose statement. Developing your mission statement takes time, thought, evaluation, and godly counsel. However, the investment pays handsome dividends. A personal mission statement can serve to direct decisions throughout your ministry.

How can a busy administrator develop a personal mission statement? We suggest the process begin with consistent prayer followed by in-depth soul-searching. It might help to identify your past roles or tasks that you felt uniquely qualified to fulfill and found great pleasure in doing. In other words, what situations "made you tick"? Consider every experience possible, not just those that earned a paycheck. Second, identify from successful and enjoyable situations the gifts that you utilized. These scenarios and gifts may point you to the mission God has uniquely called you to fulfill. At this point, gathering opinions from those who know you well and who have your best interest at heart may confirm that you're on the right track. Finally, identify the necessary steps or objectives to realize your calling. This process will project you to the desired outcomes that God has placed on you.

If constantly evaluated and followed, a personal mission statement assures that a leader assumes only those responsibilities or roles that fit within her mission statement. In many ways, it simplifies life by removing distractions and providing focus.

What benefits the leader usually benefits the organization. We cannot overemphasize that a clear mission statement is vital to the life of an organization. Without it, a school may fall into the trap of trying to become all things to all people. Yes, developing a clear mission statement can be a tedious and time-consuming task. Utilizing team members and stakeholders in the organization for ideas and purpose aids the process. In an effort to create a clear mission statement, team members should ask themselves why the school exists. Is it intended to educate students in a Christian worldview? Is the goal to evangelize unsaved children? Remember, the school's *original* intent helps define its *current* mission statement. Keep in mind that mission precedes and differs from vision in any organization.

Mentoring and Modeling

Investing in future leaders is one of the most visible and satisfying activities a school administrator does. Leaders cannot function without relationship, and mentoring may be one of the most important roles of a leader. Whether we mentor one-on-one or through large groups, we cannot avoid the visibility attached to our positions. Again, Jesus gives us the greatest example. The time He spent with His disciples proved invaluable in the success of their future ministries. We have both experienced the benefits of caring, committed, and confident mentors over the years; their involvement in our lives served to mold us in ways we never dreamed possible.

In a Christian school, effective mentoring benefits the mentor and the protégé. Investing in another lightens the task load of the leader. Likewise, the protégé benefits from exposure to the leader's tasks and responsibilities. Through appropriate modeling of skills, effective leaders provide important insight into leadership style and administrative process.

A good leader constantly works herself out of a job—training and mentoring others so that when she moves on to her next position or role, the school continues to thrive without her. But don't forget that mentoring has its downside for leaders. Investing in another and delegating tasks is time-consuming and risky. Many leaders find they do not have the time to think through a mentoring relationship, or they consider it less than beneficial for those they mentor. Some misunderstand their role as mentors and simply delegate mundane tasks without thought or purpose. When that happens, mentoring no longer benefits the protégé. Mentoring takes a great deal of energy on the part of the mentor but, if performed correctly, benefits both parties greatly.

Empowering Others

Empowering others begins with relating to them effectively. How you treat your faculty and staff correlates with the level at which those individuals perform their tasks. When leaders dictate tasks without genuine concern, team members eventually view themselves as mere tools in the leader's quest for accomplishment. In other words, *if a leader values what another can do for him instead of the person himself, disheartenment will surely follow.*

We have the opportunity to create community within our teams. Engaging in nonwork-related activities and conversations fosters a sense of belonging and importance on the part of our people. A teacher who feels valued willingly commits wholeheartedly to the mission (and usually to its leader).

Also, *empowering others requires that you release motivation.* Constantly reviewing the mission statement and objectives with team members keeps them abreast of the school's goals. It also promotes ownership. Motivating others is hard work. The administrator who knows her faculty and staff personally can distinguish how she can motivate them. You may choose from a myriad of personality inventories or assessments to aid in this process. For instance, many organizations employ inventories like the *Myers-Briggs* for new staff members. With the resulting information, they can place people in roles God uniquely wired them to fulfill. *Leaders empower others through empowerment.*

Jethro's counsel to Moses in Exodus 18 lays the biblical foundation for appropriate and necessary delegation. In leading God's people, Moses suffered near burnout until he decentralized his leadership and allowed capable men the opportunity to lead smaller groups of people within the nation. It's obvious that empowerment benefits the leader as well as the team member. In school administration, delegation is an absolute necessity because of the myriad of tasks we face on a regular basis. Giving others the opportunity to own responsibilities and outcomes assists in our mentoring and training of team members.

Given this reality, however, you should not delegate *responsibility without authority* to team members. People qualified for their tasks should be given the authority to make decisions within the boundaries of those tasks. If you cannot grant authority for some reason, you may choose to delay delegation. For example, if the team member does not have the maturity, experience, or rank suitable for a particular responsibility, you should not delegate that responsibility to him. Effective administrators must recognize those tasks that only they themselves can fulfill. Highly confidential issues within the organization may fall into this category. Remember too that tasks not under your direct responsibility should not be delegated to team members.

Finally, *leaders empower others by providing them with detailed job descriptions*. Detail specific activities and reachable objectives. Job descriptions direct the team's activities and help organize the leader's agenda. Without them, team members face uncertain expectations from others and must endure performance evaluations without a reasonable benchmark.

Foundational work for developing job descriptions includes understanding how faculty and staff roles support or define the school's mission and identifying those tasks necessary to fulfill those roles. On a personal level, you should know the team member's personality and giftedness so that her job description includes activities and objectives for which she is suited. For example, an introverted person highly skilled in computer technology might not perform well in a job that includes a lot of social interaction on behalf of the institution.

An effective job description also includes an organizational chart clearly identifying where everyone fits in the team and clearly delineating to whom and for whom each person holds responsibility. Furthermore, team members should ideally answer to one leader, avoiding confusion and possible frustration. *The most effective faculty and staff work within their giftedness as it contributes to the mission of the organization.*

Conflict Management

Regardless of the work environment—whether positive or negative, Christian or non-Christian—conflict between people will arise. Veteran administrators find both privilege and responsibility in minimizing and resolving school conflicts. However, handling conflict appropriately isn't easy. We balance many factors in the process.

Conflict, in and of itself, is not necessarily negative. In other words, organizations and leaders should not try too hard to avoid conflict. Since most school teams include both veterans and rookies, conflict may arise when the latter instigate change. Like conflict, change is not inherently negative, but it can be difficult for the problem solver, not just for those having the conflict. Including and valuing all stakeholders carefully, a good administrator must focus the entire team on the mission of the school. She must engage those involved in conflict and utilize mature listening skills in order to hear each member's concern.

April Moreton learned one of the best examples of conflict management while she served in a Christian organization early in her adult life. The staff were taught to *keep short accounts* with others. Keeping short accounts meant that the sun did not set on their anger, a scriptural lesson they already knew. If conflict existed between them, they immediately addressed and resolved it to the best of their ability. Negotiation, diplomacy, and compromise play key roles in maintaining positive working relationships. Educational leaders must be willing to confront others, and appropriate confrontation is a skill absolutely necessary to the leadership process. We must address problems quickly and lovingly.

At times, conflict arises out of expectations in a Christian school environment. We forget that Christian organizations consist of redeemed yet sinful individuals. Our expectations get the best of us: "We shouldn't have conflict if we're Christians" or "He shouldn't act that way because he's a believer." *As a leader, it's your job to recognize when expectations (real or imagined) create problems for those around you.* Your entire staff needs to remember that we live in a fallen world and that we often act in ways that reflect that status.

Although administrators may utilize confrontation, negotiation, diplomacy, and compromise to maintain short accounts, sometimes such strategies are ineffective. Face it: even difficult people work in Christian schools. They may be passive-aggressive, appearing agreeable on the outside but undermining affairs on the inside; they may be shouters, unable to control their emotions during tense moments; they may be pouters, withdrawing when their ideas or positions seem threatened; or they may be nitpickers, constantly complaining about anything and everything.

How do you handle these types effectively? First, we suggest *prayer*—much prayer! A discerning leader bathes all relationships with consistent prayer, especially the most difficult ones. Second, an effective leader will take the necessary *time to evaluate any underlying issues* that drive difficult persons. Why does team member A always respond negatively to new ideas or responsibilities? Why does team member B complain about other members? Getting to the heart of the matter gives us wisdom in dealing with conflict.

But we bring bad news as well. Despite prayer, understanding, and confrontation, we will not resolve all conflicts to our satisfaction. At such difficult junctures, good leaders are forced to weigh the troublemaker's role in the organization and act accordingly. However, difficult people, as well as all team members, must be handled graciously and lovingly.

Critical Thinking and Creativity

At a large university, a professor surveyed doctoral students regarding their opinion of the most important daily task of any educator. *Teaching students to think critically surfaced as the unanimous choice!* Teaching others to think critically means that we must think critically as well. What role does critical thinking play in educational leadership?

Suffice it to say that good decisions require in-depth critical thinking. Before a leader can make the often difficult decisions required of him, he must have the ability to formulate the problem in his mind, view it from different angles, and apply logic, knowledge, and current information in order to reach a wise decision. Many leaders make decisions off-the-cuff, relying on their intuition or experience. However, leadership is not stagnant. This fact has never been more evident than in our fast-paced, high-tech society. Today's decisions require that we consider more information and options than we did in the past.

For instance, an administrator might face the dilemma of controlling inappropriate material on the Web for students utilizing school computers. Or he might be forced to explain the effects of postmodernism to high school students who rely on relativism for personal ethics (see chapter 12). Both situations arise from today's society and require critical thinking to provide effective leadership.

Creativity forms an important component in critical thinking. "Thinking outside the box" has been a buzz phrase in the business world for many years. It becomes an important consideration for Christian school leaders as well. Given the current rate of societal change, thinking creatively as well as critically requires that we explore problems from every angle. At times, pulling from the decisions or procedures of others such as sister institutions and other leaders in the field proves highly effective. However, when traditional methods do not work for your school, you must rely on experience, problem-solving ability, and creatively instigated change.

We hasten to add one point to this discussion: *Critical and creative thinking must remain faithful to Scripture.* Decisions made outside God's revealed will, regardless of their pragmatic effectiveness, are never acceptable in a Christian school. Effective leaders must remain committed to prayer and dependent on the Holy Spirit during tough decision-making episodes.

Strategic Planning

The difference between effective and ineffective leadership often evidences itself through goal achievement. A competent leader somehow manages to meet deadlines and objectives, while an ineffective leader struggles to manage crises as they arise. Though a leader may fall short in achieving goals for many reasons, one of the most obvious pertains to lack of planning. Many busy administrators feel they do not have time to plan. They fail to realize that their lack of planning actually robs them of time. For example, if a leader schedules meetings back-to-back without evaluation and organization time in between, she may spend more time at the end of the week reviewing each meeting, poring over minutes, or contacting colleagues for clarification of information. Simply scheduling meetings with thirty to sixty minutes in between allows for reflection and regrouping.

Not only is planning essential for daily and weekly activities, but it sustains the long-term mission of an organization. Strategic planning, in most leaders' job descriptions, appears at the top of the priority list. In order to plan effectively, try employing the following steps: *reflect, review, revisit, and relate.*

1. Reflect on the past and present state of the school. What qualities characterize your school? Has it faced financial difficulty in the past? Does it currently operate in the red? Knowing the status of the organization allows any leader to plan more effectively for long-term goals.
2. Review all the information relative to the organization, including past records, minutes, written histories, and the like. Sometimes, interviewing long-term staff or board members and stakeholders may fill in the gaps. By gathering and organizing information, you can see the "big picture" of the school, past and present, and you will gain an advantage in formulating its future.
3. Revisit the mission statement, objectives, and vision. The organization's mission reflects God's purpose, and likewise, long-term planning should reflect the organization's vision. Keep in mind that mission statements are not necessarily absolute. They need periodic evaluation and even revision as the culture of the school or its constituencies change.
4. Relate strategic planning and its objectives to team members. Properly communicating and delegating key components of the plan to board, faculty, staff, parents, and alumni assures that each stakeholder embraces the vision of the school and works toward its goals.

Organizing and Prioritizing

Someone once said that if you don't control your schedule, someone else will. Unfortunately, this illness has invaded too many administrators. Leaders face direction and pressure from board or church members, faculty, staff, students, parents, and family. Establishing priorities and organizing your calendar according to your personal and organizational mission statements provide protection from the tyranny of the urgent and from crisis management. We won't tell you it's easy; we'll just say it's crucial.

Foremost, you must manage your time well. This process includes many of the skills we've already mentioned, particularly empowering others and establishing clear job descriptions.

Others have taken control of your day when you must focus on strategic planning, which requires a great deal of thinking, and yet you face constant interruptions by unscheduled guests, phone calls, and correspondence. In an effort to curb distractions, leaders must learn to say no to those activities not related to their personal or organizational mission statements.

As leaders, we face many tempting ministry opportunities every day; however, if these activities keep us from our objectives, we may need to avoid them. The first step in managing your time requires you to *identify those activities for which you are directly responsible*. Doing so automatically determines your priorities. Once you've established your priorities, then plan your day, week, or month so that you allot time for each priority. For instance, if training a leadership team for a forthcoming event necessitates thinking time on your part, add a block of several uninterrupted hours to your calendar. If you have a secretary, ask him or her to protect your scheduled uninterrupted time.

It has never been easier to manage calendars than with the recent invention of Palm Handhelds. These handy instruments allow you to schedule appointments, take notes, check email, and complete many other tasks by using a small pocket-size component. Today, many organizations provide employees with Palm Handhelds to enable them to disseminate information and communicate efficiently with one another.

Depending on the size of your school, you may need to enlist an administrative assistant or secretary to handle your correspondence, which includes electronic mail. We are quickly becoming a paperless society. Our in-boxes now appear on our computer screens instead of in the administration office. If someone can run interference with daily email, your workload may be much smaller. However, if you do not have the personnel for this task or prefer to handle your email yourself, several steps may reduce the amount of time spent on this area. For starters, make a schoolwide commitment to minimize personal email while at work. Catching up with a dear aunt on the West Coast, while important, will distract faculty and staff from thinking clearly about other tasks at hand.

We all know that electronic junk mail increases with the number of websites you visit. For instance, if you order an item on-line, you may not be aware of tiny boxes at the bottom of your order form, prechecked to send you news of forthcoming sales or events. Watch out for these tricky little tools. Some websites have the capability, through the use of "cookies," to track your Internet use and even maintain your email address. You need all the protection you can muster.

What, then, is the best solution for these time-wasters? The delete key! Don't even open them. On the other hand, managing important email for quick retrieval and reference may also reduce inefficient use of time. Most email packages include handy organizational tools similar to a standard filing cabinet. Label these electronic filing cabinets and use them on a regular basis. Your goal should be to leave the office each day with an empty in-box. We're serious! Periodically, take a moment to transfer the most important files to permanent storage via floppy disc or CD.

Learning to use technology effectively requires time. Without it, technology becomes a time-waster rather than a time-saver. Computer classes and technology vendors offer brief to comprehensive training on the latest developments in the field. And every school has at least one "techie" to help you learn what you need to know.

An organized and comfortable work environment, conducive to periods of study as well as meetings with team members, aids the leader in time management as well. Constantly working in clutter or in an environment where you cannot readily locate needed materials creates poor time management.

As is the case with many time management tools, organizing a work environment takes time and forethought. If you do not organize well, enlist another person to help you. He or she can suggest creative ways to label and store files, organize supplies, arrange furniture, and manage your work space. Once the area is organized, maintenance becomes vital! Just as you leave your in-box empty at the end of your day, leaving your office primed and ready for the next workday keeps you on track. Spending the last fifteen minutes of each day storing files and other items ensures that clutter remains minimal. This scenario is not hopeless idealism—we both practice it regularly.

Perseverance

When considering the wide range of responsibilities, commitments, and struggles of leadership, you may ask how a leader endures over time. Realistically, who wants to spend long hours on the job, dealing with difficult decisions and pesky people? Enduring leaders revisit their personal mission statements and calling at times like these. *Maintaining a commitment to the school until their work is complete separates strong leaders from those influenced by panic, unresolved conflict, or lack of vision.*

Practically speaking, certain disciplines aid a leader's ability to persevere. The most obvious one that comes to mind involves time off—time away from the school for relaxation, rejuvenation, and recreation. Many leaders fail to correlate their job performance with their lack of personal time away from the office. Protecting time off on a weekly basis as well as extended time on a yearly basis pays dividends to our performance in ministry and leadership. Those of us with families must acknowledge their need for quality time as well. Successful ministry includes a well-balanced family.

Support from "safe" people aids in long-term commitment to leadership and to the organization. Counsel and fellowship with colleagues outside your school provides a safe haven to refresh yourself and gain the necessary encouragement to continue the race. Moreton likes to tell about a mountain climbing excursion she and her husband embarked on several years ago. "Early in our trip to Colorado, we chose a 14,000-foot peak to conquer. Initially, we were excited as we approached the trailhead and began our trek to the summit. As the hours flew by and our legs and lungs ached from the stress, we began to lose our enthusiasm. However, we reached the summit after many short breaks for rest, lots of encouraging words to each other, and a determination to reach our goal. Standing on the summit as we overlooked God's creation and experienced a mission accomplished, we felt the hike was well worth the effort."

Such is the satisfaction of a leader who endures. With careful planning, forethought, delegation, and much prayer, you can be a leader who manages both mountains and molehills.

Bibliography

Barna, G. (Ed.). (1997). *Leaders on leadership*. Ventura, CA: Regal Books.

Decrane, A.C. Jr. (1996). A constitutional model of leadership. In F. Hesselbein, M. Goldsmith, & R. Beckhard (Eds.), *The leader of the future*. San Francisco: Jossey-Bass.

Eims, L. (1996). *Be the leader you were meant to be*. Wheaton, IL: Victor Books.

Gangel, K. O. (1997). *Team leadership in Christian ministry*. Chicago: Moody Press.

Gangel, K. O. (2000). *Coaching ministry teams*. Nashville: Word.

Habecker, E. B. (1996). *Rediscovering the soul of leadership*. Wheaton, IL: Victor Books.

MacKenzie, A. (1972). *The time trap*. New York: McGraw-Hill.

Pinchot, G. (1996). Creating organizations with many leaders. In F. Hesselbein, M. Goldsmith, & R. Beckhard (Eds.), *The leader of the future*. San Francisco: Jossey-Bass.

The Captain and the Crew
Building an Administrative Team

Peter W. Teague, Ed.D.

Chapter Summary

Successful team building in your school may make the difference between an excellent school and a mediocre one, between achieving your goals and not achieving them. Whether the team is made up of administrators, teachers, or volunteers, their ability to work together toward a common goal is crucial to accomplishing your school's mission.

With nearly thirty years of leadership experience, Dr. Teague articulates easy-to-apply principles for establishing leadership teams in your school, and he provides guidelines for the way they function. The chapter carefully defines the role of the head-of-school, both as a member of the administrative team and as the leader of the school.

About the author

Peter W. Teague, Ed.D.
President, Lancaster Bible College
Lancaster, PA
29 years of educational leadership experience

Chapter 4

The Captain and the Crew
Building an Administrative Team

Peter W. Teague, Ed.D.

S uccessful team leaders always remember that each person on the team has a role to play, and every role contributes to the big picture. They continually keep the mission and vision of the organization before themselves and their team members.

In *The 17 Indisputable Laws of Teamwork*, John Maxwell offers Winston Churchill as an outstanding example:

> It's said that during World War II when Britain was experiencing its darkest days, the country had a difficult time keeping men working in the coal mines. Many wanted to give up their dirty, thankless jobs in the dangerous mines to join military service, which garnered much public praise and support. Yet their work in the mines was critical to the success of the war. Without coal the military and the people at home would be in trouble.

> So the prime minister faced thousands of coal miners one day and told them of their importance to the war effort, how their role could make or break the goal of maintaining England's freedom.

> Churchill painted a picture of what it would be like when the war ended, of the grand parade that would honor the people who fought the war. First would come the sailors of the Navy, he said, the people who continued the tradition of Trafalgar and the defeat of the

Spanish Armada. Next would come the best and brightest of Britain, the pilots of the Royal Air Force who fended off the German Luftwaffe. Following them would be the soldiers who had fought at Dunkirk.

Then last of all would come the coal dust–covered men in miners' caps. And Churchill indicated that someone from the crowd might say, "And where were you during the critical days of the struggle?" And the voices of ten thousand men would respond, "We were deep in the earth with our faces to the coal."

It's said that tears appeared in the eyes of those hardened men. And they returned to their inglorious work with steely resolve, having been reminded of the role they were playing in their country's noble goal of preserving freedom for the Western world. (Maxwell, 2001)

Churchill's mind-set was precisely the kind required to build a team—dogged determination and resolve. But team building takes time. Teams do not emerge overnight. Successful administrators foster a team mind-set in others by modeling a willingness to look at the big picture.

The Administrative Team Defined

As leaders think together on this vital subject, defining terms is foundational to the process. The term "administrative" is derived from the Greek word *kubernetes*, meaning "to steer or pilot," or perhaps "to guide, govern, or master." Only three uses of the term appear in the New Testament. Once the term relates to a ship's helmsman or master (Acts 27:11); once to a ship-master (Revelation 18:17); and once to church government (1 Corinthians 12:28). In common usage, the word means "to manage or direct the affairs of a given institution."

The word "team" refers to "a number of people working or acting together, especially one of the sides in a game" (*World Book Dictionary*, 1992). An "administrative team," then, is a group of people brought together to manage or direct the affairs of a given institution or organization. However, this simple definition does not adequately portray the depth of meaning associated with the administrative team concept; leaders do more than direct the affairs of a school. The concept also includes how leaders implement that direction. In other words, it encompasses both form and process.

The administrative team concept requires that all members of a leadership group be of one accord. Wearing multiple hats for various responsibilities, superintendents or principals must lead the team yet be fully functioning members of it. The leadership team in any school must understand and embody a variety of administrative concepts. These concepts include:

1. The role of the chief administrator as school head and leader of the leadership team

2. The clarity of institutional goals and objectives
3. The clarification and coordination of individual and group roles
4. The delegation of authority and responsibility
5. The division of tasks
6. The standardization of procedures
7. The span of control
8. The stability of policies and programs
9. The flexibility of policies and programs
10. The security of individual institutional members
11. The development of proper personnel policies
12. The provision of evaluative procedures for individual and group actions with appropriate corrective measures and professional growth plans

The administrative team concept envisions a school head who surrounds himself or herself with competent people who have diverse abilities and the confidence of not only the principal but every member of the team. The team members must complement one another as they share openly and act unitedly, yet still maintain their individual integrity and uniqueness. And most importantly, their first commitment must be to the Lord Jesus.

Developing the Team

Several important considerations should arise when Christian school leaders select qualified people for a teamwork assignment. These leaders must carefully analyze the job requirements before beginning the selection process. They must probe for objective evidence of an applicant's skill, knowledge, successes and failures, dependability, attitude toward work, and response to supervision. A potential member of the team must understand the job requirements and the expected standards of performance. Everyone should assume a role that is likely to result in individual success.

Once they select an administrative team, leaders must focus on training and retaining the members. This process involves hard and deliberate work, but it is worth all the necessary effort. Christian school leadership is not for the emotionally, mentally, or spiritually immature. It requires well-adjusted people who understand faculty and staff members, enjoy their company, and respect them as brothers and sisters in Christ.

Training and retaining an administrative team requires that the team leaders understand the demands of group leadership. In his book *Group Leadership and Democratic Action*, Franklyn S. Haiman suggests three ingredients of respect and concern for other people:

1. Social sensitivity: having the capacity to discern which concerns are of greatest importance to group members and thus gain insight into their needs and desires

2. Extroversion: enjoying interaction with people
3. Belief in the value of the individual: affirming the worth of others through actions as well as attitudes (1951)

Wise leaders set a regularly scheduled time and place for the administrative team to meet. The meeting agenda makes provision for prayer, discussion items, and action items, all within a designated time frame. The school head must sense the feeling of the team and the underlying current of their thoughts, perceiving both in relation to a broader picture of events in the school. The leader must then be able to summarize these feelings and thoughts orally in a way that is easily understood by each member.

As the leader of an administrative team, I had to learn restraint in expressing personal views because the views of leaders carry more weight than those of other members. Furthermore, leaders must heed how they contribute and how they take sides—both of which may be more influential than the views they express. Leaders should exhibit an attitude of eagerness to learn from each member, thereby drawing each person into the discussion.

Kouzes and Posner claim that love is the secret of success in leadership. I agree. They define "love" as "encouragement, loyalty, teamwork, commitment, and respect of others' dignity and worth," thus indicating that successful leadership is an affair of the heart and not of the head. If any one thing will cause people to distrust a leader, it is their perception that the leader does not care. In contrast, the authors write, "When we encourage others, we give them heart. And when we give heart to others, we give love" (Kouzes & Posner, 1995). Paul further explains that kind of love: "Love is patient, love is kind. It does not envy, it does not boast, it is not proud. It is not rude, it is not self-seeking, it is not easily angered, it keeps no record of wrongs. Love does not delight in evil but rejoices with the truth. It always protects, always trusts, always hopes, always perseveres" (1 Corinthians 13:4–7).

Maintaining Team Effectiveness

In *Transforming Leadership*, Terry Anderson defines the twelve skills necessary for leaders to develop personally if they want to be effective in leading a team:

1. Grounding: Control attention to focus in the present (not in the past or future)
2. Centering: Maintain clear awareness of self in the context of events going on around me
3. Beliefs Clarification: Express and live out a clear and consistent set of beliefs
4. Purpose Specification: Identify and live out a personal statement of purpose for my life

5. Values Identification: Identify, prioritize, and live out a set of personal values

6. Life Planning: Formulate an integrated plan and live out an intentional lifestyle

7. Education Goal Setting: Specify and live a goal-driven plan for life-long learning

8. Career Goal Setting: Set and implement motivating and realistic career goals

9. Time Management: Plan and implement the best-prioritized use of time

10. Stress Management: Apply effective stress management methods to daily life

11. Health Management: Get optimum nutrition, exercise, deep relaxation, and restful sleep

12. Positive Mental Attitude: Control "self-talk" and build my own sense of self-worth (1998)

In order for the administrative team to be effective, its members must identify realistic and motivating goals. Together they explore adequate steps for implementing those goals. Teams specify and facilitate proper ownership of an issue and follow up on results with appropriate praise and rewards. The team members, whether a principal and teachers, several administrators, or any other combination, need to identify and help each other address self-defeating behaviors.

I can still remember the day and place I said something unkind about a fellow believer. My administrative assistant looked at me in disbelief and rebuked me in love. He said, "That was not a kind thing for a person who is a Christian leader to say." He cared enough to confront me, and to this day the lesson has stayed with me. The team members that can confront each other in love and candor will be successful in carrying out the mission and goals of the school.

On an effective administrative team, each member accurately assesses the needs, problems, and fears of the people he or she directly leads, usually through surveys, research, the school's information systems, and one-on-one contact with people. Each member of the team brings clear, accurate, and objective information to a group meeting. The group then discusses what specifically needs improvement and what hurdles must be overcome to bring about improvements. Together they make decisions and take responsibility for their success or failure.

Ideally, this team spirit permeates the trustees, faculty members, student body, and parents. With their values clearly aligned, they can all help accomplish the agreed-upon mission of the school.

Skills of Team Development

Anderson provides a comprehensive list of team-development skills that form the cornerstone of effective leadership:

1. Informal Assessment: Assess needs, wants, problems, and fears by one-to-one interaction with people
2. Formal Assessment: Assess needs, wants, and problems through surveys, research, and information systems
3. Problem-Management Facilitation: Facilitate effective problem-management meetings that improve performance
4. Needs Clarification: Clarify the need for change in a language others will understand and accept
5. Readiness Checking: Explore readiness for change and overcome blocks to constructive change
6. Values Alignment: Explore and facilitate team spirit and synergy through clarifying and aligning values
7. Vision Consensus Building: Facilitate consensus regarding objectives, goals, and action plans
8. Program Design: Design and implement flexible programs to achieve objectives reliably
9. Program and Team Performance Evaluation: Evaluate and report the impact of action programs and team efforts
10. Leadership: Lead teams toward continuous improvement of what our organization produces or provides
11. Building Accountability: Install accountability systems so everyone experiences "no-doubt contracting" (Anderson, 1998)

These skills provide team members with the capacity to achieve consensus-based problem solving and decision making, manage the stress of working on an administrative team, and ultimately enhance the team's performance as well as the school's. Periodically, leaders should build a discussion of these skills into the agenda of an administrative team meeting.

Further, the skills needed to develop an administrative team are lovingly born out of a clear understanding of and commitment to a Christian philosophy of education. In his book *Christian Education in a Democracy*, Frank E. Gaebelein lists six requirements for a truly Christian school:

1. A Christian educational institution must be built on a thoroughly understood and practiced Christian philosophy of education.
2. A Christian school must have faculty members thoroughly committed to its distinctive philosophy.
3. The curriculum of a Christian educational institution must be Christ centered.
4. A Christian school must have a student body (constituency) that will actively support its philosophy and aims.

5. A Christian school must recognize the two aspects of Christian education—the required and the voluntary.
6. A Christian educational institution must adhere to the truth by applying Christian ethics in all its relationships. (1951)

Each member of the team must have a long-term commitment to making every aspect of the school programs consistent with the school's philosophy. Building a strong school takes time, persistence, prayer, hard work, and adherence to biblical truth. Even when others in the school become discouraged, each member of the leadership team must be determined to stay the course and make decisions to deepen the school's commitment to quality, Bible-centered education.

One of the greatest challenges facing a school with a leadership team is developing trust among the team members. In this day of cynicism and mistrust born out of horror stories recounting how people have been mistreated—often in Christian organizations—it becomes all the more important to build and maintain trust. In their book *Building Strong People*, Bobbie Reed and John Westfall suggest three ways to affirm people and build trust:

1. Give decision-making authority to the team and let people know that you have done so
2. Stand behind the team when it is under attack
3. Believe in the team (1997)

Ultimately, the power to affect the administrative team comes from the Holy Spirit working within each member. The Holy Spirit, being all-powerful, can accomplish the plans of the team. When leaders step out of the way and release people to minister in the power of the Spirit, these leaders help empower the team. But when leaders insist on maintaining control of all plans, activities, and decisions, they may well restrict the work of the Holy Spirit in the lives of the people they are responsible for.

The leader of an administrative team makes it a personal mission to empower each team member. Even extraordinary leaders cannot accomplish a great deal without a capable leadership team. The open exchange of ideas between leaders and team members does not pose a threat to leaders who are secure in their positions. Experience and maturity help leaders realize that individual achievement and success provide the basis for team achievement and success. Good leaders know how to delegate authority, what authority to delegate, and how to make others feel authoritative. True leaders will make sure each member of the team has access to the necessary funds, information, and authority to complete tasks and develop new ideas. Such leaders encourage others to make decisions rather than making all decisions themselves.

Over the years I have told members of our administrative team that I am their servant, providing necessary resources and encouragement in order to empower them to complete assignments and carry out their responsibilities in the most productive way. Members of the team, when chosen carefully by the leadership, are passionately committed to their work. They love their jobs, whether in development, discipline, finances, human resources, or curriculum design, and they have a great deal of affection for their coworkers.

Leaders must be sure to assign to all members of the leadership team those areas for which God has given them the necessary skill and passion. If leaders fail to do so, frustration results, and the people the members serve suffer from inadequate attention. The love of leaders for their own work creates a passion, which translates into personal enthusiasm, which ultimately enables them to motivate others to perform to their highest possible level. By encouraging maturity, fostering open communication, demonstrating forward thinking, sharing responsibility, and exhibiting commitment to each team member, leaders can meet the challenge of effectively directing a Christian school into the future.

Good leaders will distribute power among the members of the team. Paradoxically, leaders gain power by empowering others. All members of the administrative team will work harder when they feel they have a significant voice in making decisions (Murray, 1991).

Sharing power also fosters cooperation among team members, and cooperation increases group accomplishment. The effectiveness of any group depends in large part on the cooperation of each member. *The genius of administrative team leadership lies in combining individual efforts in order to achieve goals that would be beyond the capability of any one person.* Leaders lose the team advantage when participation is only halfhearted. Kouzes and Posner report that enabling others offers the key to leadership; accomplishment results from the efforts of many people, not just the leader (1995).

Effective teams focus on goals that maximize team outcomes. Heads-of-school are primarily responsible for helping to define and articulate goals and for motivating each member of the administrative team. A team that works at peak performance usually has a leader who has clearly identified and stayed focused on the agenda.

Further, team members must be accountable for their behavior in all situations. Members of a successful administrative team know what is expected, and they are the agents of responsibility who make sure assignments are completed in harmony with the goals of the school and for the benefit of the students.

Through my years of leading an administrative team, I have seen a team identity emerge, one that others notice. Effective leaders set out to create that identity, which grows out of a unified support for the school's mission. Members must think through the specific actions required to achieve their collective vision for the team and the school. Effective leaders also create change, which is essential to progress. Principals who encourage the members of the administrative team to seek out new and better ways to solve problems empower the team by unleashing the talent and intelligence of all team members.

An Administrative Model

The Greek word *kubernetes*, mentioned earlier in this chapter, suggests the image of an ancient ship, an image that can serve as a tangible model for the vital concepts presented here. All analogies break down at some point, but a ship can serve to remind us of some important elements of school leadership.

The school's leader, like the ship's captain, is charged with overseeing the tasks of those who run the school or operate the ship as it moves from its current position to its intended destination. The administrative team, or ship's officers, are directly responsible to their leader. Both groups have been appointed because they have specific and diverse skills that enable them to carry out their responsibilities. The faculty and staff, like the ship's crew, perform the operational functions of the organization.

Just as the ship was built to carry its passengers, the school was built to carry its students into the future, and the leaders of both must set a course that will lead to their destination. Like a ship's rudder, the school's biblical mission statement keeps it on course as it carries its students to new and unexplored places. As a ship must be prepared to face strong winds and high seas, so the school must prepare itself for the inevitable challenges—physical, financial, social, and spiritual.

Jesus often used two other analogies—those of the shepherd and the servant—to make important points about leadership. These analogies can further enrich our understanding of what leaders should be like and of how they should carry out their tasks. Of course, no specific leadership model is necessarily right for all Christian schools, but perhaps if leaders work at seeing their role through the eyes of the ship's captain, the shepherd, and the servant, they will come to a more biblical perspective.

A number of questions may help us as leaders apply these ideas in our own schools:

1. What characteristics in our schools are effective in carrying out our mission?
2. What characteristics in our schools can we identify as ineffective and needing improvement?
3. As an administrative team, what changes can we make in our school to improve faculty effectiveness, student learning, and student spiritual maturation; and how can we make these changes?
4. How does our administrative team measure up in terms of respect for one another and positive action?

5. In what ways can we use the model of a nautical vessel or some other metaphor to define our purposes, tasks, and relationships clearly?

Summary

Leaders in Christian schools must understand and build leadership teams differently than leaders in other vocations. In my experience, while the function of leading is the same, the way Christian school leaders carry it out undergoes constant scrutiny. People who have a significant interest in schools are often quick to share their views, producing pressures and problems unique to Christian school leaders.

The administrative team concept used in Christian schools requires members to make judgments by balancing the demands of various principles. Few are the times when leaders can solve a problem by applying a single principle. An administrative team must deal successfully with various ideas. At this point, the administrative team concept makes its strongest contribution. Through multiple counselors, we find wisdom. Team members present a range of perspectives, consider the multiple facets of a situation, apply proven principles, and exercise balanced judgment.

Bibliography

Anderson, T. D. (1998). *Transforming leadership*. Boca Raton, FL: St. Lucie Press.

Gaebelein, F. E. (1951). *Christian education in a democracy*. New York: Oxford University Press.

Hackman, M. Z. (2000). *Leadership: A communication perspective*. Prospect Heights, IL: Waveland Press.

Haiman, F. S. (1951). *Group leadership and democratic action*. Cambridge: Houghton Mifflin.

Kouzes, J. M., & Posner, B. Z. (1995). *Credibility: How leaders gain and lose, Why people demand it*. San Francisco: Jossey–Bass.

Lowrie, R. W. (1984). *Administration of the Christian school*. Whittier, CA: Association of Christian Schools International.

Maxwell, J. C. (2001). *The 17 indisputable laws of teamwork*. Nashville: Thomas Nelson.

Murray, M. (1991). *Beyond the myths and magic of mentoring*. San Francisco: Jossey–Bass.

Reed, B., & Westfall, J. (1997). *Building strong people*. Grand Rapids, MI: Baker Books.

World Book Dictionary (1992). Chicago: World Book, Inc.

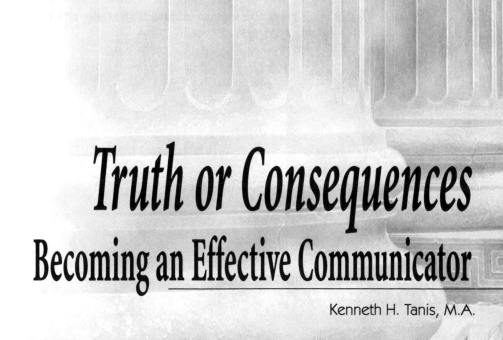

Truth or Consequences
Becoming an Effective Communicator

Kenneth H. Tanis, M.A.

Chapter Summary

Communication is one of the easiest things we do and, at the same time, one of the hardest. The writer of Ecclesiastes warns, "so let your words be few" because as words increase, so does the opportunity for foolishness. (Ecclesiastes 5:2, 3) But in the school world—where communication is vital—how do we develop the skills for effective communication so that "it may benefit those who listen" (Ephesians 4:29)?

Mr. Tanis frames effective communication for you as a Christian school leader in light of viewing people as God's image bearers. You have been called to reflect the communicative qualities of God Himself with the staff, parents, and school community. He presents many *dos and don'ts* that are as applicable for the veteran administrator as for the newcomer.

About the author

Kenneth H. Tanis, M.A.
Headmaster, Delaware County Christian School
Newtown Square, PA
37 years of educational leadership experience

Chapter 5

Truth or Consequences
Becoming an Effective Communicator

Kenneth H. Tanis, M.A.

The story is told of three octogenarians sitting on a park bench passing the time of day and engaging in light conversation. Because of the onset of advancing years, their hearing had become rather selective and far from accurate. The first gent made the observation that he thought it was a rather *windy* afternoon. His good friend responded by saying, "*I don't think it's Wednesday afternoon; it's Thursday.*" This led the third friend to reply, "*No thanks. I'm not thirsty; I had some iced tea before I left the house.*"

We find such stories humorous because they capture both the foibles of getting old and the difficulties and challenges of accurate communication. As human beings, we have been granted a huge gift and responsibility. We call it the *gift of communication*. And what a gift it is! Where else in all creation do we encounter such a sophistication of contact? Some research has documented limited amounts of communication between various nonhuman species of God's creation, but we hardly feel comfortable even calling it communication. We are more comfortable with the phenomenon when we think of it as signals or sounds made from one creature to another rather than as actual communication.

Communicating in God's Image

When we read that God created man in His image and likeness, our first thoughts often focus on other aspects of that image rather than communication. Yet that is part of the image of God. During our first encounter with God in Genesis, He *speaks*. His speech provides the very energy that brings into existence the creation itself. In *Reclaiming the Future of Christian Education: A Transforming Vision*, Albert Greene captures this unique aspect of God's gift of communication.

A Christian philosophy, therefore, begins with the assertion that all of reality had its beginning in and through the Word of God. The Lord has spoken everything that exists into being. The biblical account of creation in Genesis says repeatedly, "And God said," followed each time by the assertion that what He said came into being. We speak words; God speaks things. He opens what we suppose to be His metaphorical mouth, and out tumble trees, viruses, and moons. From His lips pour blood, water, and wisps of clouds. Tsetse flies and ptarmigans trip from His tongue. Whereas we can only say "is" or "equals," *He* utters the essential *to be*: "Let there be!" While such a thought sharply distinguishes the power of God's voice, it does not obviate the fact that we image God when we speak and transform thoughts into words of communication.

The God Who Speaks

As mentioned above, when we first encounter God's presence in the Garden of Eden, we encounter a God who spends time in verbal fellowship with Adam and Eve. The Scripture records that God comes looking, or perhaps more accurately, *calling* for Adam, His image bearer, after Adam's sin. Therefore, we unavoidably acknowledge that God is a communicating God. Hallelujah! What a cold world this would be if we had no word from God— if His gracious pursuing voice were inaudible in our universe! *We have a God who speaks*. Praise the Lord!

As we reflect on this fact, we need to remember that we have a responsibility, a command, to be imitators of God. We are to be like Him. This concept instructs us in the field of communication. It challenges us to reflect on the manner in which God communicates with us so that we can then communicate like Him to others.

The God Who Proclaims Truth

When we consider that we serve the God who proclaims truth, we face the most central concept of true communication: it is marked by *truth. All* His words are true. His Spirit is called the Spirit of Truth. God does not lie. Every word He ever uttered is true. Therefore, we have a frame for our words. As Christian educators, our words must be marked by *truth*. We cannot afford for one moment the unfortunate aberration of shading the truth or even telling a boldfaced lie. In the Christian school, the commodity of trust is indispensable. Show me a school that has lost trust between board and administration, administration and faculty, or parents and board, and I will show you a school that has failed in its ability to communicate truth. We must carefully guard the truthfulness of all communication. Loss of trust can kill a ministry. Restoration becomes possible only when we once again tell the truth without compromise.

The God Who Listens

God's communication is also marked by His listening to the heart. People look at and listen to what is on the surface, but God looks and listens to the heart. Communication always involves listening. A good communicator goes beyond words and listens to thoughts, motives, and heart. When Saul uses words to defend his actions to the prophet Samuel, at first Samuel does not hear the words. Rather, the prophet exposes the disobedient actions of Saul's heart first. Such listening affords difficult challenges for us as school administrators or board members. We need the discernment of God's Spirit to allow us to listen to the issues behind the words. Often, this type of listening can be accomplished only as we ask probing questions and avoid hasty judgments. God provides this grace for us as we seek to serve Him each day.

Scripture also impresses us with God's use of nonverbal communication. He uses symbols, stories, and examples to communicate truth. How rich the Old Testament celebrations are with their symbols of blood, lambs, circumcision, and sacrifices—all of which formed part of God's communication!

The God Who Tells Stories

Another way to communicate is through stories. God used stories to point out the lessons He sought to teach, such as the story the prophet Nathan told of the man with only one little lamb. He used this story to confront David with his sin.

Christ filled His communication with *parables*. New Testament Scriptures abound with stories of farmers, banquets, prodigals, lost coins, and lost sheep. As we communicate with parents and students, we serve them well when we can use true stories from our experiences to strengthen and encourage them. One of the great blessings of lengthy ministry experience is the overwhelming compilation of stories one has to tell others regarding the grace of God. These stories reveal how He met the needs of people who cried out for healing, for financial help, or for strength to persevere with a rebellious son or daughter. We can use these stories to imitate God's pattern of communication.

The God Who Loves

Speaking the truth in love always marks good communication. Perhaps the best example from the Old Testament is the picture Samuel gives us of God exposing David's sin and leading him to repentance. In the New

Testament, we see Jesus with the woman caught in the act of adultery, or Peter on the shore of the Sea of Galilee after the Resurrection. Both illustrate God's loving reproof. Our God condescends without losing transcendence; He meets us in our self-created messes; He speaks great words of comfort and forgiveness even as He holds us accountable for our sin.

The more we reflect on the communication of God and seek to imitate Him, the greater our effectiveness as communicators becomes. Obviously, we could review much more regarding the marks of God's communication, but perhaps these thoughts will suffice to make the point.

We all acknowledge that communication is an extremely important aspect of human activity. And yet we would also admit that we struggle with this essential administrative skill, often doing it rather poorly. Why do we find communication so difficult? We can easily think of many reasons. The most obvious problem is sin, the curse that causes us to misuse this wonderful gift. We all stand in danger of shading the truth to protect ourselves.

Those of us who have interviewed students following an incident at school have found that although a number of people witnessed the same event, the descriptions and stories of what really happened vary significantly. Often these differences occur because people want to shield us from their potential guilt. Also, they do not always say what they mean.

Some cultures are even more mysterious regarding communication. For example, they consider it impolite to say *no* to any request. Even in our culture, communication is often marked by saying only what the speaker believes the other person wants to hear, so only a portion of the truth survives. In every conversation, both listener and speaker bring a filter system through which words pass and change. For this and other reasons, leaders often find it helpful to have a witness present during highly sensitive conversations.

However, behind all the communication problems we discover an underlying fact—we are not good at telling the truth. If we were, we would likely have far more harmony in our relationships.

Improving Your Communication

Since I have had my share of experiences over many years in administration, it may be helpful to share some of the *dos and don'ts* of communication that I have learned, sometimes the hard way. While I do not profess infallibility in these principles, I have found them helpful in providing the best setting for effective communication.

Prioritize Faculty and Staff

Faculty and staff should always hear board decisions from the school head before they hear them from anyone else. This courtesy communicates their privileged position of relationship. Furthermore, administrators demonstrate both professionalism and courtesy when we announce board decisions to them before the general public hears them. To accomplish this process, board members must understand confidentiality. But we must also arrange immediate opportunities to communicate with faculty and staff following board meetings.

Communicate Hope

One aspect of our communication involves parent/teacher conferences or administrator/parent conferences. Some of these sessions can be very diffi-cult. A rebellious student may have created a hostile environment that threatens to wreck everything her family has sought to accomplish in her life. Every attempt to rectify the problem has failed. Administrators should make certain that such conferences always end with a note of hope. This hope should not result from some kind of Pollyanna sugarcoating of diffi-cult issues but rather from the stark reality that God is a part of the equa-tion in our effort to solve problems, and so we have every reason to hope.

We can remind parents that such a day may be looked on in years to come as a beginning of something new and wonderful. We may not see it now, but by God's grace and with perseverance, wisdom, and courage, we may see it in the future. God blesses such communication in countless ways.

Write It Down

Because we often misspeak, we should consistently put certain concepts and ideas in writing. This admonition applies particularly to parent/teacher conferences, teacher/administrator conferences, or any other high-level, important communication. Shortly after such events, a brief summary of the issues discussed and plans put in motion ought to appear in writing so that everyone can agree on what took place. You might be amazed at how this kind of communication can clarify important matters.

Repeat What You Hear

As discussion takes place between parties, you will want to occasionally interrupt such dialogue with summarizing statements. For instance, you may have listened to how a parent felt that a teacher handled a situation. You might interject, *"Let me try to summarize this situation as accurately and honestly as I can from what I have heard you describe. Please feel free to correct or adjust what I am saying so that we can be clear about what hap-pened."* Comments such as these can significantly strengthen clarity of com-munication.

Know When to Be Still

Effective communication allows one person to enter the mind and experience of another. During such a personal conversation in this privileged territory, I often find it helpful at the conclusion to determine what can be shared with others and what belongs exclusively to the conference setting. Such commitment fosters future trust. Good administrators and board members know how to keep a confidence.

Find the Kernel

Criticism comes to us in countless ways: some of it in anger, some of it with great unfairness, and some of it with genuine kindness. But behind all criticism, we can find a *kernel of truth* that should not be discarded. The wise administrator sets aside defensiveness and any other secondary motives, and hears what God might be teaching so that some kind of effective, beneficial action can take place.

Listen to People

Teachers and administrators gather information in numerous ways. We are all familiar with MBWA (management by walking around), characterized by always keeping our antennae positioned to receive information. Informal times such as lunchroom activities, van or bus trips with teams, late night retreats, and ordinary day-to-day living provide us with significant opportunities to pick up information and to take note of issues, perspectives, and helpful attitudes. For these opportunities to happen, we need to stay close to the action.

Ask Questions

Because we live in a "sociological zoo" in our schools, we rub elbows with people constantly. Good teachers and administrators arm themselves with questions that elicit thoughtful information. People like to give you their opinions, which need to be evaluated in the light of all other opinions. But every comment can provide useful information. Thinking administrators show up at school events, where they mingle with students and parents, and chat with them about the joys and sorrows resulting from family life or school experiences.

Communicate Thanks

If truth be told, few of us would say we spend a significant amount of time each day sending notes of appreciation. Yet short notes sent to students after they play their instruments in chapel, share a testimony, help out in some exceptional way, supply a piece of art for your office or bulletin board, or act in any other way that you wish to acknowledge and encourage become a powerful leadership tool. I have been astounded over the years at how many students or parents will make a point to thank me and tell me how they appreciated a personal note. *Never underestimate the power of the positive.*

Name Names

An important part of communication is connecting personally with the other party. Whenever possible, we should seek to know the names of the people with whom we speak and to use their names throughout the conversation. Perhaps we should not automatically use first names of people unless they grant us that permission. But parents and students like to be greeted by name when they dialogue with us.

Protect Yourself

In some instances, you need the Holy Spirit's wisdom in determining whether an observer ought to be present. When you choose to have an observer, let the other party know. It is unfair to surprise people with an audience when they arrive for the conference. Don't become paranoid in such matters, but sometimes the testimony of another person can be critically important—if not career saving.

Communicate Through Prayer

Our offices need to be places of prayer, the highest kind of communication. What a blessing to conclude a conference with meaningful, specific prayer regarding the matter just discussed! Such prayer can happen over the phone as well. Even when we do not know how to pray, the Holy Spirit can take our jumbled conversation and translate it into spiritual language (Romans 8:26, 27).

Avoiding the Potholes

In addition to these positive suggestions, it might be helpful to reflect on the negative as well. Sometimes we can understand an issue more clearly when we identify what we don't want to do so that we avoid some of the traps involved in this minefield we call *communication*.

Don't Be Defensive

It is hard for us to hear people whom we admire and love criticize the school to which we have dedicated ourselves, or complain about our own handling of a situation. However, defensiveness shows an unwillingness to listen to another perspective and to weigh its value carefully. Sometimes we need to remind ourselves that the ministry and our own reputations are not as fragile as we may think.

Often our egos feel under attack, and we discover that the old nature is alive and well within us. Perhaps a more helpful perspective is to trust God to teach us through the criticisms of those whom we consider either our friends or our adversaries. When we trust, we open ourselves to new ways of carrying our ministries forward and of building positive relationships with those willing to confront us with their criticisms.

Don't Be Too Proud

Christian school administrators should place a very high value on servanthood. However, one of the best tests of servanthood is to see how we react when we are treated as servants and not as masters, whether we are head administrator or not. In my years of administrative experience, I have observed that it seems difficult for us as leaders to humble ourselves before others. We cannot control the hearts of others, but we are certainly responsible for controlling our own hearts. We gain credibility, as well as model our Christian faith, when we willingly say to a colleague or parent, "I was wrong, and I need your forgiveness." Amazing things begin to happen in conferences and in relationships when this spirit prevails.

Recently, a parent berated one of our administrators after a National Honor Society induction. This incident lasted for an extended period, depriving the administrator of time he needed to spend with other parents at such a wonderful event for our families. We set up a meeting to resolve these differences. To my surprise, the parent began the conference with a total humbling of himself and with a genuine desire to be forgiven for his completely inappropriate conduct. I assure you that this conference resulted in praise to God for obvious and essential grace.

Don't Pursue Everything

We need discernment regarding communication. Rumors can often fester in our ministries. Over the years, I have learned that Romans 12:21 can serve us well. This passage reminds us that we should not be overcome by evil, but we should overcome evil with good. Each day offers limited time. Head administrators make choices about how that time will be used. We can spend it tracing down every rumor and making every effort to put out fires that may be better left to burn out by themselves. We can use our time much more productively in building others up and sending notes of encouragement. These testimonies themselves become a backdrop against which rumors have a way of fizzling out. However, we cannot ignore some rumors. Pray for discernment in knowing which ones to tackle.

Don't Make Assumptions

Our work as administrators often requires us to make decisions and set plans in motion that perhaps have not had the full benefit of everyone's participation. We should not assume that everyone understands the reasons why an action has been taken. At such times, it is critically important that reasons for an action be explained carefully.

Consider a conference in which a parent and a teacher have disagreed over a dealing with a student. A wise administrator does not assume everyone remembers that we all seek the same goal. In such cases, we may want to remind the group that we are here because we want to find the best solution for the student, not to get our own way. This assumption seems reasonable, but reviewing reality almost always enhances communication. We serve the whole resolution process well when we give voice to things that we might have assumed.

Don't Talk About Others

We face the danger of speaking about other students or other families during parent conferences. We may imply negative attitudes toward other students who we think are a bad influence on the student we are discussing. Such conversations come back to us and will require us to do some explaining to the student or parents whose child we identified. In Christian schools, we should speak well of one another in all circumstances. Only an unwise administrator speaks disparagingly of a teacher's handling of a situation in the presence of a parent. There may be a time for this criticism, but only in private with the offending teacher. Such a conversation can damage our credibility, and people could view it as a total lack of appropriate leadership.

Don't Ever Use Reprisal

One of the strange phenomena that I have witnessed over the years is that parents who openly criticize a teacher to an administrator fear reprisals against their children. It does not matter how many ways we try to explain that this situation will not happen; parents believe it will. Herein lies one of the great inhibitors of communication between parents and educators. I don't have any *silver bullets* to resolve this issue; I just identify it as a reality. Such a fear on the part of parents should always be groundless in Christian schools. We must never give parents a reason to suspect that any action in defense of their child will result in negative treatment.

Don't Use Your Children

Many of the students in our Christian schools are the offspring of our faculty, staff, and administration. Many of the largest families in our schools come from this segment of our school community. It is typical to have almost ten percent of the student body made up of employees' children.

These children have special challenges. At times, especially if they are middle school or high school students, they may feel uncomfortable in certain social situations on campus. They may overhear a discussion about how their parents handled a matter. This discovery creates difficult days for these children.

However, the problem worsens when we as their parents take the opportunity to "pump" them for information regarding situations that may have happened in school. Such questions put our children in the terrible dilemma of choosing between loyalty to their friends and loyalty to us as their parents. Our children carry enough baggage without having additional burdens placed on them. Yet I have discovered over the years that most of these children have an amazing resilience and that they handle these situations very well.

I have also known employees in our school who attach unreasonable credibility to the words and opinions of their children; one might conclude that their children's wisdom exceeds that of all others. Generally, we tend to give greater weight to the accuracy and truthfulness of our own children's perceptions than to those of our professional colleagues.

Don't Be Afraid

Don't be afraid to ask specific questions. Gather information from students, parents, and your colleagues regarding their concerns. Ask students whether they were blessed in chapel and why. Ask a colleague about a policy that needs clarification. Gain the insights and opinions of people around you. Parents welcome the opportunity to respond to a specific question regarding how activities at the school impact them. When you ask questions of others, you indicate that you value their responses. This process builds relationships and broadens your understanding of the issues.

Don't Play Favorites

While it may be a good idea for your local radio station to play favorites, wise leaders do not gather around themselves an inner circle of people they trust in some exclusive manner. They build broad relationships with others. Don't always "hang out" with the same people. To some degree, we do have special friends, and that's not inappropriate. *But* we leaders need to connect with a large variety of parents, colleagues, and students so that we do not gain the reputation of listening only to certain people.

In the final section of this chapter, let me suggest a variety of practical ideas that we can implement in our Christian schools to provide an effective setting for good communication. Obviously, each school needs to know its own dynamics and fashion its programs in response to those dynamics. But a wise school constantly reviews and redeems the ways communication takes place within its ministry.

Parent Communication

Communication with parents presents the most critical challenge. While this task may seem easy, it is not! Printed materials sent home are rarely read. Handbooks of over 100 pages of policies and practices are rarely opened. Each fall generates about twenty percent new families who have no background with the school. These are among many reasons that meaningful communication between home and school is a constant necessity.

Reregistration Meeting

Require all the school's families to personally turn in reregistration materials on a designated night. Such a policy provides a direct line of communication between the administration and the families and between the board and the families.

Koinonia Groups

Larger schools can divide, on the basis of student ages, the overall school organization into groups that are somewhat specific. Koinonia groups composed of parents in each respective division can be a great source of input to the administration, and they can provide lines of communication to parents. Organizing Koinonia groups according to grade levels might result in the following groups: kindergarten through second grade, third through fifth, sixth through eighth, and ninth through twelfth. Ask a parent or a couple from each grade level to serve with an administrator in designing programs that benefit parents and specifically serve as a sounding board for parental opinions, which the administration can review.

Home Meetings

Some schools have found that a home provides an outstanding setting for personal and effective communication. Perhaps on a three-year cycle, home meetings can be held in the various geographic regions represented by the student population. The administration simply contacts a family in that area and asks them to host a home meeting. Parents who plan to attend the meeting (conveniently located near their homes) are asked to bring a small amount of finger food for ten to twelve people. The host provides the beverages.

At the meeting, a representative for the faculty, board, or administration listens to input from parents, and later provides information about the meeting to those who did not attend. Home meetings indicate to parents that the school values them enough to spend evenings in homes talking about Christian education and the effectiveness of the school.

Dedication Service

At the start of the school year, preferably during the first week, some schools provide a special occasion to commit the year to the Lord. This event, which should involve all the students, might include a cookout or box supper, depending on the size of the school. Keep the program brief. Ask new teachers to share their testimonies; hold a time of corporate worship and praise; and most importantly, pray for students, parents, and all those who serve the school. Such a program launches the year on a high spiritual tone, and it gives you opportunity to highlight and explain the theme verse of the year.

Utilize Surveys

Schools need an established cycle of surveying the opinions of parents. These surveys need to be well designed and representative of a large segment of the constituency. Some schools mail surveys with registration materials and require that the surveys be returned when the family reregisters. This method usually guarantees a sizable response.

These surveys can include every aspect of the school's ministry, such as the effectiveness of its various programs, the spiritual climate, discipline, dress code, and financial policies. Keep the survey relatively constant from year to year so that you can compare responses over time. Remember, parent surveys diminish in their effectiveness if people do not believe their comments are read or seriously considered. Each school needs to find the best way to communicate survey results to parents.

Board Reports

Some boards find it helpful to provide a written summary of board decisions and discussions on a monthly or quarterly basis. Not all families are interested in this material, but some consider it extremely important.

Exit Interviews

Each year schools discover families that choose not to reenroll for the coming school year. We need to know why that happens. Interestingly, a board member is often more successful than anyone else in discovering the reason. Sometimes parents seem reluctant to divulge to a school administrator or employee issues that caused them to withdraw. Furthermore, since board members may come with a more objective perspective, they can often be a good source for gathering this information.

Schools should categorize the responses of nonreturning families in order to assess whether any trends need to be addressed. This kind of communication, while often related to negative matters, is of critical importance to the communication process. We have a responsibility to a family that has entrusted us with its most precious possession, its children.

Materials Audit

We produce an amazing amount of paper in our effort to communicate with parents. On a regular basis, I like to take all our published materials, both those created commercially and those produced in-house, and spread them out on a large conference table. Then I ask several questions about the items: *Is there a common logo? Is there a common typestyle? Does the photography show excellent quality? Is the mission of the school prominent? Do these pieces have a corporate integrity that speaks well of the school's ministry?* These questions help us make certain that our printed materials provide the quality of communication we desire to have with our current parents, the entire constituency, and the community.

A school that treats communication as a serious responsibility has taken a giant step toward having an effective ministry. The hallmark of our communication must be *truth*. Politically correct language has become a standard for communication to such a degree that all of us run the risk of elevating style above integrity. Our schools need to be refreshing places where the truth is told with great joy. Excellence in Christian school education can accept nothing less.

Why Umpires Wear Masks!
Making Tough Decisions

Ellen Lowrie Black, Ed.D. and Robert M. Miller, Ed.D.

Chapter Summary

It seems that all you do is make decisions—about student enrollment, teacher hiring, discipline problems, unsatisfactory teachers, the instructional program, and so on. School policy dictates some decisions, but others fall into that gray area where the right course of action is not as evident. Although there is no cookie-cutter formula applicable in every case, there are certain principles of good decision making that you can apply to any situation.

Drs. Black and Miller outline tried-and-true principles found in God's Word and validated by research. These fundamentals will provide you with a strong framework for handling the tough decisions so much a part of the life of an educational leader. You can easily apply these practical suggestions to your own decision making. Your school community is looking to you as a Christian leader for timely and appropriate decisions.

About the authors
Ellen Lowrie Black, Ed.D.
Board Member, Columbia International University and
Educational Consultant
Lawrenceville, GA
19 years of educational leadership experience

Robert M. Miller, Ed.D.
Director for Administrative Leadership Development, ACSI
Colorado Springs, CO
40 years of educational leadership experience

Chapter 6

Why Umpires Wear Masks!
Making Tough Decisions

Ellen Lowrie Black, Ed.D. and Robert M. Miller, Ed.D.

It was the bottom of the ninth inning, and you could feel the tension as the batter stepped to the plate. With one out and a runner on third, the score was tied. The batter hit a sharp grounder over second base, miraculously fielded by the second baseman. In the fielder's attempt to prevent a run, he threw the ball home. Ball and runner arrived at home plate together in a swirling cloud of dust. For an intense moment, the game seemed to come to a complete halt as all eyes in the stadium turned to the umpire and awaited his call. Was the game over or would it go into an extra inning?

The Importance of Decisions

While a Christian school leader's decisions may not be quite as dramatic, the baseball analogy still applies. For people, departments, or institutions, momentum stops as they wait for a leader's decision. That decision determines what's next in their particular situations.

Central to the success of any school or organization is the nature and process of decision making. Decisions reflect values. Decisions reflect power. Decisions tell the story of who and what we value. It is appropriate to look first to Scripture to get a perspective. While many biblical characters provide insight, two key models are Nehemiah in the Old Testament and Jesus Christ in the New Testament.

The book of Nehemiah offers a manual for strategic planning and vision. Nehemiah faced an incredible task and showed passion to fulfill his God-given vision. However, Nehemiah did something that has become unusual in Christian circles. He took time to pray and fast before he made any decisions. He chose to get alone with God and then decide how to proceed. His vision came from God. Often organizations get so caught up in the "doing" that they do not value the time needed to seek God.

As a strategic thinker and leader, Nehemiah recognized his need for God's wisdom. He was not indecisive but rather was quiet before God. How often do we plan and work round the clock, taking two minutes before a board meeting to ask God to bless our plans? It could revolutionize school leadership if we were to take a three-day retreat to pray and fast before making decisions.

Just like Nehemiah (or the umpire), leaders must be trustworthy. Their integrity must be above reproach. Proverbs 11:3 reminds us, "The integrity of the upright guides them, but the unfaithful are destroyed by their duplicity." Leaders must not be perceived as self-serving people in their decision making, but rather as servants deciding in the best interest of the team and the school. Any lack of integrity or any suspicion of the leader's desire for personal gain casts a serious cloud of doubt over the legitimacy of the final decision.

In Christian school administration, leaders must consistently be guided by integrity and a biblical worldview. Such leadership, geared to principle rather than emotion, will often be predictable. Predictability in decision making encourages a staff's confidence and builds their sense of security. It reinforces the assurance that they know their leaders and that their decisions are not arbitrary.

Jesus demonstrated very clearly His views on decision making. He empowered people and willingly included mere mortals in the process. Jesus, who embodied all power and authority, chose to give power to others. As Bolman and Deal state, "hoarding power produces powerless organizations. Giving power liberates energy for more productive use. When people feel a sense of efficacy and an ability to influence their world, they seek to be more productive. They direct their energy and intelligence toward making a contribution rather than obstructing progress. The gift of power enrolls people in working toward a common cause" (1995).

In many Christian organizations, small groups of people commonly control all decisions and assume that this method models strong leadership. While that control may be efficient, it is not how Jesus led. Mary Beth Jones discusses this in *Jesus, CEO:*

> Taking action means making decisions, and making decisions is painful. Jesus gave his staffers authority to act in his name even before they seemed ready for it. When he first sent them out with this newfound authority to heal the sick and raise the dead, he must have paced by the sea wondering what they would come back with. Sure enough, they came back with tales of success, but also stories

about how they sometimes couldn't quite get it.

Yet he gave them authority, and eventually they became quite good at carrying out the mission. By giving them authority to act, he was delegating power. There was much work to be done that could not humanly or even divinely be done without them. So, he took the workers he did have and gave them authority. (1992)

Every school faces circumstances that involve tough decisions: dis-enrolling a family, expelling a student, dismissing a teacher, relocating a campus, or resigning a position, just to name a few. None of us is immune. We tell new administrators, "In every good school, someone is making the tough decisions," suggesting that some schools face their tough decisions, while others find ways to avoid them. Tough decisions do not just go away. You can face them today or tomorrow—but you will ultimately face them. Unfortunately, often the longer you wait to deal with problems, the more difficult the resolution.

Christian leaders must carefully observe biblical principles that will enable and direct them in the day-to-day decision-making process.

Biblical Principle

A. Be certain of your facts.

"If you hear it said about one of the towns the Lord your God is giv-ing you to live in that wicked men have arisen among you and have led the people of their town astray, saying, 'Let us go and worship other gods' (gods you have not known), then you must inquire, probe and investigate it thoroughly. And if it is true and it has been proved that this detestable thing has been done among you, you must cer-tainly put to the sword all who live in that town" (Deuteronomy 13:12–15a). Leaders must thoroughly investigate their facts. Rumors and partial reports must prove true before we can confidently act on them.

B. Avoid partiality or intimidation.

"Do not pervert justice; do not show partiality to the poor or favoritism to the great, but judge your neighbor fairly" (Leviticus 19:15). We compromise when our decisions are influenced by partial-ity resulting from the approval of powerful members of the commu-nity; we also compromise when we allow ourselves to be influenced by their possible disapproval.

C. Don't violate known biblical principles.

"Though I constantly take my life in my hands, I will not forget your law. The wicked have set a snare for me, but I have not strayed from your precepts. Your statutes are my heritage forever; they are the joy of my heart. My heart is set on keeping your decrees to the very end. I hate double-minded men, but I love your law" (Psalm 119:109–113). The efficacy of spiritual truth means doing, not simply knowing. The Scriptures must shape and guide our decisions.

D. Seek God's guidance prayerfully.
"Show me your ways, O Lord, teach me your paths; guide me in your truth and teach me, for you are God my Savior, and my hope is in you all day long" (Psalm 25:4, 5). God can provide us with the needed guidance and discernment for wise decision making.

E. Commit to do the right thing as God enables you to understand it.
"Teach me, O Lord, to follow your decrees; then I will keep them to the end. Give me understanding, and I will keep your law and obey it with all my heart. Direct me in the path of your commands, for there I find delight" (Psalm 119:33–35). As God reveals His truth, we incorporate it into our decision making.

F. Trust God with the consequences.
"Offer right sacrifices and trust in the Lord "(Psalm 4:5). Leaders must first obediently honor God with their decisions and then trust God for the consequences that result from those decisions.

Finding the Most Appropriate Style

While there are different decision-making styles, there is often a more appropriate style to use for each situation. Some decisions may require you to be *authoritative*. You make the decision without seeking any assistance. This method is appropriate when you have the necessary experience and information to reach the decision and when others lack the ability, willingness, or confidence to help. If some team members do have that ability, leaders may choose the *consultative* style, asking for team input but making the final decision.

Two additional styles allow leaders to share the decision-making process. *Facilitative* decision making is a cooperative effort in which leaders and followers work together to reach a shared decision. This process works well when leadership team members have sufficient ability and experience to participate in decision making. The final style, *delegative*, could be used when followers can actually make the decision. In such instances, the leader turns the decision over to these capable followers.

Each style would follow the decision-making process presented earlier. The difference lies in the level of group involvement. Research shows that effective leaders with well-selected, well-trained teams prefer to delegate as many decisions as possible.

Mistakes to Avoid

A. Don't undermine the facts.
This mistake occurs when leaders bring certain biases or expectations to the facts. This preconception can cause leaders to see or hear only what they anticipate or prefer.

B. Don't undervalue your instincts.
A leader's intuition emerges from her training and experience. Intuitive insights should not be overlooked. Christian leaders may experience the promptings of the Holy Spirit, which must not be ignored.

C. Don't over- or underestimate the value of other opinions.
Some people are generally more verbal and vocal in an institution, while others carry substantially less influence. Wise leaders take care to prevent one opinion from being more or less valued because of the influence of the source.

D. Don't limit your alternatives unnecessarily.
Even yes or no answers may have more than those two alternatives—"yes, and" or "no, but." In administration we must work to see all the possible alternatives. Adopting parts of different alternatives may often create the best solution.

E. Don't rely too much on the experts.
Rarely do your circumstances match the hypothetical situation of the experts. Value their counsel but always apply it selectively to your school setting.

F. Don't procrastinate.
Once you have arrived at your decision, implement it. Generally, expeditious decision making will encourage your staff. Needless delay can frustrate them.

G. Don't overlook the spiritual implications of your decision.
Not only what you decide but how you decide has spiritual implications. Your school community wants to know that their leaders search the Scriptures and practice prayer.

Three Key Levels of Decision Making

The Role of the Administration

In schools, the chief administrator provides daily leadership and is directly responsible to the board. The culture of the school and style of its leader significantly impact how decisions are made and perceived. Again, the biblical model of empowerment must be viewed as optimal, even when contrary to common practice. Administrators function in the decision-making process at many levels:

- Staffing
- Scheduling
- Cocurricular activities
- Discipline
- Instructional materials
- Budget management
- Board communication
- Community relations
- Fund-raising
- Space allocation
- Instructional design
- Troubleshooting
- Staff development
- Technology
- Spiritual formation

While administrators do not hold exclusive authority in these areas, their leadership is required in order for the decision processes to function effectively. The cooperation of many people is essential for schools to run well. Authoritarian cultures tend to have people working in isolation with a lack of collaboration (Fogg, 1994).

A strong decision maker must have access to accurate information. Because of this need, trust and personal relationships are very significant. DePree states, "Effective influencing and understanding spring largely from healthy relationships among members of the group. Leaders need to foster environments and work processes within which people can develop high-quality relationships" (1992).

Administrators who have developed healthy relationships are inclined to hear the good, the bad, and the ugly. Decisions made in a vacuum have the potential of being dangerous. Hudson T. Armerding, president emeritus of Wheaton College, writes, "It is an obvious advantage to have associates who speak and live the truth. It is an administrative blight to be told what others think you want to hear, rather than what really is" (1978).

Leadership by walking around (LBWA) is an adaptation from the business world concept of management by walking around (MBWA). LBWA provides thousands of pieces of information that we file away, both consciously and subconsciously. When we make decisions, we process both informal data and personal observations. We could compare it to information contained in a still shot and information contained in a video—two dimensional versus three dimensional.

Daniel Goleman, in his bestseller *Working with Emotional Intelligence*, clearly articulates this concept:

The emotional tone set by any leader ripples downward with remarkable precision. While average leaders tend to be invisible, the best leaders frequently walk around and strike up conversations with their staff, asking about their families and other personal matters. They let it be known that they want to be informed, creating an atmosphere of openness that makes it easier for communication to take place (1995).

One of the most difficult decisions leaders face today relates to the issue of change. Administrators determined to fulfill their missions must be willing to do some things differently. And not all people handle change well. Furthermore, schools are greatly influenced by the rapid changes in culture.

Consider, for example, the use of technology in the school. This issue has huge budget and staffing implications. To decide not to move forward because we "aren't quite ready" abdicates responsibility. Students who do not attain technical skills will leave our schools in one of two ways: they either choose to go to different schools, or they enter the next chapter of their lives ill prepared.

Change is inevitable, and decisions require flexible navigators. *AQUA Church*, written to discuss the leadership arts needed in these volatile times, states:

> Every leader needs to create his or her own map. But no leader dare create a map in isolation. Leaders learn from other explorers about their maps. A river's course does not change quickly, but the character and complexion of the river changes daily, even hourly. When white-water rafting, a change of even an inch can change a river drastically. (Sweet, 1999)

Veteran administrators and teachers all know that days at school can change in a second. The ability to make wise choices quickly is becoming more essential for effective leaders. Flexibility has become a precious commodity.

The Role of Faculty and Staff

The faculty and staff are the frontline soldiers who hour by hour implement the policy decisions of the board. They also make important decisions in cases such as:

- Personal attitude
- Nature of the learner
- Instructional strategies
- Organization/grouping
- Time management
- Room design
- Involvement of parents

• Role of technology

These decisions have the most immediate and direct effect on learners. Determining what, how, and when one will teach is always an outgrowth of personal attitudes and belief systems. For example, a teacher's belief regarding the kind of world the students will live in impacts the emphasis on literacy, verbal skills, and technology.

Classroom teachers decide how much autonomy to give students as well as what learning experiences should look like. Emphasizing fill-in-the-blank education and rewarding conformity indicate that we do not challenge students to reason at high levels.

It is time to determine how serious we are about preparing the next generation. Making the decision that Christian educators have a significant role to play leads to some core faculty choices. We may have to confront our teachers with serious and difficult self-assessment, which forces them to determine that they:

• believe they are called to teach
• allow their fellow teachers to do it their way
• accept students where they are
• provide experiences that create a bridge for students to go where God desires
• allow students to ask difficult questions
• plan activities to develop higher-order thinking
• provide outlets for students' natural giftings
• empower students to try new things
• facilitate student-led ministry opportunities
• love their students
• have fun

Teachers who have established rapport and work closely with administrators, staff, families, and students embody up-to-date leadership traits. According to Sweet, "Leadership in the postmodern world is collaboration and interaction. Everybody has it. These are learnings. The leadership art of collaboration transforms everything—from how leaders behave to what leaders believe and become" (1999).

Teachers and staff members must be involved in decisions that affect themselves as well as their students. They cannot properly collaborate with students if they themselves have been blocked from involvement. Choosing to empower others always carries a risk. Choosing not to brings even greater risk.

The Role of Students

The decision to empower and involve students more openly poses a dilemma for many educators who were raised during more authoritarian times. The need to respond to each generation seems obvious, and yet these decisions are often met with quizzical looks and even scorn. Nowhere is this need more visible in our schools than in decisions related to worship.

Students today are much more participatory, and they will choose music that closely reflects who they are and how they think. A Christian school administrator recently told me that the administration had turned chapel music over to the students. The music was louder, had more bass than before, and was not well received by many teachers. However, the decision to involve students led to increased cooperation as well as student excitement about chapel.

Choosing to involve students implies that one has decided to work with students and allow room for mistakes. (Why should our students be any different from us? We surely make mistakes. Perhaps we have refined the art of covering our mistakes.) Their learning and spiritual growth accelerate when students have a voice.

Steps in Decision Making

Much of our daily decision making requires primarily common sense, and we make this type of decision spontaneously. However, more substantive decisions may require a decision-making process. That process will include most or all of the following steps:

Step 1: Tough issues stir up emotions and seem to demand a resolution. However, in spite of the perceived urgency of the matter, effective leaders make sure they are legitimately charged with the responsibility to make the decision. *As a leader, note that recognizing the issues does not necessarily empower you to make the decision.* Information gathering may result in a recommendation to other decision maker(s), such as the trustees, pastor, headmaster, or an executive committee.

Step 2: Once you determine that you are authorized to make the tough decision, consider the decision-making style. Will the decision be shared with colleagues and/or the board, or will it be made alone? Unless you can share sensitive details, you may have to make the decision alone. Sharing partial information often skews the judgment of other decision makers. One group of leadership experts suggests, "It is important to remember that, although you may choose to give others a degree of authority in making decisions, the ultimate responsibility is yours alone" (Hersey, 1996).

Step 3: Even if the decision must remain only with the leader, the Scriptures encourage the use of a "multitude of counselors." Good leaders not only involve other people in gathering information, they seek their advice. Such counsel expands our perspective and helps us gain a broader understanding of the issues involved. Remember to neither undervalue nor overvalue counsel simply because of someone's position or institutional influence.

Step 4: Determine the amount of time available to make this tough decision. You may face a clear deadline or (less frequently) enjoy an ideal window of time in which the decision should be made. You must not hurry the decision needlessly just to gain quick closure or relieve your emotional discomfort. The psalmist offers the admonition, "Wait for the Lord" (Psalm 27:14). Give the Lord the necessary time and space to work in you and to work out the problem.

Step 5: Commit to a decision that will honor the Lord, will serve the institution's best interest, and will treat the people involved with love and respect. Do not sacrifice any one of these elements for another. God can provide a solution that will meet these conditions.

Step 6: Within the time constraints, proceed to gather the necessary facts. The main concern rests not in the number of facts, but rather in whether or not crucial questions have been answered. If they have, you probably have the vital details needed to make the decision.

Step 7: Work hard to withhold judgment until you have collected the needed details. Don't undermine facts with partiality or intimidation and thus create emotions that cloud objectivity. Details that you have improperly weighted because of their source will corrupt tough decision making. The Scriptures urge us to investigate to ensure the accuracy of our facts (Deuteronomy 13:12–15).

Step 8: You are now ready to weigh all the possible alternatives. Make every effort to generate all the plausible possibilities. Don't forget that tough decisions often include a multitude of variables not available to a consultant or other outside authority.

Step 9: Test the most viable solutions. If they violate a known biblical principle, revise or discard them. Having completed this testing, you will usually arrive at the appropriate decision. However, sometimes two alternatives seem equally advisable. In that situation, you may test these options by asking, What are the consequences if this decision is wrong? One set of consequences may be easier to live with than the other. If so, that determination may help eliminate one of the existing alternatives.

Step 10: Eventually, you arrive at the best course of action. From the beginning, you have been committed to doing the right thing. Now you may trust God with the consequences of your decision. Since this decision has been the focus of meditation and prayer, you trust your instincts and the promptings of the Holy Spirit in finalizing the decision.

Step 11: But you're not finished yet. You must still decide whether any part of this decision is negotiable. This determination may affect the opportunity for a more gracious application and reception of your decision. If possible, try to identify those parts of the decision that will *not* be negotiable.

Step 12: Once you make the decision, do not procrastinate beyond the time you need to "sleep on the decision." Practice the principle of deciding early and announcing on time. For example, although the process may be finalized on Friday, you might announce the decision on Monday.

Step 13: Carefully decide the best time and place to announce the decision. Also determine who should be present for that announcement and in what form the decision will be presented (written and/or oral). While the decision may be presented orally, because of the emotions and complexity surrounding tough decisions, it is usually wise to write out the decision in detail.

Step 14: Include the following in the announcement of a tough decision:

- Candor: While you may choose not to share all the considerations surrounding the decision, everything you say must be accurate.
- Calmness: Remain calm and don't allow excitement or emotion to detract from the decision.
- Confidence: Biblical leaders believe that God has directed them to the wisest decision. We convey this conviction by our confidence and competence.
- Compassion: Compassion conveys love for those who are affected or those who have a different opinion. Humility and a soft spirit should characterize all administrative demeanor.
- Concern: Communicate your continuing concern for the school, the people, and the Lord's honor both in the decision and through its implementation.

Step 15: If possible, allow for feedback following the decision, especially questions that will help clarify some aspect of the decision.

Implementing Tough Decisions

Every decision must be implemented. Implementation should include the same careful thought and planning that went into making the decision. Decisions often stir strong emotions among followers who harbor conflicting ideas on the issues. That fact is part of what makes some decisions tough. We can face criticism because we understand that emotional people tend to vent their anger or disappointment. Nevertheless, the leadership team must remain united, and they must stand firmly in support of the decision. They must never become defensive in the face of critical comments.

We understand that while the decision had to be made, the complexities of the situation create powerful arguments for other possibilities. We stand firm in our decision, but still remain gracious. *Our humility acknowledges our humanity in the midst of a tough situation.* Leaders make tough decisions. Nevertheless, we understand that others might have decided differently and perhaps even more effectively.

Once we announce a decision, additional information may come to the surface. For a variety of reasons, these details were not available at the time we made the decision. If the newly revealed information clearly contradicts the decision, leaders must not be afraid to revisit the decision. This scenario happens rarely. Usually it is best to avoid second-guessing decisions. If we have been careful in the process, we can trust God with the outcomes.

We close by suggesting ten general principles for you to consider in making tough decisions in your school:

- Follow Nehemiah's example and pray more for direction.
- Be like Jesus and empower people before they have all the skills.
- Apply biblical principles at all points in the process.
- Understand the fifteen steps and make them part of your administrative style.
- Don't be thrown off stride by tough decisions; trust the Holy Spirit.
- Ask for honest input and listen to it!
- Gather information by increasing time spent with others.
- Maintain the vision but be flexible regarding plans.
- Embrace the energy and power of faculty and students.
- Intentionally implement collaborative decision making.

Leaders must not linger too long over stressful or painful decisions. Often, other duties have suffered during the period of deliberation, and they now demand your full attention. You need to return as quickly as possible to the business at hand. Rapid and cheerful rebounding can be contagious and will encourage the rest of the staff to do likewise. Thus you can help to put the crisis behind you and once again move forward.

Though you return to normal activities, keep an ear open to the aftereffects of the decision. Watch for behavior and listen for comments that suggest collateral damage. The dismissal of a popular staff member may stir up a confrontation with sympathetic supporters. Expelling a student may require the leadership team to revisit the school's disciplinary policies and procedures. Effective leaders stay sensitive to any further steps needed to bring full closure to the crisis.

It is here that the Christian executive has the tremendous advantage over his secular counterpart. Each one of us as sons of God can be assured that God is working all things together for good on our behalf. But those of us who are privileged to work as part of the organizational life of His body have the right to assume that this applies equally to the organizational task (Engstrom & Dayton, 1976).

Time is a leader's ally. The Spirit of God can take care of the consequences of a controversial decision. "And we know that in all things God works for the good of those who love him, who have been called according to his purpose" (Romans 8:28).

Bibliography

Alexander, J. W. (1978). *Managing our work*. Downers Grove, IL: InterVarsity.

Armerding, H. T. (1978). *Leadership*. Wheaton, IL: Tyndale.

Baird, K. R. (1990). *Creative leadership*. Fullerton, CA: R. C. Law & Co., Inc.

Bolman, L., & Deal, T. (1995). *Leading with soul*. San Francisco: Jossey-Bass.

Brubaker, J. L. (1987). *God's servant leader in the Christian school*. Winona Lake, IN: BMH Books.

DePree, M. (1992). *Leadership jazz*. New York: Dell Publishing.

Engstrom, T. W,. & Dayton, E. R. (1976). *The art of management for Christian leaders*. Waco, TX: Word Publishing.

Fogg, C. D. (1994). *Team-based strategic planning*. New York: Amacom.

Gangel, K. O. (1997). *Team leadership in Christian ministry*. Chicago: Moody Press.

Goleman, D. (1995). *Working with emotional intelligence*. New York: Bantam Books.

Hendrix, O. (2000). *Three dimensions of leadership*. St. Charles, IL: ChurchSmart Resources.

Hersey, P., Blanchard, K. H., & Johnson, D. E. (1996). *Management of organizational behavior*. Upper Saddle River, NJ: Prentice Hall.

Jones, L. B. (1992). *Jesus, CEO*. New York: Hyperion.

Roberts, R. (Ed.). (1999). *Lessons in leadership*. Grand Rapids, MI: Kregel Publications.

Sanders, J. O. (1967). *Spiritual leadership*. Chicago: Moody Press.

Sweet, L. (1999). *AQUA church*. Loveland, CO: Group Publishing.

The word on management: A topical index of scriptures for managers and employees. (1989). Virginia Beach, VA: Regent University, College of Administration and Management Graduate School of Business.

The Heart of the Matter

Recruiting Quality Faculty

Robert E. Gustafson Jr., M.A.

Chapter Summary

How do you select a teacher to serve in your school? Where do you find that gifted instructor, able to communicate content as well as model Christian living in a genuine and winsome manner? What qualities and characteristics, beyond those listed in the job description, do you look for in a prospective faculty member?

As one intimately involved in the process of hiring faculty, you know the joy of employing the exceptional teacher. Unfortunately, you also know the heartache of dismissing the one who "didn't work out." Mr. Gustafson communicates the simple yet profound principles that mark great teachers, adding to our understanding through examples from his own experience as a Christian school leader. These important principles can be easily adapted to your school's hiring process.

About the author
Robert E. Gustafson Jr., M.A.
Headmaster, The Stony Brook School
Stony Brook, NY
17 years of educational leadership experience

Chapter 7

The Heart of the Matter
Recruiting Quality Faculty

Robert E. Gustafson Jr., M.A.

I am a problem solver, a person who loves the challenge of tackling a situation and trying to bring order out of chaos. At work I gravitate toward seemingly unsolvable problems that demand the expertise of a determined sleuth. I'm not sure exactly why complicated problems interest me, but I have a hunch. It all goes back to a certain teacher who fascinated and motivated me during my sophomore year in high school.

Most of us have had a teacher or two who affected our development at a young age in significant ways. For me it was Ms. Bollinger. Sophomores tend to be, as their name literally suggests, "wise fools." They know everything (or so they think) and absolutely nothing at the same time. With this sophomoric aura, I entered Ms. Bollinger's class.

I determined from the beginning not to enjoy the class. After all, Algebra II did not sound like a thrilling course. I bucked the system from the start. As Ms. Bollinger required more and more, I did less and less. When she asked us to show all of our work, I figured the answer in my head and gave her the answer and nothing more. When she took points off for my unwillingness to follow directions, I protested.

Yet sometime early on, this master teacher won me over. Maybe it was her uncanny ability to explain even the most difficult math problems in terms I could understand. She activated my competitive nature; every test included a bonus question, a real challenge. If I could solve the bonus question, I could score over 100 percent on the test. Maybe I sensed she really did care about me. She even asked me about football and came to see me play. Win me over she did.

Before long my Algebra homework became the highlight of my evening's study. I wanted to do my best and tried to solve all the problems meticulously. I had the best school year ever, and I learned to love a subject and a teacher in a way I never thought I would. Henry Adams said it best: "A teacher affects eternity; he can never tell where his influence stops."

Those of us involved in education know intuitively that teachers determine the success or failure of the learning process. Technology and facilities impress us, but nothing can replace a master teacher who affects the hearts and minds of young people for the rest of their lives. A recent study confirmed the centrality of teachers to the success of students in the classroom:

> Teachers are clearly the most important factor affecting student achievement. We looked at class size, at whether schools were urban, suburban or rural, at per-pupil expenditures, at ethnic make-up, at the percentage of kids eligible for free and reduced lunch and at whether students were in heterogeneous or homogeneous groupings. Teacher effectiveness is ten to twenty times as significant as the effects of other things. It surprised me, quite frankly. (Marks, 2000)

How do we find such gifted teachers, these miracle workers who touch the hearts and souls of young people? What makes great teachers? What motivates them? Once we find them, how do we encourage them to pursue their profession with creative passion, often with very little pay and long, grueling hours?

Because we realize the critical importance of building quality Christian schools, we must hire and develop the finest teachers possible. Dynamic teachers provide the key to successful schools. Christian educators must find not only great teachers but also role models of faith for our young people. Here are the qualities we look for as we hire our faculty at Stony Brook.

Great Teachers Are Lifetime Learners

Teaching as an Art

Over the years, I have come to realize that teaching is an art, not a science. I understand educators who require prospective teachers to take a series of courses for certification. After all, it looks good on paper, and often parents and boards are concerned that teachers be certified. Yet I have observed teachers with impeccable résumés struggle in the classroom. If forced to make a choice, particularly at the secondary level, I would much rather hire teachers with a degree in the subject area they teach rather than those who have taken only education courses.

Contagious Enthusiasm

More often than not, prospective teachers who have chosen majors and pursued them have done so because of a love for the subject. Their personal passion is evident in the classroom as they share their love of learning with their students. Their contagious enthusiasm motivates children and young people to join them in the pleasure of classroom discovery.

In interviews, I always ask candidates what they have been reading recently. The ones who love their subjects never fumble for an answer. They are exploring a new discovery in their fields or a new approach to teaching their disciplines. Out of this reading comes a new curriculum unit or a relevant field trip. Lifetime learners make the most creative teachers. They establish a classroom setting that stirs students' curiosity and excitement by appealing to all five senses, and they can often reach even the most difficult students.

An English teacher who also writes, either with the class or for wider publication, a science teacher who personally explores the local marine ecosystem, and a math teacher who finds fascination in the new chaos theories of mathematics—these teachers will walk into their classrooms and ignite the fire of interest in their students.

I remember my own daughter's thrill in taking a course here at the Stony Brook School from Dr. Louis Simpson, a Pulitzer Prize–winning poet. As the students opened the anthology of poetry for the year, they discovered a prominent section of Dr. Simpson's own poetry. How motivating it was for my daughter to study with a real poet! As she explored her own poetic interest, she remained fascinated throughout the year with the love of language and the ardor for good writing that Dr. Simpson not only taught but also demonstrated. His passion became her passion.

Learning from Your Students

Great teachers also learn from their students. They realize that learning is never a one-way street. I remember a discussion in a ninth-grade Bible class at a highly regarded school in Atlanta, Georgia. Working through the book of 1 Samuel, we came to the narrative of David and Goliath. As the class pondered the story of David's courage, a boy in the back of the classroom raised his hand. I had taught this narrative for years and did not expect the question he asked: "Mr. Gustafson, why didn't Jonathan kill Goliath?" I paused as I contemplated the question. I then stopped the class and repeated it for all to hear. Responding thoughtfully, I simply said, "I do not know, but your question is worth some extended time."

I sent those ninth-graders home to think about what they knew of Jonathan in order to answer this question. We spent two days in a lively discussion, exploring possible answers. We looked at the question from every angle. I learned much from my students in those two days. Certainly

Jonathan was brave enough to kill Goliath. After all, hadn't he climbed a steep cliff to defeat the Philistine army against all odds just a few chapters prior to the Goliath story? Jonathan loved God and was committed to Him so much that he gave up his claim to the throne of Israel when it became apparent that God had anointed David.

From our discussion, I learned that sometimes God calls us to take a secondary role. He calls some to lead and others to support those leaders. The graciousness of Jonathan in accepting his role as David's servant speaks clearly about Jonathan's character and faith. We never answered the question definitively, but for two days the students taught me in a rich learning experience that opened up this biblical narrative in fresh ways.

Great Teachers Are Gifted Communicators

Making the Difficult Easy

A prospective teacher with a master's degree or even a Ph.D. who has an abundance of head knowledge but little rapport with students will flounder in the classroom. We all know that knowledge alone is insufficient.

One of the greatest traits that a teacher can have is the ability to make difficult topics understandable. I reserve my highest compliments for the teacher who can do this. Creative teachers who grapple with the traditional learning process and constantly explore new approaches usually have this gift.

Conversely, all of us have known those frustrating teachers who take a relatively simple concept and make it difficult. As students ask questions, the teacher's answers muddy the waters rather than making them clearer. By contrast, the master teacher who uses an appropriate illustration or provides a helpful hands-on experience often illumines what at first seemed impossible to grasp.

Over the years, I have had the privilege of working with a variety of gifted teachers. I will never forget a first-grade teacher named Ellen Voelker. Working in a situation where the eighteen students she taught came from a variety of backgrounds, she created an atmosphere of fun and excitement about learning. In teaching science to her first-graders, Ms. Voelker admitted that science was not her strength. Yet she unleashed such curiosity and excitement that her weekly science time captivated her young students.

I remember walking past her room one day wondering about the buzz of excitement. I opened the door and realized that she was teaching a lesson on arachnids (spiders). A group of students huddled in the room as she described the characteristics of spiders, illustrated by the tarantula she held in her hands. Not only were the children wide-eyed, but so was the headmaster! She had named the tarantula Maggie. The teacher encouraged students to hold Maggie for a minute and stroke her fuzzy back if they wanted to.

One of the young girls looked at me and asked boldly, "Mr. Gustafson, would you like to hold Maggie for a few minutes?" They all laughed when I quickly declined, and they joked for the rest of the year that Mr. Gustafson was not as brave as some of his first-grade students. Ms. Voelker smiled when I declined to hold Maggie, and then she put her gently back in her spider cage. Little did I know that tarantulas are generally mild tempered and their bite is harmless to human beings. I'm not suggesting that anyone copy this teacher's idea, but it worked for her and created excitement and curiosity in her classroom.

What Ms. Voelker may have lacked in her knowledge of science she compensated for by her creativity and natural love for the world God created. Her bold hands-on adventure became a rite of passage and a badge of courage for many of the first-graders as they learned about the world of science in unforgettable ways.

By contrast, I am dismayed by the difficulty many high school students face in navigating upper-level science courses successfully. The challenging vocabulary and extensive factual information in a rigorous introductory biology course often baffle them.

When I took my first upper school director's position years ago at a school in the South, I worried about the science department's ability to deliver necessary rigor to the students. My fears were alleviated when I walked into the biology lab. I entered a small animal sanctuary and a beautiful greenhouse known to those who had never ventured in as simply the biology room. Mr. Adams, the biology teacher, had created an amazing environment of reptiles, fish, fossils, and plants ready for the curious learner to observe and explore.

I later found out that many students had joined his science club, which included not just a common interest in God's created world but a commitment to the maintenance and care of the biology room. They fed the animals, cleaned the cages, and watered the plants. Even over holidays and summers, many students committed to the upkeep of this indoor nature world. Mr. Adams knew that this opportunity for hands-on work would overcome many of the obstacles to the book learning that students would have to conquer during the year.

His famous "bug collection" assignment each year sent curious learners scurrying to far points of the region to find, capture, and carefully mount different varieties of beetles, spiders, butterflies, and other "bugs." They learned this process so well that a local natural museum accepted the best specimens each year and added them to its collection. Our students' "bugs" were better than the museum's own! Biology with Mr. Adams transformed this difficult course from the drudgery of mere book learning and memorization into real-life experience. Caring for the animals and mounting their collections in a professional way helped make biology live.

A Multisensory Approach

As I interview teaching candidates, I broaden the definition of a great communicator to one who can not only give a great talk but who can create a multisensory approach to learning as well. Too often we think of education as learning that takes place only in the formal classroom. Tools such as textbooks, white boards, computers, and worksheets immediately come to mind.

Lawrence Cremins, the president emeritus of Teachers College, Columbia University, opened his lecture on the history of American education with the following statement: "Education happens wherever you are." As he expounded on the hundreds of ways all of us learn, including museums, historical landmarks, and cross-generational discussions around the family dinner table, it became apparent that master teachers naturally realize that the classroom simply affords a home base for learning.

Great Teachers Love the Age-Group They Teach

Teaching the Age They Love

Having taught and administered at several different schools, I recognize the importance of matching teachers with the age-group they love. A few master teachers can move from the elementary grades into high school without faltering, but in general each age-group has particular needs and requires a particular kind of teacher.

For many years, educators assumed that sixth- through ninth-graders were simply a smaller version of high school students. We rarely considered the special needs of this age-group, and often junior high was just what its name suggests, a watered-down version of high school.

In my thinking about the hiring of teachers, I no longer assume that a gifted calculus teacher can necessarily teach eighth-grade math. For many high school teachers, a move to the middle school classroom is impossible. The reverse holds true as well.

Ideally, a teaching candidate ought to have the opportunity to teach two or three classes or units during the process of the interview. This component affords a perfect opportunity to see the teacher in action, and the experience can reveal strengths not observable in the more formal interview process. I have often seen a rather sedate and quiet teaching candidate come alive when given a chance to teach.

For teachers, this ingredient of loving the age they teach is vital, since some love their subjects but seem unable to communicate that love to others. Outstanding teachers have a deep love for children and young adults, and students feel this love the minute they walk in the classroom. The teacher does not have to say much. Intuitively the students will know the teacher is for them. When students feel this care, they will do their best for that teacher. Look for teachers who demonstrate a rapport with the age-group they teach. When you find these teachers, nurture them and appreciate them; their students will be stretched and loved at the same time.

As I surveyed the science wing corridor one hot Friday afternoon, I was surprised to hear a song coming from one of the rooms. I slowly approached and peeked into the chemistry room. There my chemistry teacher was sitting on a lab stool, guitar in hand, singing a song he had written for the occasion called "The Sixth-Period Chemistry Blues." The students enjoyed the break and appreciated his sense of timing. Dr. Stribling instinctively knew that sixth period, the end of the day, was a tough time to teach anything, let alone chemistry. He let them know he understood. For a few moments, he became one of them, struggling to learn this difficult subject at the end of a long day. A simple demonstration of empathy often encourages students to enter more fully into the teacher's world of learning.

This fact was illustrated for me a week later when Dr. Stribling announced in an assembly that there would be a rare conjunction of planets over the weekend. Dr. Stribling offered to set up the school's telescope for a viewing that Saturday night. I doubted that any students would come on a Saturday night! Yet thirty students showed up to learn more about this amazing phenomenon. Dr. Stribling, by communicating that he understood his students with something as simple as a song, used their affinity with him to draw them into his love of science. Great teachers do that naturally.

Great Teachers Provide Role Models for Their Students

Teachers: The Architects of School Culture

In a very real sense, when we hire teachers for a Christian school, we search for much more than just intellectual ability and the gift of communication. Parents have often asked me how I would evaluate a Christian school. Would I look at programs? How important are extracurricular activities? Does a strong record of test scores indicate excellence? Would I explore textbooks or curriculum?

In a thorough evaluation, all these form important pieces of the puzzle, but they do not complete the puzzle. My evaluation would probably look different from that of most parents. I want to know what happens in what I call the unguarded moments of the school day. In other words, I am less concerned initially about the formal program than about the informal tone and culture of the students and faculty.

To evaluate a school accurately, I would arrive before the day begins and watch students as they arrive. What do they talk about? How do they treat each other with no adults around? Do they show a healthy respect for the adults in the community, or do they reveal an underlying dislike of the teachers and the administrators?

I would go to the lunchroom and listen to the conversations, watching how students decide where they will sit. In the afternoon after athletic practice, I would observe the interaction between coaches and players. I would go on a second-grade field trip and see what happens in the unguarded moments as children wait in line to enter the museum exhibit. I want to see evidence that God is at work through teachers who take advantage of the teachable moments.

I consider these observations important because in the hiring of faculty, one must remember that teachers are the architects of school culture and tone. They form the adult community of the school, and our mission is only as strong as the community of adults who work with students. In his book *The Death of Character*, James Hunter is concerned that character building can happen only in a community where young people "inhabit a social world that coherently incarnates a moral culture defined by a clear and intelligible understanding of private and public virtues" (2001). The teachers we hire must incarnate the gospel for our students. In a recent article, William Bennett put it this way:

> Schools are helping to cultivate moral sensibilities, to shape character, every day. Students notice whether teachers go about their work conscientiously or lazily, enthusiastically or begrudgingly. They see how the adults in the school address one another, the students, and their parents.... In all these ways, habits of feeling, thought, and action are being cultivated: Character is being formed. (Bennett & Delattre, 2001)

The Importance of Role Models

Too often in Christian schools, we pay close attention to the textbooks, the chapel programs, and the curriculum through which we desire to impart a Christian worldview to our students. One can hardly fault that intent, but we need to remember at the same time that the "living gospel," the adult community life, communicates this worldview even more strongly. This hidden curriculum, this daily positive interaction of teachers and students, makes a fertile environment for young people. If teachers are deep, wise believers walking with Christ in the humility of the gospel of grace, character education will happen each moment of every day. If not, if adults in the community are at odds with each other, the students will quickly forget the wonderful chapel lessons. As William Bennett so aptly states:

> But if character education is understood to occur inexorably through the ordinary workings of schools, then the salient question is not whether schools have an influence on character, but what kind of influence it is—i.e., what qualities of character a school is helping to form. To answer this question, one must look closely at

the particular ways a school goes about its daily business, apart from any formal programs of character education. (Bennett & Delattre, 2001)

In the hiring of faculty, we must never forget that administrators assemble a community of adult believers who will become the main witnesses of the gospel to students. If we desire our students to treat each other with compassion, they must see adults treating each other with compassion. There is no getting around it. If we want them to forgive each other, we as teachers and administrators must do the same.

Every Christian school should display an intentional Christian community of adults who love Christ and want to share that love with students. Too often we busy ourselves with formal programming and close our eyes to any problems in the adult community. We need to hire faculty who understand the demands of living in a faith community, who humbly admit fault and forgive each other, and who accept their responsibilities as role models prayerfully. Only when faculty members live the gospel can a Christian school dramatically influence students' lives. Only then will the school be a vibrant intellectual and spiritual community.

Great Teachers Are like Gentle Parents

For a number of years, I have been thinking constantly about the keys to effective Christian schooling. Increasingly, I find myself less interested in the jargon of education and more interested in knowing what really works and why. Theory is wonderful, but nothing teaches better than personal experience. It alone weaves wisdom into the fabric of our inner souls.

Having had the responsibility of working with students and teachers in the area of discipline and behavior, I have become thoroughly convinced that teaching is more like parenting than anything else. Even the most talented young teachers grow tremendously as they gain the experience and wisdom of parenting.

Gentleness: Teaching as Parenting

Recently I became acquainted with the writings of Father Jacques, the headmaster of a school in France during the years of the Holocaust. While he directed this small school, he enrolled Jewish students, often risking his life to give them a home during those troubled times. Needless to say, he was a man of great faith who learned about education in the crucible of social crisis.

In his series of essays entitled *Selection*, Father Jacques writes a wonderful short essay called "The Education of Youth." I have never read anything that so profoundly and succinctly explains the calling of Christian educators.

The school should be an extension of the family. It should reproduce, as fully as possible, the shape, spirit, and warmth of the family. It should reflect the whole range of subtle characteristics that produce what we commonly call a "family atmosphere." There should be nothing to prompt a child to utter the word "prison." There should be no ugly, drab classrooms where the child feels all alone, no faded soiled walls; no tasteless, predictable monotonous food that takes away the child's appetite. Instead everything should laugh and sing from the basement to the attic ... to reaffirm all day long that those who live within the walls are members of a family, filled to the brim with confidence and love. (Murphy, 1998)

I cannot think of a better way to describe a Christian school. Before hiring prospective teachers, the administrator should ascertain whether or not they understand their parenting role in the school family. Parents empathize deeply with the emotions and struggles of their own children, and the great teacher, the one who will impact the lives of her students most profoundly, will see in the face of every student her own child. Teachers attached to their students desire the best for them. They learn to treat students as they would their own children and thus shape their hearts and minds for eternity. As Father Jacques states, "To the child who is entrusted to them, the teachers owe the same affection, devotion and care that parents themselves give to their children ... educators in effect adopt them as their own children. If this adoption is true, sincere, and meaningful, a current of mutual affection becomes established between teachers and students" (Murphy, 1998).

A Family Atmosphere

How often we design Christian schools with rules clearly defined and structures carefully set—but no family atmosphere! The teachers all seem competent enough, the curriculum appears well planned, the chapel program has all the right ingredients (prayer, a scriptural talk, and singing), but the most important element is missing. Without family spirit, the school community feels less like home and more like prison. I look for teachers willing to "adopt" students as their own children, to parent them as true parents would—loving them, disciplining them, and caring for them with the heart of the father for the prodigal son.

Isn't this a picture of the Christian family? Aren't we all adopted sons and daughters of our heavenly Father? Doesn't He love us unconditionally in Christ? How can we talk about hiring quality faculty unless we talk about emulating our heavenly Father? If I can find teachers who instinctively understand the ingredients of great parenting and who demonstrate the ebb and flow of gentleness and tough love, then I have found adults who will have significant influence on young people's lives. Anything less minimizes what the Christian school should be.

Understanding Biblical Gentleness as a Teacher

Agreeing with the thinking of Father Jacques, I am looking for teachers who understand and live out a biblical sense of gentleness. In his essay "The Education of Youth," he states, "True gentleness is neither weakness, nor softness nor timidity.... Gentleness is above all a 'tranquil force'" (Murphy, 1998). Certain teachers have amazing ability to challenge their students with high standards and to be tough when necessary—while always being gentle. Students know instinctively that this teacher loves them enough to challenge and encourage them.

> Genuine, strong and serene gentleness can only reside in those hearts that forget about themselves in order to think of others. That gentleness knows no greater happiness than to pour out all of its time, all of its energy, and all of its devotion on those who need a kind word, a friendly bit of advice, or a helping hand. (Murphy, 1998)

Each of us needs a helping hand, and such a model of gentleness reflects our understanding of the gospel and of the need for the school to be a caring family.

I received a phone call recently from a parent of one of my students. In the course of the conversation, we talked about the school and the atmosphere created by the teachers. His caution still rings in my ears: "Rob, the rules of the school are very important. But when one of your students comes to class out of dress code and the first words from the teacher's mouth are 'Go to the office! Do not return until you are properly dressed,' that teacher has set a negative tone, one that does not reflect a family setting. Maybe a friendly greeting and later a quiet talk about the need to follow the rules would create a better atmosphere." Family atmosphere includes thinking before speaking, finding the right time and the right words to communicate concern about rules. It includes being gentle and having a tranquil force that upholds standards in a way that also upholds students' dignity. It means seeing in every student the heart and soul of one's own child. "True educators touch the hearts of all their students, and thus touch their entire lives. Such an approach requires a calm, firm, and balanced spirit. In one word, it requires gentleness" (Murphy, 1998).

Hiring the right faculty rests at the heart of successful Christian schools. As Paul Girard states, "The problem of education is the problem of the educator" (Murphy, 1998). No matter what else we do as administrators, we need a clear vision of the mission of our schools, hiring adults who love what they teach and who communicate with creativity and clarity. At the same time, we need adults who love the age-group they teach, adopting each student as if he or she were their own child. When we establish a family atmosphere, the school becomes a fertile place to educate the hearts and minds of the next generation.

What practical steps can administrators take to identify and hire well-qualified teachers? There is no simple answer to this practical dilemma. Great teachers are difficult to find. Yet the following suggestions might be helpful as we look for quality teachers, the key to great schools.

1. *Get to know the leaders* of the Christian groups located on the campuses of local and regional colleges and universities. Take them out to lunch and let them know your needs.

2. *Stay in touch with the pastors of local churches.* Often teachers in local congregations would be interested if they knew about a position from an announcement in the church bulletin. Periodically invite local pastors to speak in chapel or to have lunch with you on campus.

3. *Develop a relationship with the Christian colleges.* Stony Brook has always had a strong relationship with Wheaton College, and many of our faculty received their degrees there. Since we have close ties, we call Wheaton when a position becomes available.

4. *Be actively involved in Christian and secular educational organizations.* Often even in a secular setting, Christian teachers participate in conferences and seminars. Some of these organizations have prayer breakfasts at which administrators can meet Christian teachers from all over the country.

5. *Network with a number of other headmasters.* All of us get applications from interested teachers. If you develop a strong relationship with other headmasters, you can often share the names of applicants. For example, one school may need a math teacher, and another may need a history teacher. Sharing names may help fill the positions.

Be persistent, and when you find gifted teachers, nurture them as your most valuable asset.

Bibliography

Bennett, W. J., & Delattre, E. J. (2001, August 20/August 27). Character, the old-fashioned way. *The Weekly Standard*.

Hunter, J. D. (2001). *The death of character: Moral education in an age without good or evil*. New York: Basic Books.

Marks, M. (2000, January 15). The teacher factor. *New York Times: Education section*.

Murphy, F. J. (1998). *Pere Jaques: Resplendent in victory*. Washington, DC: Institute of Carmelite Studies Publications.

Training a Terrific Teaching Team

Developing and Retaining Faculty

Byrle Kynerd, Ph.D.

Chapter Summary

The most valuable human resource in any Christian school is the faculty you've employed. Each teacher stands before students every day, impacting tender lives for eternity. But how do you as the school administrator make certain that each teacher is adequately prepared for this responsibility? How can your school train and retain quality instructional leaders?

With more than twenty years of experience as a Christian school superintendent, Dr. Kynerd articulates your crucial role as the school leader in all faculty-related activities. Nurturing your faculty requires a purposeful and consistent effort, intended to encourage each member to grow and develop to his or her fullest potential as individual teachers and as an important part of your faculty. Dr. Kynerd presents practical ideas that you can apply to your specific school setting.

About the author

Byrle Kynerd, Ph.D.
Superintendent, Briarwood Christian School
Birmingham, AL
34 years of educational leadership experience

Chapter 8

Training a Terrific Teaching Team
Developing and Retaining Faculty

Byrle Kynerd, Ph.D.

C hristian education may be on the brink of influencing more students
and more families than ever before. The potential for impact is significant because these students could infuse culture with biblical values
and a biblical perspective. The effectiveness these students can have as "salt
and light" in a decaying culture will be determined, in large part, by the quality of the leadership over faculty in Christian schools. Christian schools can
have the most meaningful and lasting impact by attracting, training, and
nurturing instructional leaders who encourage, teach, and guide students.

Henry Adams wrote, "The impact of a teacher may go to eternity." A
recent letter from a parent to a Christian school administrator conveyed
appreciation for outstanding teachers and stressed the challenge to remain
vigilant in developing and supporting quality faculty:

I believe that the future of excellent Christian education depends upon
recruiting and retaining excellent faculty, Christian men and women who
live out the life of Christ in their lives, who energetically serve their students, who keep up in their academic fields, who know how to motivate students to want to learn and to think and to solve problems with a Christian
mind-set, who can come alongside all students in their classes whether they
have the highest or lowest academic ability and challenge them. We have
been blessed with many such teachers and administrators. (William
Whitaker, personal communication, August 2001)

This communication confirms the close relationship among school excellence, meaningful impact on students, and faculty leadership. Effective training and retention are closely linked and require the intentional focus of school officials.

Faculty Training Demands Intentional Purpose

Each faculty-related school activity should reflect clear, intentional design. We must anchor faculty training in biblical wisdom designed to encourage, equip, and strengthen those privileged to convey truth to a generation of students. Effective faculty training includes several essential building stones.

Intentional Design

Effective faculty training follows a pattern that reflects a clear purpose and specific goals. Careful assessment of the school's instructional program will define the areas of need. Training should strengthen the faculty's capacity to deliver the school's mission effectively. The following example illustrates how careful school assessment can define the goals of faculty training.

Bethel Christian School had a sound academic program, but school officials noticed a declining pattern in its achievement test scores and other measures of the academic program. In the three years of decline, the school experienced major faculty turnover. This combination of events encouraged the school staff to reexamine the instructional reading program. They were surprised to find:

- Time for teaching reading had been reduced to forty minutes a day. No one intended that to happen, but it did.
- Several new teachers acknowledged they did not know phonics and had no specific training for teaching reading.
- The majority of teachers believed comprehension is best taught through testing on facts from stories in basal readers.
- The school had abandoned small-group reading instruction when a new administrator complained that it improperly grouped students. No one questioned the change.
- Because of the absence of focused leadership and effective supervision, teachers handled reading in a variety of ways. The lack of effective reading instruction reflected the low interest level and lack of training of each teacher.
- The school offered teachers no reading training in the four years under the new administrator, who was effective in several areas but lacked strong skills in curriculum and instructional leadership.

The assessment revealed major deficiencies in the reading program. A thoughtful, thorough evaluation produced the information needed to develop faculty training that would equip teachers to meet the learning

needs of the students at Bethel Christian School. As a result of the assessment, school administrators were able to encourage, equip, and guide the
faculty in correcting the reading deficiencies. The school set up a faculty
training program with meaningful content that would lead to improved
reading instruction. Because of the prior assessment, the training reflected
intentional design.

Faculty Sensitivity

Quality faculty training, though rigorous and conducted by stimulating
leaders, must also reflect careful planning and thoughtful consideration of
the time pressures teachers face. Bethel Christian School realized that extensive training would be required to strengthen the reading program. The
school scheduled three "faculty friendly" training segments.

The first segment provided a general overview of the assessment conclusions; analysis of recent research about effective reading programs; discussion
about stewardship responsibilities to students; information on the importance of reading, comprehension, and thinking skills; and the presentation of
an action plan. The session, which lasted three hours, divided faculty by grade
level to encourage meaningful dialogue and interaction. The school provided
lunch, and substitute teachers handled afternoon teaching responsibilities to
demonstrate the administrators' understanding and appreciation for the faculty and to convey a spirit of unity and team building.

The second segment, held over two days in July, gave teachers clear guidelines, methodologies, and objectives. These sessions focused on how to teach
reading and provided specific instruction so teachers would understand the
blueprint adopted by the school. Experts demonstrated and modeled classroom instruction for the full faculty, for smaller grade-level groups, and for
individual teachers. Support materials were provided to ensure that teachers
did not have to use valuable time pulling these together.

Because change can feel threatening, all faculty training should encourage teachers and help them understand the goals and expectations of the
training. Some find it difficult to learn crucial skills, so patience and wisdom must characterize any training program.

Bethel systematically scheduled the third segment of training throughout
the first year of the reading initiative. They offered constant support to individual teachers and to groups at each grade level. Periodic grade-level meetings took place as substitute teachers handled afternoon teaching duties.
These meetings included answering questions, sharing experiences, and
revising the program.

Near the end of the school year, grade-level meetings created further
opportunities to critique and improve the program. Besides constructive
suggestions, these sessions produced resounding affirmations that the new
reading program worked well. A careful review confirmed that God had

honored faculty faithfulness and that the extensive training had helped significantly to make it a wonderful school year.

The focused faculty training for the reading program continued the next summer, with further analysis of the fruit of the faculty's labor. Several examples of the powerful impact of the faculty training were identified:

- Achievement test scores, which were excellent already, improved significantly. The improvement was especially dramatic when the increases were compared with those of the preceding five years!
- All thirty-seven teachers in the elementary school reported a significant increase in the number of books their students read. More students acquired good reading skills than ever before.
- Comprehension and thinking skills *soared* in every classroom.
- Unprecedented numbers of parents gave unsolicited comments about their children's new interest in and enjoyment of reading.
- Every teacher agreed that the reading initiative had given them a much more effective and stimulating way to teach reading!
- Representatives from several states, including some from cross-cultural schools, came to evaluate the reading program. Several of these schools sent teachers to a three-week summer institute so they could implement the reading program in their schools.
- A stimulating learning atmosphere characterized each classroom, and all teachers better understood the reading skills of their students. Revitalization characterized the instructional program in the school.
- The greatest fruit from the program may not be known for years. Consider the increased attention that good readers will give to reading God's Word!

> When it comes to serious meditation, we have sometimes belittled the importance of education to prepare the way for this crucial habit. One basic and compelling reason for education—the rigorous training of the mind—is, very simply, so that a person can read the Bible with understanding.
>
> This sounds too obvious to be useful or compelling. But that's just because we take the preciousness of reading so for granted or, even more, because we appreciate so little the kind of thinking that a complex Bible passage requires of us. (Piper, 2000)

Biblical Base

Effective training must reflect a heart for the faculty, for students, and for the community. We anchor training in wonderful passages such as Psalm 133 and Psalm 127:1 and 2:

> How good and pleasant it is when brothers live together in unity! It

is like precious oil poured on the head, running down on the beard, running down on Aaron's beard, down upon the collar of his robes. It is as if the dew of Hermon were falling on Mount Zion. For there the Lord bestows his blessing, even life forevermore. (Psalm 133)

God bestows His blessing on those who work in unity! Faculty training serves as an essential instrument for developing a Christ-centered school climate. It can bring focus to a school program, present a dynamic witness to students and community, and define a school climate.

Spiritual Formation

Every school that provides intentional, focused faculty training in philosophy and mission as related to the spiritual formation of students will sound a clear trumpet that conveys the heart of the school to faculty, students, and community. Faculty training may cultivate spiritual formation in students by:

- Recognizing the defining quality of an impact school.
- Defining the components of a divinely directed school climate.
- Helping faculty understand the importance of building relationships with students.
- Acknowledging faculty responsibility for spiritual formation.

The training can begin with several key questions asked of the faculty:

- How does spiritual formation happen in Christian schools?
- What happens to students when a school fails to prioritize spiritual formation?
- What traits mark Christian schools that successfully convey biblical truth through their students to the next generation?
- Why do some Christian schools succeed in impacting their students with spiritual formation, while other schools fail?

Discussion of these and other issues can heighten faculty interest in the spiritual formation of their students and create eagerness for training. Quality training involves the faculty as participants. Dialogue sets the stage for instruction that gives schools great spiritual impact on and through their students. Psalm 78 illustrates the impact of schools that teach truth:

O my people, hear my teaching; listen to the words of my mouth. I will open my mouth in parables, I will utter hidden things, things from of old— ... We will not hide them from their children; we will tell the next generation the praiseworthy deeds of the Lord, his power, and the wonders he has done.

... so the next generation would know them, even the children yet to be born, and they in turn would tell their children. Then they would put their trust in God and would not forget his deeds but would keep his commands. (Psalm 78:1, 2, 4, 6, 7)

Christian schools that impact their students spiritually have a divinely empowered school climate. This spiritual power transfers to countless people, including the next generation.

We must encourage the faculty to prayerfully consider how a school can have such a climate. As a group, they can define the components of this kind of school environment and assess the value of each one. Components should include:

- Priority on teaching and honoring the Word of God(Hebrews 4:12, Psalm 119:105)
- Policies and practice that reflect a devotion to God (Matthew 6:33)
- Desire to honor the preeminence of Christ throughout the school
- Reliance on the Spirit of God for all things
- Relationships that demonstrate God's emphasis on love and kindness.
- Prevailing prayer that characterizes all faculty and staff

We achieve faculty ownership of these priorities through group discussion, trainer guidance, and God's grace.

Another training session can deal with the role and responsibility of the faculty in the spiritual formation of students. During this session, we focus on understanding how impact is transferred. The teachers identify the teacher(s) who had the greatest influence in their lives and explain why. This exercise will quickly underscore the lasting value of personal relationships, emphasizing how building positive relationships greatly increases learning and impact. This discussion can include strategy-building sessions to explore biblical ways to build and strengthen personal relationships. Testimonies about people who profoundly impacted the lives of others can magnify the enormous potential of relationship formation in classrooms, activity events, and athletic endeavors.

Faculty training must give knowledge, understanding, perspective, responsibility, and appropriate challenge. The training can conclude with a personal challenge to all teachers to accept responsibility for helping with the glorious task of shaping the spiritual climate within their spheres of influence. Servant leaders need to express gratitude for the privilege of being God's instruments that shape school climate so that God may be honored by present and future generations of students.

Faculty Training Requires Sincere Evaluation

Effective faculty training includes opportunities for constructive feedback. Administrators may feel confident about the training, but faculty feedback can be instructive, insightful, constructive, and confirming. This evaluation can take the form of written appraisals, group discussions, summary testing, and individual conferences with teachers. Constructive assessment should guide future training.

Tender Truth

Christian educators should use biblical guidelines for all their professional and personal relationships. Philippians 2:1–11 provides a framework for Christ-honoring relations between teachers and administrators. The phrase "tender truth" conveys a clear picture of balance in communication: We are responsible to tell the truth to one another, and we should reflect the fruit of the Spirit (Galatians 5:22–26) throughout our communication. Good relationships provide a firm foundation for meaningful impact from faculty training, and all parties should honor the tender truth principle.

Written Records

In training faculty, leaders need to provide some information in writing. Effective administrators recognize the value of written messages:

- Written communications tend to be clearer and more precise than oral messages.
- Written communication can complement and highlight the most important points of faculty training.
- People move, new teachers come, administrators change, and memory fades, but a written message provides a lasting record.

Consistent Modeling

School administrators can use faculty training to model good teaching strategies as they deal with other primary training goals. Modeling the use of technology through presentations; demonstrating the value of developing thinking skills by asking questions; and teaching to auditory, visual, and kinesthetic learners will help teachers see the value of sound teaching strategies. Quality teaching by those directing faculty training will move teachers closer to adopting effective teaching strategies. "A student is not above his teacher, but everyone who is fully trained will be like his teacher" (Luke 6:40).

Faculty Retention

A quality, experienced faculty distinguishes and defines a school. Frequent faculty changes make it difficult to build excellence, continuity, tradition, and lasting relationships between the school and its graduates. Concerted efforts devoted to retaining well-trained, faithful teachers will yield strategic and lasting benefits for every aspect of a school.

Excellent faculty retention results from a school climate sensitive to the Holy Spirit and committed to building and retaining distinguished faculty.

School leaders convey sensitivity and commitment to faculty in a variety of ways.

Continual Prayer

"The prayer of a righteous man is powerful and effective" (James 5:16b). Wise administrators trust God to bring and keep the faculty they need; they do not depend on their own leadership. They recognize that "Unless the Lord builds the house, its builders labor in vain" (Psalm 127:1a). Administrators must appropriate God's promises and trust God's sufficiency to provide His servant leaders for Christian schools. Yielding to the leadership of God's Spirit through prayer and supplication will help build an attitude of trusting God for everything: "Call to me and I will answer you and tell you great and unsearchable things you do not know" (Jeremiah 33:3). Such passages encourage administrators to trust God for their faculty.

Ephesians 3:20 promises, "[God] is able to do immeasurably more than all we ask or imagine, according to his power that is at work within us." Prayer is the greatest privilege and the most valuable resource we have for building faculty retention in our schools. God both invites and commands us to pray!

Prayer also builds bonds of unity within a faculty. Faculties that pray together daily before school begins develop a deep level of love and caring for one another. Bearing one another's burdens by praying for each other, for families, and for personal needs strengthens cords of unity. Nothing builds a climate of brotherly love like the bond of prayer.

Biblical Focus

School administrators cultivate an environment that encourages continuity in their faculty when they extend contracts and encourage all teachers to reexamine their calling, to reconsider the blessings of their ministry, and to invite God to guide their decisions. Giving teachers time to evaluate these items promotes a God-centered focus throughout the school. All school decisions, including faculty retention, must be subject to God's plan for the school.

Administrators build strong relationships with their faculty when they demonstrate a desire to surrender to God's will for faculty decisions. Both having pure motives about faculty employment decisions and helping the faculty with their own employment decisions build an environment that invites long-term relationships between faculty and school.

Clear Communication

Leaders who build high faculty retention are proactive in faculty relations. One of the most effective ways to be proactive is through communication to and from the faculty. Good communication should be:

Frequent	Encouraging	Helpful	Open
Sensitive	Positive	Uplifting	Courteous
Thoughtful	Kind	Considerate	Articulate
Effective	Accurate	Gracious	Well timed

Weekly email messages or notes build security and confidence between faculty and administrators. These brief messages might convey appreciation for faithful service, prayer support for the week, or a verse of Scripture to encourage them. Personal notes are meaningful to people because they reflect caring and love for the individual teacher. Faculty find security and joy in a caring, open environment. Schools that prioritize meaningful communication between teachers and administrators usually experience positive faculty retention.

Encouragement and Exhortation

People respond well to communication balanced between encouragement and exhortation. Administrators win respect from their faculties when they demonstrate respect for them. One tangible means of conveying respect is through words: "Do not let any unwholesome talk come out of your mouths, but only what is helpful for building others up according to their needs, that it may benefit those who listen" (Ephesians 4:29). Such passages provide a standard that calls for balance and care in shepherding the faculty. Encouragement must be genuine and deserved, or it will become meaningless. Exhortation must be clear, justified, timely, and tempered with encouragement. A school climate that blends encouragement and exhortation will stimulate a faculty to deeds of love and mercy. People find such a milieu attractive, and they tend to remain there.

The following example of a brief email from an administrator to his faculty illustrates the power of sincere, brief messages:

> "Your Word is a lamp to my feet and a light for my path" (Psalm 119:105). May we be guided by and reflect the eternal Word in all the ways we live and serve today. Oh, for the opportunities to trust God for this day to make a difference in a person's life. Continue to be a blessing for God's glory.

The message is filled with instruction, focus, and encouragement. This type of brief message should be sent regularly.

Note some common responses:

- Thank you for the incredible blessing.
- Thank you for doing this for us. I've kept copies of the ones from last year and always appreciate the time it takes you to send these. You have no idea how meaningful it is for you to put these thoughts into words, and as God would have it, they usually are timely and poignant; as I've

tried to express before, it means so much for you to keep reminding us of the love, power, and majesty of Jesus, and our completion and strength through Him. His Word does not return void, indeed.

Purposeful Professional Development

Excellent teachers provide stimulating learning environments for students because they know that children and young people enjoy and learn best under such conditions. Good students, eager to learn, value stimulation. Teachers also enjoy quality professional stimulation. Good teachers are learners, and they value quality professional development opportunities.

Schools should equip their teachers with resources, mentors, and encouragement so that parents recognize them as instructional leaders. The school community will, in turn, value and affirm faculty for their excellence. Strong community approval of teachers strengthens ties between teachers and their school. Relationship building and faculty satisfaction flourish in a stimulating learning environment. Faculty retention improves when schools provide meaningful professional growth opportunities.

A Culture of Excellence

Philippians 4:8 encourages an attitude of excellence, exhorting believers to think about whatever is true, noble, right, pure, lovely, admirable—"if anything is excellent or praiseworthy, think about such things." Schools of excellence attract competent, dedicated teachers, who often seek out exceptional Christian schools precisely because those schools are committed to biblical excellence. Schools that promote a culture of excellence can encourage faculty retention by providing leadership opportunities for their teachers. For example, schools can encourage teachers to serve on school accreditation committees, teach at professional conventions and conferences, write for professional publications, develop curriculum ideas for publishers, and develop or participate in summer institutes. Schools may consider developing a faculty endowment that promotes excellence by making grants to teachers for enrichment opportunities. A culture of excellence stimulates and encourages creative, innovative ways to promote quality, Christ-centered education. This environment is attractive for faculty, and it fosters high retention.

Recognition and Protection

A faculty usually thrives in a safe, secure school environment. Teachers tend to remain loyal to the school that affirms, protects, and supports them. Affirmation may be conveyed by a personal letter of appreciation for faithful, caring service; fellowship meals; a break from class handled by an administrator; expressions of appreciation for faculty in front of students and parents; nominations for professional awards; prayer support; an occasional appreciation lunch or dinner; and daily affirmation. Consistent and sincere recognition is more valuable than infrequent big events.

Teachers feel secure when administrators reflect the fruit of the Spirit (Galatians 5:23) and honor the Matthew 18:15ff principle in all relationships. Faculty confidence and respect develop when administrators promote a positive climate for parental relations. Teachers must work closely and responsibly with parents, and they appreciate knowing that their administrators will support them when necessary.

Compensation and Benefits

Quality compensation and generous benefits are very important to developing long-term retention, and these must be supported by a host of intangible benefits. Competitive salaries alone are usually insufficient to maintain high faculty retention.

Quality compensation begins with a salary competitive with the local school employment market. Other core benefits that encourage high retention include premiere insurance provisions, excused absences for illness, personal leave opportunities, financial support for professional development, retirement provisions, and tuition assistance for children of faculty members. A consistent history of salary increases is also an incentive for faculty retention.

Personal Relationships

People are of supreme value to God. They are the only part of creation made in His image and the only part that is immortal. Cultivating personal relationships should be a priority for administrators. An environment that prioritizes and values relationships develops a special community. This community has a service focus designed to help people meet one another's needs and to provide outreach to unbelievers.

Unity, peace, and joy characterize the people of this community as they see God working in their lives and in their community. Teachers tend to remain in school environments that impact culture with biblical values and a biblical perspective. Yes, Christian schools stand on the brink of influencing more students and more families than ever before, but they must have strong instructional leaders. Faithful servant leaders who abide in Christ and use the Word of God as their compass will be thoroughly equipped to help instill a biblical soul in their schools. Christian educators come to and remain in schools with a strong biblical soul.

Bibliography

Birman, B. F., Desimone, L., Porter, A. C., & Garet, M. S. (2000, May). Designing professional development that works. *Educational Leadership*.

Castetter, W. B. (1981). *The personal function in educational administration.* (3rd ed.). New York: MacMillan.

Danielson, C. (2001, February). New trends in teacher evaluation. *Educational Leadership*.

Darling-Hammond, L. (Ed.). (1994). *Professional development schools: Schools for developing a profession.* New York: Teachers College Press.

Darling-Hammond, L. (1998, February). Teacher learning that supports student learning. *Educational Leadership*.

Gorton, R. A. (1983). *School administration and supervision* (2nd ed.). Dubuque, IA: William C. Brown.

Keenan, D. (2001). Cultivating belonging in the school staff. *Christian School Education 4(5)*.

Lykins, C. (2001). How professional development influences school culture. *Christian School Education 4(5)*.

McLaughlin, M. W. (1992, September). Building a community for learning. *Educational Leadership 50(1)* .

Piper, J. (2000). *The pleasures of God*. Sisters, OR: Multnomah Publishers.

Tells, C. (2001, February). Appreciating good teaching—a conversation with Lee Shulman. *Educational Leadership 58(5)* .

Tennies, R. H. (2001). Promoting faculty body life. *Christian School Education 4(5)* .

Is Your Mission Showing?
Attracting Students—
Quality and Quantity

Janet Stump, M.A.

Chapter Summary

As a Christian school administrator, you face the essential yet delicate issue of student admissions. You have probably sensed a tension between enrolling the right students for your school and filling every student desk. Are these goals mutually exclusive? What can you do to establish an admissions process that will not sacrifice quality for quantity?

Mrs. Stump describes an admissions procedure that every Christian school can embrace. By focusing on mission, the heart of the admissions process, she proposes an admissions philosophy and procedure that can strengthen your entire school program. She identifies numerous ways you can apply these principles and practices immediately.

About the author

Janet Stump, M.A.
Director of Development and Public Relations, ACSI
Colorado Springs, CO
11 years of educational leadership experience

Chapter 9

Is Your Mission Showing?
Attracting Students—Quality and Quantity

Janet Stump, M.A.

Setting down the telephone receiver, I glanced at the clock and was surprised at the lateness of the hour. I was engrossed in my lengthy but rewarding conversation, so I hadn't noticed that the activity in the halls was waning. The prospective school family—anticipating a job transfer to our city—plied me with questions, first about our school and then about our community. Their children were thriving in a Christian school, and the parents were calling each private school in town. Eager to find a compatible experience for their young children, they asked informed questions, and as we discussed their hopes and dreams for their children, the conversation warmed and flowed. "Perhaps," I reflected, "this is the beginning of a lasting relationship."

It had been a busy day, and between routine administrative work and several unscheduled visitors, I had fielded numerous inquiry calls. My thoughts turned to my conversation with a dad about his eleventh-grade son. Clearly frustrated, this gentleman wanted just the facts: cost, availability, hours, graduation requirements, and enrollment standards. When asked if he was familiar with our school and its mission, he hesitated, saying that his son's counselor recommended us. Soon he revealed his motive for calling. Expelled from the public school with one quarter remaining, his son was in danger of losing his credits if he did not enroll in another program. I gathered that he would tolerate our "religion" requirements if his son could somehow salvage his high school career.

Two calls and two completely different conversations! My thoughts, however, drifted to a third—very delightful—inquiry. The ten minutes were filled with the hopeful questions of a parent eagerly wanting to provide for and protect his young child. As I jotted down the pertinent family information on the contact sheet, I asked for the child's name. There was a pause. Sheepishly, this eager parent admitted that his wife was presently in labor and that the child was due to be born that day. His forethought both amused and heartened me. What a great opportunity I had to educate him, as well as kindle a desire for Christian schooling!

The Potential of the Admissions Process

Whether realizing it or not, most of us Christian school leaders face incredible opportunities daily to strengthen our schools and the families within our communities. Too often, we do not give time and priority to phone calls and visits, instead leaving them to be addressed on the run by overworked or unprepared staff. For schools with admissions staff, budgetary necessity, not mission focus, often drives the process. We pressure staff to enroll students in order to strengthen the operating budget, rather than to enroll those who will most likely thrive in our schools. It takes time to nurture relationships, to listen to hearts, and to educate families about the school's mission.

It may seem contradictory, but a full school is not the primary objective of the admissions process. Instead, we want to draw and keep families who understand and support our God-given mission to their children. Therefore, schools must clearly understand their educational and spiritual goals and accomplish them—increasingly over time—in the lives of their students. A unique and well-articulated mission guides the admissions process and gives the staff a game plan for cultivating relationships with mission-appropriate markets such as churches and feeder schools through daily calls and visits. My three phone conversations with prospective parents not only illustrate the variety of circumstances in which families inquire; they also highlight the importance of a prepared and defined philosophy that can guide such discussions.

Those who respond to each inquiry have the potential over time to shape the school and move it closer to its stated purpose. A thoughtful and caring staff member can cultivate a desire for the compelling fruit of a Christ-centered education while gently redirecting those who inquire for various misguided reasons. An insightful, proactive board and administration will allocate resources, however modest at first, to begin a thoughtful mission-directed approach to the cultivation and eventual enrollment of students. When we elevate the admissions process, from the time of the first inquiry through assimilation into the school's culture, we elevate the Christ-centered mission as well.

Defining Mission-Driven Admissions

At this point, some might ask, "What do you mean by 'mission-driven'? Isn't the mission of the Christian school obvious?" Yes, many of us would agree that our overriding mission brings the person of Christ and His Word to every facet of the learning process. However, few schools see the direct relationship between specific standards and practice, and the ability to achieve mission objectives.

Although a full philosophical discussion remains beyond the scope of this chapter, I want to stress the importance for every Christian school of having a thoughtful, diligently researched, and carefully formulated biblical philosophy for what it hopes to accomplish in the lives of its students. This philosophy should spring from an awe-filled and ever increasing awareness that in Christ "are hidden all the treasures of wisdom and knowledge" (Colossians 2:3) and that only by having the mind of Christ can we become truly wise (1 Corinthians 2:16). Although our schools should be protected places, they do not exist primarily to protect. Many of our schools outperform their public school counterparts, yet superior academic preparation alone does not secure our uniqueness.

Finding a Specific Niche

Each school, however, has a distinctive niche within its community, and its specific mission derives from a careful analysis of that niche in light of its history and educational philosophy. Some schools focus strongly on college preparation, an essential emphasis for many contemporary families; some offer special resources for students with learning challenges; some serve families primarily of a specific congregation or denomination; and some target the unsaved, while others seek to partner only with Christian families.

Even in this short list, we can see that some of these mission focuses appear at odds with each other. In fact, families choose schools for contradictory reasons. If we take a shotgun approach to admissions, enrolling students with divergent needs and expectations, we make little progress toward achieving excellence or accomplishing stated objectives. Year after year, schools suffer poor morale when teachers struggle to meet a spectrum of needs, when parents grow disgruntled and withdraw, when fiscal health deteriorates, and when student behavior clones the prevailing cultural norms. A watching community observes this instability and forms opinions about the efficacy of Christian school education.

Before we implement a mission-driven admissions approach, we should engage in careful institutional soul-searching, answering the following questions: Why were we founded? Why do we now exist? Whom do we serve? What, specifically, do we hope to accomplish in the lives of our students? Are we accomplishing our goals? To answer these and other questions, we must engage in institutional archaeology, as we attempt to dig up the founding vision of our school. Although the school may have intentionally changed course over the years, understanding the past provides insight for the present. If the school has drifted from its original mission, this exercise can serve as a caution and prescription for future decisions. Consultant Jean Crawford summarizes our challenge:

> Identifying who we are, what we do, and what outcomes we expect to achieve is one of the most challenging roles an organization has to accomplish. If [it] was accomplished some time ago, it may be appropriate to review the vision and mission statements to ensure they accurately reflect the current organization.... The culture of the organization reflects how we carry out our work. The vision and mission tell us what we aspire to be. Not-for-profits should receive input from stakeholders and the community. What values guide us? Are we customer focused? Are we a learning organization that adapts to change and makes improvements? (2001)

Stating the Mission

If we intend to reach unchurched youth in our community, then outreach should be a part of the mission statement. If we desire to provide a nurturing environment and/or rigorous college preparatory academics, then these specifics should appear as well. We should clearly articulate spiritual distinctives. What specific attitudes and actions do we desire to nurture? Do we expect our students to transform their culture, live lives of service, transition into a traditional classroom, or excel in the university or workplace? If so, we must include these objectives in our mission. Thus, our mission becomes the tool by which we evaluate our progress toward our goals.

Given the spiritual importance of the task, we as Christian school leaders and educators should focus on building effective and spiritually productive schools to the glory of God. Dependence on the Holy Spirit can make us willing to enlarge our vision, focus our mission, and take the courageous steps necessary to bring them to fruition.

Refocusing Resources

A prayerfully focused mission allows us to channel our resources toward achieving targeted outcomes. Rather than providing a broad but mediocre program, we concentrate on accomplishing limited and prioritized goals. If, for example, the school wants to partner with Christian families in the education of their children, the recruitment budget should target the Christian market and not the entire community. Similarly, the admissions staff should invest their efforts nurturing relationships with mission-appropriate families rather than with those whose children are less likely to thrive or even be admitted to the school.

Envisioning the Mission-in-Action

When my children were very young, I hoped to nurture sons who would have open and sweet countenances. In times of discipline, training, and celebration, I monitored their heart attitudes through their expressions. What do we look for in the lives of our students? Faculty and staff must discuss what students and alumni "would look like" if the school's mission were being accomplished. Of course, this description should include actions, attitudes, passions, and priorities. As we spend time envisioning our mission-in-action, excitement and unity of purpose will grow. As the faculty adopts a unified philosophy and direction for their instruction, the mission will move increasingly toward accomplishment.

The admissions process does not exist in a vacuum. It links fundamentally to the philosophical framework of the school. Enrolled students and their families will eventually shape the school. The more purposefully we articulate our mission, attract families that understand and support it, and gently distance those that don't, the more surely we can achieve our God-given mission. When we administrators guide this process proactively and diligently, our schools move incrementally toward their objectives.

Mission-Driven Admissions Starts Internally

Recruiting new students begins by satisfying and retaining the mission-appropriate students we already have. Amid the pressures of operating a viable program (often on a shoestring budget), we can easily lose sight of the fact that as a school we render a service for fees paid. Our schools belong to the service industry, and we must provide worthy service. The more effectively we accomplish our mission, the more effectively we will retain our students. It does little good to enroll scores of new students if just as many withdraw.

High student turnover has a deleterious effect on the entire program because disgruntled families leaving the school generate negative publicity in the community. Often, departing families justify their decision to withdraw by criticizing the school, and their injurious comments are given credence because the critics have experienced the program firsthand. Hostile evaluation moves faster than positive evaluation and has greater impact. We must take student attrition very seriously.

According to Independent School Management's (ISM) newsletter *To The Point*, "Any time a student or family initiates the move to a competing school, [we] should consider that [our] school has failed in its promise" (1996). Although financial struggle is often stated as the reason for student withdrawal, ISM suggests that parents really mean that the education is no longer worth the cost. Thus, student retention should be a priority for the enrollment strategy. We must consistently demonstrate competent and Christlike service.

A mission-driven admissions program carries a dual focus—*internally* striving to satisfy and keep mission-appropriate school families, and *externally* attempting to draw new families who understand and support that mission. Many schools cannot consistently enroll the quality of students they desire because they have relaxed their admissions standards. Therefore, they struggle with discipline problems, with families at odds with the school's mission, or with students whose academic needs they cannot meet.

Internal Mission Focus

Before a proactive admissions program can be successful, the board and administrators must evaluate current programs and establish or reaffirm mission-driven standards and policies. The annual reenrollment process can keep the parents aware of the school's mission. Providing an annual means for parents and students to reaffirm their commitment to the school's core values gives the school opportunity to monitor changes. Then it can deal expeditiously but carefully with enrolled families who are no longer mission-appropriate.

Some Christian schools struggle with a "reform school" image, and sadly many have earned it. They have lost sight of the profundity of their task, and they often react out of desperation rather than vision. It takes courage and faith to enforce policies and standards at the risk of losing families, and thus much needed revenue. The author of Hebrews writes, "No discipline seems pleasant at the time, but painful. Later on, however, it produces a harvest of righteousness and peace for those who have been trained by it" (Hebrews 12:11). It takes discipline to make wise decisions consistently. We must esteem the mission enough to uphold standards that will strengthen the school.

Once we establish the school's specific mission and put supporting policies in place, all publications and procedures should be evaluated accordingly. If, for example, the mission is to partner with Christian families, then all written and spoken communication should clearly convey this message, thus drawing mission-appropriate families early in the enrollment process. An effective admissions brochure presents the school's mission clearly and compellingly in words and pictures, and does so in a way that attracts like-minded families while deterring those with other priorities.

Role of the Faculty

Faculty must be consistently encouraged and trained to see their essential role in the admissions process. Not only do they affect student retention; they play a crucial role in welcoming and educating new families. Veteran faculty and staff can adopt a bunker mentality, assuming the beleaguered position of the overworked, underpaid, and underappreciated. Throwing open their classroom doors to welcome parent volunteers and prospective parents can prove difficult for many.

I remember my first attempt at shifting the focus of our school culture from inward to outward. The initial resistance I encountered eventually crumbled because of persistent education and encouragement, as well as the wonderful reward of the unleashed support and resources of incredible school families. Our school parents need to spend time in the classrooms to witness the Spirit of God at work through dedicated teachers. They will leave encouraged in their commitment to Christian education. Some weak teachers or demanding parents challenge the wisdom of this *open-door policy,* but problems are less likely to be swept under the carpet and ignored when such a policy is in place. Problems rarely resolve themselves; they only grow. Together, faculty and parents can create a compelling atmosphere in which the school's mission can flourish.

The Foundation

Where do we start? Creating a strategic plan is an important process and tool to identify and affirm our mission and core values, to identify strengths and weaknesses, and to recognize opportunities and threats. Fisher Howe asserts that the strategic planning process "calls on an organization to think through and articulate its mission—the purposes, programs, and priorities; and the values—not what it does but how it does it; and its vision—what kind of an organization it wants to be in the coming years" (2001). One- to five-year goals derive from this plan, and include action steps delineated and prioritized. Such a process brings ordered perspective to what can be an overwhelming task of sorting needs and tackling issues. It takes godly wisdom and vision to begin operating from a mission-driven perspective while addressing weaknesses and minimizing threats. Strategic planning guides an institution to increasing levels of maturity and effectiveness.

Attracting Mission-Appropriate Students

Let's consider a practical example. It takes time to plan and implement change effectively, and our school needs thirty more students *now* to balance the budget. In the meantime, how and where do we find the students we need? In his book *Mission Based Marketing*, Peter Brinckerhoff explains, "Market segmenting is the technique of looking at your larger markets in more finite parts, and then deciding which of those parts your organization can, should, and wants to serve. It is a technique that will really focus you on what you do best" (1997). Thus, market segmentating enables us to prioritize our markets on the basis of our mission and core values. Where are we most likely to find mission-appropriate students?

Mission-Appropriate Markets—A Place to Start

Once we identify key markets, we should prioritize those that are most closely connected with us, and we should strengthen the bond by consistently demonstrating our mission-in-action. For example, if our school serves families attending fifty churches, it makes sense to cultivate relationships with the families who attend the ten churches most represented by our student population. We can enlist satisfied families as ambassadors in their churches to build bridges between the school and potential school families. Similarly, we should prioritize outreach to preschools and other feeder schools on the basis of their relationship to our program.

While we continually expand our network to more distant markets, we will reap greater results from those already impacted by our mission. Satisfied school families generate positive word-of-mouth advertising, which is the most effective tool in attracting other mission-appropriate families. Schools with full enrollment and waiting pools know the power of satisfied parents. If we take the time to build nurturing relationships with parents and accomplish our mission in the lives of their children, we will produce effective ambassadors. Christlike service is always the first step in becoming mission driven.

Our outreach can now expand to fringe markets. We should ask the following questions: Who and where are the mission-appropriate markets that already know of our existence but have no connection with us? Who and where are the mission-appropriate markets that don't know we exist? Now we must catch the attention of those who would share our mission and thrive in our program—if they knew we existed. This extended marketing outreach is selective and controlled so that we use resources strategically and frugally.

Effective Use of Marketing Tools

Marketing tools, such as view books; tri-fold brochures; postcards; newsletters; videos; and print, radio, or TV advertising should clearly communicate the school's mission in words and pictures. Often our school's marketing tools focus on the institution and its history and achievements, not on how we accomplish our mission vibrantly in our relationships and faith/learning interactions. Whatever the budget, we can tell our story compellingly through lively prose that conveys both the life of our school and its engagement in Christ-centered learning. Statistics and charts have their place, but documented quotations, first-person stories, and close-up photographs draw in more readers.

Each admissions tool should have a stated goal before production begins.

We must consider the audience and what they value. All communication should target a mission-specific audience by appealing *only* to families that would fit within the context of our mission. It should also have a tone that reflects the school's style and culture. It is also notable that if no one reads our brochure, it doesn't matter how brilliant its content is, so let's keep it concise and readable, with lots of white space surrounding the narrative.

Every communication with the school family, constituency, and surrounding community should communicate the mission in one or more of the following areas: academics, spiritual development, service and outreach, athletics, fine arts, extracurricular activities, and fund-raising. Every external and internal communication becomes a marketing tool, therefore painting a verbal picture of the mission-in-action in each newsletter, report card, memo, and press release. Over time, the consistency and volume of this targeted information will educate and strengthen our constituency and thus our mission.

Prioritizing Admissions

Attracting and keeping quality mission-appropriate students will not work with a hit-or-miss process; it must be a prayerfully and strategically orchestrated process—no matter the size of the school or the budget. Not an isolated program, the admissions process draws its vitality and message from a healthy and visionary school; in turn, it perpetuates that health as we enroll quality students and nurture relationships. This cycle cannot take place unless the board and administration embrace this mission-driven approach, educate faculty and staff, allocate resources, and prioritize goals.

Our schools can begin by equipping an outgoing, relational staff member to answer every new student inquiry. This person takes time to listen to each family's heart, to involve them when appropriate in the mission of the school, to guide them through the process, and to strengthen their bond with the school until their children are fully assimilated. Admissions personnel require the full support of the faculty and administration so that prospective families feel warmly received during classroom visits and open houses. A spacious office, stunning brochures, and a professional video can help the recruiting process; however, a staff person who loves people and believes in the school is a priceless resource. Even small schools can have a successful recruiting process through careful use of well-trained part-time or volunteer help.

The Mission-Driven Admissions Process

The phone rings. You promptly answer it, finding a rather tentative caller on the line. Not sure where to start, the young dad asks the standard question: "How much is tuition?" Although you answer it, you also draw him into a conversation. His bright son, growing bored with school, has begun to get into mischief. As you listen and respond with questions, you hear his fears and hopes for his child. He asks about academics and discipline, and you answer each question within the context of your school's mission.

Although uninformed about Christian schooling, he listens and learns because of the newly perceived need in his child's education. By the end of the conversation, he begins to sense what he is missing. Later that day, you add a personal note to the information packet you send him, addressing his concerns and inviting him for a personal visit. You nurture this budding relationship through a mission-guided process that leads to the enrollment of his son and eventually to the bonding of his family to the school community. Two years later when his preschooler prepares for kindergarten, there is no question where she will attend.

Relationships Rule

Vibrant relationships form the foundation of a fruitful admissions program as well as a profitable development program. As we draw families to the school through Christlike relationships and they experience the mission firsthand, they will eventually give time, energy, and finances, thus producing a strong support base for the school. It takes time to build relationships with prospective parents, but the investment will reap bountiful rewards. We need to listen for families who are not mission-appropriate or whose academic needs cannot be met in our school. Once we establish rapport, we can redirect families who are not appropriate candidates for admission to other schools more suited to their priorities or needs.

Families appreciate a straightforward approach. If desired programs are not available for their child, we must be honest with them. If we wish to enroll families active in their churches, we need to communicate that clearly in the first conversation. It will not only save time and perhaps embarrassment; it will also keep expectations in line with reality, preventing damaging repercussions. Families inquire because of perceived need, not always because they understand the Christian philosophy of education. Through relationship, a family's needs and desires may come to match the school's mission and program.

Establishing an Admissions Process

The student application should clearly state the school's educational philosophy, its distinctives, and its enrollment procedures. It should define the mission and provide enough information for families to make an informed decision. Applications can require any or all of the following elements: pastor's reference, administrator's reference, personal reference, answers to a student questionnaire, grades and transcripts, personal essay, personal testimony, and signed parent-student cooperative agreement. Each aspect of the application needs to provide the information necessary to make a mission-directed decision.

Family interviews should be a part of every school's admissions process. Although they require considerable time and effort of several staff members, they provide an essential step in the screening and bonding process. In many schools, grade-level administrators conduct interviews. While this method works, it is wise to involve two or three additional staff members. We need continuity between interview teams, but having several interviewers provides a balance of personalities and perspectives. Bridging the possible information gap between faculty and administrators, teachers become invested in the process as they connect with new families and communicate with their colleagues.

We should plan interview questions derived from our specific mission, and we should plan the objectives and tone of the interviews as well. If we grill potential applicants in order to "skim the cream" off the waiting list, the interviews will not be effective as a relational tool. However, if admissions personnel have completed a thorough screening through mission-directed brochures, phone conversations, and site visits, most of those interviewed will enroll. Valid objectives for the interview can include the following: observing family dynamics, assessing student attitudes and actions, educating families, conveying information, answering questions, and assessing ability to meet academic needs. These objectives inform the tone and content of the interview.

We need to choose interview questions prayerfully. Five or six well-designed questions can elicit a discussion that can last up to an hour. The questions should be tested to determine whether they are easy to understand and likely to evoke the desired information. We must carefully scrutinize the mission statement, breaking it down into elements that form the core of the interview questions. Each interview should be consistent and well documented, with some objective component to rate the mission-appropriateness of applicants. We can evaluate the interview process annually, garnering input from all those involved.

Let us consider a school that undertakes a thorough self-study and recognizes that its college preparatory program is good but far from excellent. While the majority of its parents desire a college-preparatory emphasis, some require a resource program for students with special needs. The school has neither the space nor the budget to meet the needs of students with moderate to severe learning challenges. It is better to do a few things with excellence rather than to do many things with mediocrity.

Considering demand in light of resources, we as school leaders narrow our focus and build excellence into our core academic program in order to meet the needs of the majority of school families more effectively. This decision informs our admissions process; now we can test all applicants to see if our school can meet each student's learning needs. In the future, our strategic plan may guide us in another direction, but for now we can concentrate our resources in one direction.

Evaluating and Protecting the Process

The enrollment process should be uniquely tailored to each school. It should strengthen effectiveness, not become a bureaucratic nightmare. We must evaluate the process annually by obtaining input from those who interview as well as from the general faculty. What trends have they observed? Are new students more or less prepared? Are there fewer or more behavior problems? Are families cooperative and supportive?

We have to guard the admissions process from two enemies: pragmatism and legalism. Pragmatism can threaten the process during times of high and low student interest. When we need students, we may be tempted to fill openings just to meet financial obligations, regardless of the fit. During times of high demand, we can also stray from mission-driven criteria and enroll those with the best test scores or the ability to pay, rather than families who align with our educational objectives. Over time, these daily decisions profoundly impact the spiritual vibrancy of the school.

The second enemy is a legalistic mind-set that can result from a well-honed process. Too often we quantify students by their responses and select them by points earned. While objective measures help balance subjectivism, we must humbly seek God's wisdom throughout the entire process. Sometimes when every answer is correct and every requirement fulfilled, we sense a red flag signaling that a family may not fit. Other times, a family may stumble through the questions, yet we reach consensus that they need to be brought into the life of the school. God's grace must continually control the admissions process.

Bonding Families to the School

The admissions process does not end when students enroll; it continues until students and their families bond firmly to the school. Most children have anxiety about starting a new school, particularly secondary students. It is just as stressful for parents since they want their child to adjust to the school they have carefully selected. We do well to invest considerable planning into assimilating new students into the school family. We can host a new-family orientation, which can prepare parents for coming adjustments and assure them of the school's concern and partnership. Pertinent information reduces anxiety and increases a sense of partnership. We reassure new students when we give them opportunity to preview their classrooms, find their lockers, and orient themselves to their schedules. Pairing students by grade also relieves their anxiety since they don't have to face lunchtime alone or stand out in isolation.

Truth in advertising applies to the marketing process of admissions. By promising too much, we set up new families for disillusionment or failure. It disarms disgruntled school parents to hear staff acknowledge areas of weakness and share strategies for change. Most parents don't expect perfection; it encourages them to see problems identified and addressed.

Fiscal Foundations for a Fruitful Admissions Program

Collateral issues, such as tuition policies, scholarship programs, and faculty salaries, impact a school's ability to draw and keep mission-appropriate students. Christian schools have an obligation—whatever their mission distinctives—to provide excellent schooling that reflects the mind of Christ. It takes excellent Christian faculty to reach this standard, and often excellent faculty are difficult to keep because of substandard wages. In too many schools, dedicated teachers subsidize the cost of education because boards fear that if they raise tuition, families will leave.

We should establish tuition rates on the basis of the true cost of service. However, the result could eliminate many families who desire Christian education for their children. This complex issue needs to be addressed carefully by individual schools, contextualized within their missions and constituencies. A number of models are available, but boards and administrators must carefully discuss the pros and cons of each. At the very least, we must elevate our thinking about tuition in light of the eternal value of our school's mission. We enforce our tuition payment policy so that we can meet our obligations. Where applicable, schools should keep tuition in line with the fees parents pay for other educational services, such as daycare, preschool, or tutoring.

In some schools, tuition is nearly impossible for parents to afford. Schools that desire to serve a broad socioeconomic spectrum must rely on funding from grants and charitable contributions to allow for their tuition fees, which are less than their expenses. Every school needs a mature, sustained development thrust to consistently acquire funding needed to augment tuition (see chapter 17). Since development is built by sustainable relationships and fueled by mission and vision, the admissions process can initiate and foster institutional development in the Christian school.

Scholarship programs, which serve and strengthen a school's mission, should be in harmony with all funding programs. The objective for a particular scholarship thrust should derive from the school's mission; it should never thwart it. Scholarship programs can honor students who demonstrate the mission-in-action within the school and the community. Other awards may honor academic or athletic achievement, and they should also acknowledge spiritual and character excellence.

Need-based programs must have objective, well-articulated guidelines administered by a committee. If we intend that all families who desire a

Christian education should receive it, we must realistically face the challenge of providing adequate and fair scholarship assistance. We resist the charge of being elitist when it comes to our fiscal demographics; we embrace it when it refers to our mission-driven distinctiveness.

School boards and administrators make many decisions that may indirectly jeopardize the admissions process and policy. If we take on debt for a new facility, that decision puts extra stress on the admissions office to keep the school full. An economic downturn resulting in lower enrollment can pressure a school with a high monthly mortgage to lower admissions standards in order to meet obligations. Commitments to special interest groups within the school and its constituencies, promises to donors or alumni, and alliances or partnerships can all divert our school from its core values. To keep our mission focused, we must make short-term decisions within the context of our God-given mission.

Is Our Vision Big Enough?

If we measure the accomplishment of our mission by our students' test scores, their attendance at prestigious colleges, or their successful employment, our vision is too small. If we aim to compete with the biggest and best public school in town—even if we do it for the glory of God—our vision is woefully constrained. Perhaps the right techniques and strategies could help us fill our schools with students. The question remains: Is our vision big enough? That question propels us beyond the confines of this topic to the epistemological, teleological, ontological, and cosmological questions that Christian schooling must address. The answers are found in the person of Christ, in the Bible, and in creation. In his book *Reclaiming the Future of Christian Education*, Dr. Albert Greene states eloquently:

> The Word of God is God's powerful way of revealing and giving Himself to His human image bearers in and through His creation. In each way God's word comes to us—the creation, the Bible and the Person of Christ—it comes through the power of the Holy Spirit.... Everything we have for curriculum has been created by the Word of God ... God intends to speak to us in and through the creation if only we have our hearts open to hear.... If as Christian [educators] we can internalize this alternative consciousness and begin to communicate it to our students, the possibilities of Christian schooling are breathtaking. (1998)

Can we envision these breathtaking possibilities? Does the content and quality of our instruction instill a growing love for the Word of God in all its fullness, and thus a passion for learning, loving, and serving? Do we study our culture enough both to critique our own institutional assumptions and practices and to prepare our students to engage the culture and flee the world? As leaders we must be passionate in our love for Christ, love for learning of all kinds, and love for our postmodern students. Our vision can expand. Our mission can be defined. Our schools can accomplish their God-given tasks.

Bibliography

Brinckerhoff, P. (1997). *Mission based marketing*. New York: John Wiley & Sons.

Crawford, J. (2001). The balanced scorecard: A performance measurement tool for not-for-profit organizations. In J. Greenfield (Ed.), *The nonprofit handbook* (3rd ed.). New York: John Wiley & Sons.

Greene, A. (1998). *Reclaiming the future of Christian education*. Colorado Springs: Association of Christian Schools International.

Howe, F. (2001). The board's role in fundraising. In J. Greenfield (Ed.), *The nonprofit handbook* (3rd ed.). New York: John Wiley & Sons.

Independent School Management. (1996). How to retain students beyond grade one. *To the point*.

Traveling the Road
to Excellence
Developing Curriculum

Kathy Ralston, M.A.

Chapter Summary

How would you respond to the question, What is your school's curriculum? If your answer is to name the textbooks you use, then you have probably relinquished very important curricular decisions to a publisher who doesn't know the philosophy and mission of your school.

Mrs. Ralston will walk you through a systematic procedure for developing curricula that will allow you and your staff to determine what is to be taught, when it is to be taught, and how to teach it. This collaborative process will enable you to design a curricular program that accurately reflects the goals and priorities you have established for your students. Such a plan for purposeful and ongoing evaluation and refinement of the curriculum will be hard work, but it will become one of the most meaningful and rewarding activities you and your teachers will ever do together.

About the author
Kathy Ralston, M.A.
Assistant Director, ACSI Southern California Region
LaHabra, CA
10 years of educational leadership experience

Chapter 10

Traveling the Road to Excellence
Developing Curriculum

Kathy Ralston, M.A.

"When a new teacher is hired, how does he or she know what to teach?" This was the first question posed in a graduate class I took on curriculum and instruction. I looked forward to an insightful answer, one that would give me useful direction as I began my job as curriculum director. The immediate response to the professor's inquiry was silence. He tried again, asking if perhaps a novice would be given a curriculum guide to ensure instructional success. We all laughed quietly, and someone commented that such a tool would probably sit on a shelf gathering dust because it had no relationship to classroom reality. After a short discussion, the class members reached this conclusion: At the secondary level, teachers are handed a textbook and told to cover the material. At the elementary level, they are told to find another teacher who has taught that grade and ask that person what to teach!

The job of directing the school's instructional program ultimately belongs to you as the school administrator. You decide what is to be taught, when it should be taught, and how it should be taught. Because many administrators do not have expertise in curriculum development and do not have a specialist on their staff to handle curriculum coordination, they rely on textbooks to determine the instructional program. But another solution to this dilemma can produce a quality instructional program that is uniquely designed to support the mission of the school. All Christian schools are equipped to implement this solution immediately if they follow the simple steps outlined in this chapter.

Defining Curriculum Development

The Definition of Curriculum

What is your curriculum? is a common question heard by school personnel talking with parents of prospective students. Do they really mean, What textbooks do you use? The interchange of the terms "curriculum" and "textbooks" is frequent, not only by parents but within the educational community as well. Because people use the two words synonymously, the definition of "curriculum" must be clear in a discussion about curriculum development in Christian schools.

What is curriculum? A broad but useful definition is *the planned instructional program delivered to the students*. The word "planned" implies that at the heart of the program lies a designed sequence of learning experiences in the instructional areas chosen by the school. The word "delivered" indicates what *really* happens in the classroom.

Perhaps "curriculum" is defined most effectively by establishing what it is not. It is neither *a textbook, nor something bought or borrowed*. Often administrators give teachers textbooks alone for instructional direction, so these teachers then believe that their primary objective is to complete the books. But if textbooks determine the curriculum, publishers have made the important curricular and instructional decisions for your school. No thinking administrator wants to choose that option.

If curriculum development means more than just teaching the textbook, what is it? Curriculum development is the means by which a school *formulates, evaluates*, and *implements* a planned instructional program. *Formulating* consists of devising a plan for documentation and annual review. *Evaluating* involves looking at what your school teaches and determining what it should teach. *Implementing* includes ensuring the teaching of the designed curriculum and assessing the effectiveness of the instructional program.

The Benefits of Curriculum Development

Each school has a unique philosophy, mission, and community. The curriculum must align with the philosophy and mission of the school and meet the needs of its students. A successful curriculum development process brings coherence and cohesiveness to the school's instructional program. Effective curriculum provides the focus and orientation of instruction and clarifies assessment for teachers, students, and parents. It provides a basis for systematic adjustment and review because both its clear definition and its written plan include frequent assessment to define strengths and weaknesses.

Teachers confined to one area of study and/or one grade level have limited information on which to base decisions. Administrators and teachers need to have a clear vision of the school's educational process from beginning to end. Because every academic discipline contains more content than a school can teach, someone has to decide what to include and what not to include. Schools need to make those decisions in advance, in an informed manner, so that what their faculty members teach will be part of a larger plan that builds—fact upon fact, skill upon skill—toward overall school objectives.

Let me share a story about a school that did *not* take this approach. A local church had started a successful preschool program, and when the first class of four-year-old students approached "graduation," their parents came to the director and said, "We love your school! We don't want to send our children anywhere else! Please add a kindergarten class." Both church and school leaders decided that offering another class would meet a need for their school families, so they included kindergarten on the roster for the next school year. At the end of the kindergarten year, those same parents came back to the administration and said (you guessed it), "We love your school! We don't want to send our children anywhere else! Please add a first-grade class."

As a result, the school then offered classes through fourth grade, and the kindergarten had grown to two classes. In the middle of the school year, the principal learned that the two kindergarten teachers dramatically disagreed philosophically. One teacher had her kids reading, writing, and ready to drive a car, while the other had been nurturing her class and preparing them to start an academic program in the *first grade*. The administrator finished her story and said to me, "What should we do?"

This problem has no easy solution. The school would reap the consequences of this dilemma for many years. The administrators let the individual teachers make decisions on the basis of personal opinion instead of developing a unified school philosophy and working collaboratively to bring all instructional experiences into alignment with it.

As faculty members work together to decide what should be taught, when it should be taught, and how much should be taught, their involvement develops an ownership of the curriculum plans. Such cooperation helps ensure implementation of the designed program. *Intentional* education empowers teachers to be effective educators and allows students to receive complete education, not just hit-and-miss instruction based on the likes and dislikes of each teacher.

A well-designed curricular program improves the teaching-learning process. Notice that I did not use the word "teaching" by itself. Someone gave me a cartoon that explains my statement. The illustration in the cartoon shows two little boys and a dog. The owner of the dog tells his friend, "I taught Stripe how to whistle!" The friend looks at the dog and says, "I don't hear him whistling." To which the first young man responds, "I said I taught him. I didn't say he learned it!" A teacher has not really taught unless the student has learned!

The teaching-learning process improves when you give teachers appropriate tools to support classroom instruction. You furnish assistance when you cultivate teaching skills and techniques by providing more time for teachers to focus on designing creative, meaningful, and effective learning opportunities. When educators do not have to decide *what* should be taught, they can focus on *how* best to teach to the objectives. Curriculum development does not mean the elimination of teacher flexibility and creativity. Good teachers take the designed curricular framework and personalize methods and activities to meet the needs of their students and to reflect their own personal teaching styles.

In addition to addressing academic concerns, planning the curricular program can also contribute to the success of a critical and defining element of Christian education: *biblical integration*. Biblical integration is not just biblical correlation, that is, bringing God's truth *alongside* content. True biblical integration *weaves* God's truth into the life of the school in every possible way. This incorporation does not happen by chance, nor does it come naturally to most educators. Many teachers in Christian schools are not trained to integrate a Christian worldview into their instruction. If you consider biblical integration essential, you must plan the curriculum to incorporate and support it.

The Participants in Curriculum Development

Curriculum decisions should involve the school community—the school board members, administrators, faculty, students, and parents. Although all these people should be involved, the degree of input and control should not be equal. Curriculum development is primarily the responsibility of administrators and faculty; the professional staff should make the instructional decisions. Administrators and teachers should determine the overall curriculum collaboratively, and they need a process that encourages cooperation and teamwork.

Involving the Professional Staff

Select a Leadership Team

You as a school administrator are not necessarily the "point person" in curriculum development; a better description depicts you as the coach of the team. When you formulate a plan for shared leadership, you take the first step toward developing a school curriculum. A team of educators, representing the needs of all grade levels and subject areas, *leads* the decision-making process. This process does *not* have teachers from every grade level and subject area serving on the leadership team. It *does* have, for example, one teacher from the primary grades participating on the team and representing all kindergarten through second-grade teachers.

Likewise, one or two teachers represent the groupings of the upper elementary grades (three through five), the middle school (six through eight), and the high school (nine through twelve). These representatives communicate with the other faculty working at those levels. All team members are responsible for soliciting the input of the teachers they represent and then sharing those thoughts with the leadership team. At the secondary level, team members can represent an assigned subject area rather than a grade level.

Define the Responsibilities and Authority of the Leadership Team

As you choose the members of the leadership team, you must also clearly define their responsibilities, which you align with board policy. The success of a shared leadership approach will rest on the willingness of the administrators and board members to trust the wisdom of the leadership team and implement its recommendations. This process will succeed because all concerned parties have had the opportunity for input and have considered all limiting conditions, such as philosophy and budget.

Create Subject Area Subcommittees

Essential to the success of the leadership team is the involvement of all faculty members on subject area subcommittees. A subcommittee for each core subject area (Bible, language arts, mathematics, science, and social studies) should consist of *at least* two teachers who have indicated an interest in and/or have knowledge of that subject. Again, you must ensure cross-grade-level representation on the subcommittees, just as on the leadership team. The subcommittees will assist in making decisions related to their specific subject area assignment.

Producing Effective Curriculum Documents

The Process of Documenting the Curriculum

Guiding the entire teaching staff in writing curriculum documents is the first assignment of the leadership team. A successful curriculum development plan begins with what you are doing now and moves systematically through the improvement process. Documenting identifies what you are teaching, giving you information that will allow you to determine what you *should* teach.

Curriculum planning provides the basis for ongoing review and adjustment of the instructional program. Documentation of the curriculum requires time and energy from your faculty, but the people involved in teaching the curriculum *must* take part in documenting it.

The Purpose of Documenting the Curriculum

Why are curriculum documents important? You create them because the process of writing them is invaluable and the documents themselves play a critical role in the life of the curricular program.

The curriculum plan will help you develop your instructional program because it assists the faculty in identifying the strengths and weaknesses of the educational program. In addition, by referring to these written guides, new teachers can readily adhere to the school's instructional program. The documents become a framework for *all* teachers by ensuring that the *planned* program is the *implemented* program and by providing a basis for accountability. This design forms a vital part of the school program. It provides specific information that allows the instructional staff to implement the school mission and philosophy in their daily instruction.

The Products in Documenting the Curriculum

Curriculum writers utilize a variety of formats to record the instructional program. In a school just beginning this process, two basic documents provide the necessary information for identifying and evaluating classroom experiences: the *scope and sequence* and the *course outline*. Producing these documents for each of the five core subject areas is the minimal goal. This chapter contains descriptions of these documents; samples can be located in *Curriculum Development for Christian Schools* by Dr. Derek Keenan.

Scope and Sequence

The leadership team collaboratively writes the scope and sequence, which is a good beginning that provides necessary information for continuing documentation in a subject area. The team starts by organizing what is to be taught according to grade levels (at the elementary level) or according to courses within a discipline (at the secondary level).

The team then compiles for the teachers a list of skills and/or topics within each subject. They need not reinvent the wheel; they can glean suggestions for the skills/content areas from several available resources: the scope-and-sequence documents of publishers, frameworks and standards of states, models from other schools, and information from educational vendors found on the Internet. They use these resources as a starting point and revise the information to reflect the school's instructional program.

When the team completes the skill/content listing, they give all teachers a copy. The teachers then identify skills/topics included in their instruction during the year and the sequence in which they teach them. They do not need to indicate the depth of instruction; they can designate with a check mark any part of the grade-level or course curriculum.

Not only do teachers use their experience as they complete the chart, but they can also use their lesson plan books and core resources to make sure they correctly identify what they *currently* teach in the instructional program. At this point, the teachers must be completely honest about what they teach. (Should I put down what I teach or what I think they want me to teach?) Note that if you have not given clear direction on content, you cannot hold the instructional staff accountable for gaps, overlaps, and omissions. Be sure to encourage an atmosphere of "no blame and no shame."

The team compiles this completed work from each teacher onto one sheet and distributes it to the entire faculty for review. Before meeting together, individual teachers note areas of concern or inconsistency within their grade levels/courses and across the grade levels/courses. After the teachers have had opportunity to look over the combined information, they discuss areas of concern in a large-group setting, which includes the leadership team and you, the administrator.

The large group decides the desired depth of instruction for each skill/topic appearing on the listing (introduction, development, mastery, and/or reinforcement). The goal at this point is to reach consensus, not resolution of concerns. Delay any major revision issues until you address the subject area in the evaluation and adjustment phase of curriculum development (to be discussed later).

Course Mapping

Following the scope-and-sequence development, the next task will enable teachers to organize the information from the scope and sequence so they can prepare to write the second report, the course outline. In order to align the subject area scope and sequence with the course outlines written for each subject, the teachers create a course map for each grade level and/or course.

A course map/chart takes the content components from the scope and sequence and organizes them within the appropriate grade or course. The faculty must work collaboratively within each grade level (elementary) or subject area department (secondary). They place the content into topical units and determine a time frame for instruction (when in the school year each unit will be taught and how long the instruction will take).

The process of mapping helps teachers take information from the scope and sequence and clearly identify which content/skills are their responsibility. The course map can also include information that identifies to what depth the information is taught (introduction, development, mastery, and/or reinforcement). At this point in the process, teachers can also develop a list of mastery concepts for each grade level. After completing the mapping for each grade level and course, the teachers are ready to write course outlines.

Course Outline

Creating a course outline provides a unit-by-unit description of what a teacher includes at a grade level or in a course in the identified subject area. Using the course map is helpful because the material is already organized into units.

In developing a scope and sequence, teachers write one document for each subject area. In producing course outlines, they create one outline for *each* grade level and course within that subject area. Again, the teachers should author the outlines. If you have more than one teacher at a grade level, the teachers can divide the work, as long as they review each other's outlines so that the finished product reflects their collective ideas.

A course outline includes important pieces of information for instruction. In it, teachers identify the *content and objectives* as well as the *biblical integration concepts* woven into each unit. They note the *approximate time* it will take to complete the unit, and describe the *methods and activities* used to meet the objectives. They also specify the *materials and resources* that support instruction, and the *evaluation techniques* that assess student progress.

Writing *objectives* is one of the most difficult parts of completing the course outline. The writers must remember that the objectives should identify the important content components. A list of seven to ten objectives for a two- or three-week unit is appropriate. A day-by-day, lesson-by-lesson list of objectives is not necessary; less is better as long as teachers identify the target concepts in objective form. The objectives describe student behavior, not teacher behavior. If the text resource that was used does not contain good objectives, the writers need to find another resource for that topic to help determine the main ideas.

The next component of the course outline identifies the *biblical integration concepts* that will enable teachers to weave God's truth effectively into the unit. This portion is especially important for new teachers, who may not be skilled at this aspect of instruction.

Ask the staff to share strategies for effective integration. Veteran faculty can assist by explaining their techniques, or offering suggestions for specific units. As they work on this component, teachers should look for ideas that identify biblical principles and for biblical concepts that will genuinely surface from the content. Integration in some subject areas is more difficult to plan than in others. Materials from the publishers of Christian textbooks provide good resources for completing this section of the course outline.

For a comprehensive volume with integration suggestions, see the *Encyclopedia of Bible Truths for School Subjects* by Dr. Ruth Haycock. If you need to train teachers to integrate a Christian worldview, explore *How to*

Develop a Teaching Model for World View Integration by Dr. Martha E. MacCullough. Dr. J. P. Moreland has written a thought-provoking book titled *Love Your God with All Your Mind*, which includes sources for integration in a variety of subject areas. Other chapters in this book will also serve you well.

The *activities and methods* section of the course outline is the component that reflects the teachers' creativity. The information in this portion should include learning opportunities that enable students to meet identified objectives. This section should also explain for new teachers strategies that can successfully engage students and meet the objectives. Encourage experienced teachers who wish to do so to develop new activities not included in this section, as long as they continue teaching to the identified objectives.

The *resources and materials* section helps teachers locate items that will support instruction. It contains the textbook or main resource information as well as the details for locating any other items necessary to complete suggested activities. Especially helpful are bibliographic citations of resources, both written and electronic.

Evaluation techniques should include ideas for traditional and alternative assessments. The writers do not need to include details such as percentages. Instead, they should recommend effective evaluation approaches that are appropriate for the suggested activities.

Completing the Task

As mentioned earlier, writing curriculum documents will take much time and energy on the part of your staff, so everyone must be convinced that the process is worthwhile and valuable. Administrators and faculty must commit to this project and to a realistic timeline. (Can you finish in one year? Possibly, but you won't have a teaching staff when you've finished!)

As you formulate a timeline and schedule for developing the documents, remember to take on this project in manageable chunks. (Teachers still have to teach!) Taking longer to finish and do a better job is more profitable than concluding quickly but producing unusable documents. You need to allow time for staff to do quality work. Setting aside paid workdays for writing, or providing released time through the use of a substitute teacher shows the faculty that the board and administration understand the commitment and time involved.

Implementing a Cyclical Review

After you have spent considerable time and energy producing your curriculum documents, the next question might be, Now what? The following steps can enable you and your staff to design and implement a curriculum review cycle.

A Three-Level Review Cycle

You need a process—one the entire faculty understands—for making decisions, addressing problems, and implementing changes. Establishing a curriculum review cycle will allow the instructional staff to develop an effective learning program as they focus on one major subject area at a time for the purpose of evaluation, examination, and implementation.

I suggest a three-level plan that provides the time needed to complete the review effectively while keeping the budget impact at a minimum. When reviewing a subject area, a subcommittee will accomplish the three goals of evaluation, examination, and implementation. By doing so, they can identify the areas of strength and address the areas of weakness, thus providing a foundation for improving the instructional program.

The multilevel review cycle will take a subcommittee three years to complete, but the financial impact (to purchase new materials, offer training, etc.) for a single subject area will be felt only in the last year of review. Since you will assign a subcommittee and not the entire faculty for a subject area review, three different subcommittees can work at the same time on the three levels of the process. You can determine the order of the subject area review according to the needs that surfaced during the writing of the curriculum documents.

Year of Evaluation

During the evaluation year, a subcommittee will gather and analyze data related to their assigned subject area. Information for this analysis can come from surveys, and feedback from parents and students related to the effectiveness of the instructional program in that subject area. In addition, the subcommittee can look at work that students have produced, achievement test statistics, and curriculum documents. Members of the subcommittee should look for evidence of curricular effectiveness and appropriateness. They need to identify where the curricular program is now, determine what changes need to be made, and plan how best to implement those changes. Remember that there will be few, if any, quick fixes. You are making plans for changes that will happen over time and are designed to produce meaningful and lasting improvements.

Year of Examination

During the examination year, the subcommittee will research, evaluate, and select the materials and the staff development opportunities that will allow the plans for improvement to be carried out. They will examine new instructional materials, alternative teaching methods, and information about additional content or skills to incorporate into the current instructional program. Solicit input from all faculty members who will implement the changes, especially if the changes involve new teaching materials and/or new teaching techniques.

Year of Implementation

Continue to support your teachers as you implement plans for improvement. The subcommittees must be available to hear concerns and find ways to solve the problems that arise.

During this implementation year, provide training about new materials and new programs. Allow individual and collaborative planning time for the faculty. Continue to assess the effectiveness of the curricular program and make changes as necessary. Administrators must empower the leadership team to do whatever it takes to make the improvements successful. In addition, the subcommittee takes responsibility for the revision of curriculum documents as needed, keeping them current, practical, and useful.

Ongoing Assessment

Not only do you need to keep looking at the success of the instructional program; you also need to keep evaluating the effectiveness of the curriculum development process itself. How can you ensure the success of the curriculum development process? Make sure the process is and continues to be an integral part of the professional life of the staff. Keeping the process effective will empower the school to continue in the cycle of self-evaluation and self-improvement. Remember that an effective process will be thoughtful, intentional, and reflective.

A Journey That Never Ends

I'd like to conclude with the reminder that curriculum development and design is an ongoing, continual, "living" cycle that can allow your school to accomplish its mission and ministry successfully.

Curriculum development allows you to journey on the road to excellence. You travel to a target, accomplish that goal, and then continue to the next target. The road never ends, and that is the bad news. As you progress down the road, your school becomes a better institution, offering programs and opportunities that help you accomplish your mission. That is the good news. You do not seek the *destination* of excellence but rather the *process* of moving in the direction of excellence. With God's help, you will minister effectively to the students He has placed in your care. My prayer for you is that God will give you courage, strength, and wisdom to take this journey toward excellence as you seek to minister for His glory.

Bibliography

Haycock, R. (1993). *Encyclopedia of Bible truths for school subjects.* Colorado Springs: Association of Christian Schools International.

Keenan, D. J. (2001). *Curriculum development for Christian schools.* (Rev. ed.). Colorado Springs: Association of Christian Schools International.

MacCullough, M. E. (2000). *How to develop a teaching model for world view integration.* Langhorne, PA: Center for Leadership Development.

Moreland, J. P. (1997). *Love your God with all your mind.* Colorado Springs: NavPress.

Marksmen or Painters?
Achieving Accreditation

Derek J. Keenan, Ed.D.

Chapter Summary

How long have you wrestled with the question of accreditation for your school? Is it important? Are you able to become accredited? Are you ready? The list of questions goes on. Regardless of your questions, you must face the issue addressed by accreditation—the assessment of your school by sympathetic peers according to reasonable and objective standards. Only after your school has undergone this kind of assessment can you honestly answer the question, Is my school doing what it claims to be doing as an educational institution?

Dr. Keenan presents a clear challenge for every school not yet accredited—When will you make accreditation a priority? He defines in practical terms what it takes to become accredited. He also tells why accreditation should be a priority—not for the sake of saying your school is accredited but for the value added to your entire school community through completing this arduous but rewarding task.

About the author

Derek J. Keenan, Ed.D.
Vice President for Academic Affairs, ACSI
Colorado Springs, CO
28 years of educational leadership experience

Chapter 11

Marksmen or Painters?
Achieving Accreditation

Derek J. Keenan, Ed.D.

Q uality ... you know it, yet you don't know what it is. But that's self-contradictory. Some things are better than others; they have more quality. But when you try to define "quality," apart from the things that have it, it all goes poof!

But if you can't explain quality, how do you know what it is, or how do you know that it even exists? If no one knows how to define quality, then for all practical purposes it doesn't exist at all. But for all practical purposes it really *does* exist. What else are the grades based on? Why else would people pay fortunes for some things and throw others in the trash pile? Obviously some things are better than others ... but what qualities make up "betterness"? ... So round and round you go, spinning metal wheels and nowhere finding any place to get traction. Quality ... what is it? (Pirsig, 1974)

In *Zen and the Art of Motorcycle Maintenance*, Pirsig wrestles with some of the challenging issues of life by utilizing the ethereal to explain the mundane. One of those issues is the variety of terms that we use to indicate that something is of high quality. The word "excellence" has the same mix of clarity and ambiguity. Just a few days ago, a school forwarded to me its literary-art magazine called *The Artisan*. Thumbing through the first few pages, I could not help entertaining thoughts about outstanding work. This wonderful collection of photography, poetry, short stories, art, and pictures of drawings, paintings, and sculptures spoke volumes about this school and how it has answered Pirsig's pithy, penetrating question. What is quality?

All our schools face the challenge of finding some means of quality assurance for parents who plunk down thousands of dollars with fairly ambiguous expectations. If pushed, most parents will resort to generic terms such as "quality," "excellence," or "good education." Others may speak in terms of future outcomes related to college admissions, test scores, or even career goals. Sometimes the reputation of a school will answer the quality control questions, but the acknowledged measure of quality in educational institutions is accreditation.

A Brief History of Accreditation

The American system of schools developed in the colonies around a variety of models. These models grew and expanded into a heterogeneous mix. Having no ministry of education, schools recognized a need for some system of organization and standards. In the years between 1890 and 1920, four regional associations were formed. The geographical boundaries were established so as to limit travel within the region to two days or less. These four "standardizing associations" began to identify formally the features of well-functioning educational institutions. They avoided becoming an arm of governmental authority; rather, their assurances of institutional integrity would come from a *peer* review process. The members of the peerage would agree on the standards and then apply them to each institution in a collegial process that would verify the integrity of the schools. Credits would be transferable among the peerage institutions because of the readily identifiable features common to the membership.

The term used for this process was "accreditation." The word has long roots that pass down though Middle French and Old Italian, and into the classical languages. Although the Middle French *accredit(er)* has been applied to acts of ascription, credentialing, and approval, the Old Italian *credito* and Latin *credentus* (past participle of *credere*) were applied primarily to acts of belief, trust, or faith (Stoops, 1998).

The Old Italian and Latin words form the root of our English word "credible" and connect closely to our word "creed." Accreditation signifies that an institution is one of integrity as reviewed by members of its peer group who understand the standards for a quality institution and yet *respect a particular school's unique setting and mission*. The accreditation process provides both internal and external checks on the trustworthiness of an educational institution. As Alexander Pope noted, "Tis with our judgments as our watches, none go just alike, yet each believes his own." Too many brochures and advertisements for schools contain terminology of quality assurance, yet in too many cases, rigorous assessment fails to confirm the claim.

William J. Abernathy, writing in *Industrial Renaissance*, had this to say about quality assurance in the automobile business:

> Many domestic consumers regard a car with a luxurious interior, stately dimensions, and "boulevard" ride as being of high quality; others attach that label to a car with functional interior, aerodynamic styling, quick acceleration, and responsive handling. How to choose between them? In point of fact, there is no reasonable way to do so, for these cars were designed for quite different purposes and were intended to satisfy quite different sets of preferences. Evaluations of quality based on workmanship, reliability, and durability, however, would apply to both cars. It requires no leap of faith to believe that most consumers would view a car with obvious streaks in the paint job, windows that do not roll all the way up, doors that do not hang right, an engine that leaks oil, and an electrical system that fails after 500 miles, as being of lower quality than a competitor's product without these failings. (as cited in Bogue, 1985)

Some agencies that bear the name and sell the product called "accreditation" have no interest in credibility. These organizations are to be scrupulously avoided by schools that wish their accreditation to be accepted by peers in the greater educational community. Leadership that looks for the shortcut or the appearances of quality without the demands of process and the rigor of attaining results is not exercising integrity.

Should Schools Become Accredited?

Schools avoid engaging in the process of accreditation for various reasons. Sometimes their philosophic premise is that the process has nothing positive to contribute to the organization, or that they should avoid scrutiny and disclosure. Some view this as the faith-as-foolishness argument, which advocates that knowing less is more pleasing to God since He is impressed with our bumbling as long as it is "spiritual." In other cases, schools minimize the importance of standards, and defer the process of meeting them and of engaging in a formal improvement process. Sometimes the financial commitment, time demands, and leadership energies needed to take a school through the accreditation process are given lower priority than the press of daily routine.

Every school should be interested in quality, and its governance (board) and leadership (administration) must take the responsibility for achieving effectiveness. One of the most reasonable ways to achieve quality is to engage in the process of accreditation. A Lutheran school memo to board members states it this way: "Where else can schools like ours receive objective evaluation, commendation for superior performance, and a master plan to make necessary improvements, all in one package" (Abernathy, 2000)? The term "effectiveness" rather than the more subjective word "quality" may well bring into focus whether or not we value the excellence that is the goal of the accreditation process.

In measuring our professional or organizational effectiveness, we all tend to embellish the obvious strengths, and diminish or dismiss the flaws. One of the reasons that we do not accomplish strategic or long-range planning relates to this same matter. In planning, we need a clear assessment of the present in order to project the future. The fear of discomfiting change that may come from thoughtful appraisal, strategic analysis, and indicated gaps in performance can incapacitate leaders from moving their organizations forward. A great deal of what Olan Hendrix says about why leaders do not plan applies well to why many school leaders do not engage in the accreditation process.

> [W]e do not plan because most of us prefer to do things rather than think about them. Planning is thinking. Planning is coordinating. Planning is analyzing. Planning is communicating. Planning is interacting. Planning is revising, appraising, and it is easier to plunge into action than think. One of my clients refers to this as, "Ready, fire, aim." (2000)

I remember an old story of a mountain man, reputedly the best shot in his entire area. After hearing of his reputation, a marksman from another part of the country traveled to meet the mountain man and see how good he really was. Some said that the mountain man regularly came to a general store and often did some shooting while there. After finding the general store, the marksman looked at all the bull's-eyes on the store fence and the bullet hole in the exact center of each one. Accosting the clerk, the marksman asked about the mountain man and marveled at the quality of the shooting. The clerk remarked, "T'wern't nothing." To every expression of amazement by the marksman, the clerk had the same reply. Frustrated, the marksman said that the dead-center shooting was the greatest he had ever seen. With drawling nonchalance, the store clerk said, "All that guy does is come here, shoot a hole in the fence, and then paint a bull's-eye around it."

This humorous story illustrates how easily impressions mislead. Perhaps the mountain man was a better painter than marksman. How easy it is, within the confines of the Christian education community, for schools to publish literature that proclaims their quality and excellence, and to have these claims accepted by a trusting constituency! Accreditation makes it possible for schools to assure their constituents, their staff, and the greater watching community that they are, in fact, marksmen and not painters.

Preparation for Accreditation

Two things must mark any leader worthy of the position: caring and courage. Overcoming inertia in schools that have not seriously considered becoming accredited demands that the administrator express care for her institution and its staff by facing an effort that invariably leads to some level of change. She must have the courage to affirm the board and faculty in the worthiness of what they will undertake. At times, implications for staff not only involve the work of the accreditation process but also involve their positions. Accreditation studies the school staff in light of their training and qualifications. If staff members teach far outside their realm of preparation or if they do not have the appropriate degrees or credentials, the unveiling of such information can be traumatic. Leaders must be well prepared to answer questions about the standards and their implications for the school.

Leaders must have the capacity to present any growth, change, and development initiatives in a manner that motivates and invigorates the staff. A school that exists as a learning community tends to have much less difficulty with change than one that has stagnated. Taking a school from inactivity to healthy engagement is one of the great benefits of the accreditation process. No true teacher is completely satisfied with her own effectiveness, and that attitude should also govern school quality. Only ineffective teachers repeat the same lessons in the same way year after year; only careless schools continue to function without some regular process to ensure that they achieve their goals.

An administrator who wishes to take her school toward accreditation must first prepare the school culture for the process. In order to achieve accreditation, a mark of any good community of educators, she must get the faculty into the habit of exploring issues. Every school has matters of practice and conduct that need thorough airing and the combined counsel of the staff to seek well-reasoned solutions. The failure to delve into issues that characterizes most mediocre schools produces a lack of honesty about significant issues. Worse, it results in an absence of thoughtful, reflective dialogue by the staff about any issues at all.

Foundational Steps

Every school entering the accreditation process expects to fulfill the requirements and receive the benefits. The initial step, either with one of the six regional accrediting bodies or an organization such as ACSI, requires an institutional commitment to the process. Generally the entire school should seek accreditation, but at times there are good reasons to complete the process in steps, for example, first the high school and later the middle or elementary school.

Effective leadership brings informed opinions, accurate data, and a solid consensus in favor of the accreditation process. A visit with an administrator who has taken a school through the process can help you get a sense of where resistance or obstacles may appear. Then you can take anticipatory steps to prevent distractions. Often, especially if you face some measure of resistance, it helps to bring in a colleague from an accredited school to meet with the faculty and others. Some schools take key staff members to visit a school that has recently completed the process; others prefer that a person or two observe another school's team visit. These suggestions have budget implications, but wise investment is rarely poor stewardship.

An informed commitment to accreditation requires that school leaders obtain the appropriate materials from the association. Typically, these materials include the *standards document* that lists the threshold requirements for becoming a candidate, and an *evaluative criteria booklet*. The latter document guides the school through a series of questions and exercises; the compilation of the resulting responses is called the *self-study*. The board, administrators, and faculty should review both the materials and the process, and address significant questions or areas of concern to the accrediting association. At first, some schools perceive insurmountable obstacles in the standards, but they learn they can explore favorable options with the association.

For a variety of reasons, Christian schools often find it beneficial to become jointly accredited with a Christian association and with a regional (secular) group. In some states, participation in high school activities requires regional or recognized accreditation. Each of the six regional areas of the country has its own association (see appendix) with its own standards and evaluative criteria. ACSI and some other accreditors have agreements with these groups to conduct a joint candidacy, self-study, and school visit. A school may also choose to become accredited by a specialized organization and then add regional accreditation later. As a school administrator, you should take time to investigate the merits of a joint- or individual-association accreditation. You will probably decide that initial accreditation with a single organization offers the least complex approach.

Beginning the Process of Accreditation

After thoughtful analysis of the issues, your school will formally apply to the accrediting body. Typically this process is not particularly rigorous, but it often requires a resolution from the board and the payment of a candidacy fee. In response to this application, the association schedules a "candidate for accreditation visit" to review the application, peruse the standards, meet with the faculty and/or board, and establish the timeline and first steps toward accreditation. The candidacy period, depending on the association, lasts from two to three years. During that time, the school completes the self-study and develops the required supporting materials, after which it is ready for a team visit.

The Consultant

During the candidacy period, the accrediting body will provide a consultant to work with the school. In some associations, such as ACSI, this consultant becomes the chairperson of the visiting committee. However, with other organizations, the chairperson of the visiting committee may not have been associated with the school in its candidacy period. The number of visits to the school and the extent to which the school must rely on the consultant vary with the expertise and experience of the staff.

The Administration

Administrators almost always take the critical role in the process. This responsibility requires strong leadership including effective delegation of management roles within the accreditation process. In schools, leadership and management overlap in many arenas. But one critical difference is that leadership focuses on the ideas, vision, influence, integrity, and values of the organization. Management is more goal, control, delegation, and task-achievement oriented (Hendrix, 2000). For some schools, the accreditation process provides great opportunities to discover the wealth of leadership talent and management skills already available on their staff. In too many cases, these talents and abilities have functioned only within the classroom and have not been utilized to their fullest extent (see chapter 3).

The Documents

The school's leadership team organizes the parts of the accreditation process within the candidacy timeline. They must pay particular attention to areas of the standards where the school has significant work to do. In many schools, the most significant work takes place not so much in the questions and data required for completing the self-study but in the required supporting documents. The two areas of supporting materials most often outdated, incomplete, or nonexistent are *curriculum guides* and *policies and procedures manuals.*

These two documents are critical to any well-functioning school. The first gives teachers guidance, direction, and accountability for the curriculum—not meaning textbooks alone—in each grade and subject throughout the school, *as defined by the school.* Policies and procedures manuals, which may have a variety of titles, lay down the policy structure established by the governing body (board) under which the staff functions. Typically staff functions are further delineated in an administrative policies and procedures manual. This management tool denotes how the administration implements the policies of the board and ensures consistent functioning of the school on a day-to-day basis.

The Steering Committee

Given the magnitude of developing current and accurate curriculum guides, this task should be one of the first assignments for the school staff. Such assignments come from the accreditation leadership group, or steering committee. In many cases, an administrator chairs this team, but there is wisdom in appointing someone else with strong consensus-building and delegation skills to fill this role. As a member of the group, you can attend as many of the meetings as your schedule will permit. Remember, you face many responsibilities in the accreditation process. The increasing regularity of steering committee meetings may put unnecessary pressure on you when your energies may be better spent encouraging the staff and addressing major needs in the accreditation process.

The steering committee has the responsibility of assigning all staff duties and of finding members for each of the committees that will complete the self-study. Board members, parents, and student groups all have assignments, but the self-study is the major responsibility of the school staff. Depending on the timeline, it is typical for every faculty member to serve on at least two committees—a section committee of the evaluative criteria, and a subject discipline committee for the instructional program.

The Self-Study

Design an organized system of accountability and of reporting to both the steering committee and the entire faculty. This system creates the "pleasant tension" needed to get all the work finished in a manner that serves the school and the process well. Staff members need regular reminders that the self-study has the greatest value in the accreditation process. The visiting committee will use the study to compare the school's stated objectives with what the school is actually doing. More than that, the completed self-study becomes influential in the strategic planning and development of the school. You should require the best level of thinking about and responding to matters in the criteria so that this document becomes the valuable asset it ought to be.

The Process

Wise educational leaders engaging in the process of accreditation look at the school calendar, and then they schedule time for the quality of work the process warrants. Finding sufficient time slots can be accomplished with early dismissals, delayed starts, or additional professional development days. In the first two years of the candidacy period, an allowance of forty hours within the year in addition to faculty meeting times is a general guideline.

The first summers of the candidacy period are also important times to make strong progress on the self-study materials. If possible, employ some key steering committee members who can work with the various self-study section committees and the instructional area committees. That work will take some of the pressure off the staff during the school year. Expect a great feeling of accomplishment as sections of the report begin to take shape and become available for faculty perusal. Seeing their colleagues' work reach its final form also helps motivate other committees who need to make some additional progress.

Completing the Self-Study

As the sections are completed, the increasing mass of the document indicates your progress toward the important visit of the accreditation committee. As you complete each self-study section and compile the requisite support data, make sure that the school staff carefully read and become familiar with the sections of the report that involve them. You will likely see a greater involvement by the staff as well as by board members and parents as they hear these reports and get the opportunity for any additional input. For efficiency, you can divide these readings among faculty groups. The more diverse the construct of these groups, the better the quality of insight.

At times you may see some sharp disagreement about how the questions were answered and what data were used to support the answers. These matters need to be resolved, and in this setting your group leadership skills come into play. If an issue becomes a debate during report reading, you should probably define the disagreement and plan a time to resolve it. A word of caution is necessary here: As with any situation of competing ideas, do not allow the matter to fall into a black hole and be forgotten, or worse, adopt a decision without involving those with strong opinions on the issue (stakeholders). Every effective school has a forum where dissent is cultivated and pursued to a positive conclusion. If such a process has not been a part of the ethos in your school, accreditation will surface ample opportunities to develop and incorporate it into your school culture.

The final steps in the completion of the self-study include editing, proofreading, and compiling into bound documents. The quality of the final product can have a profound effect on the visiting committee since they receive this document four to six weeks before visiting the campus. You should create a sense of anticipation as team members read their assigned sections and gain a perspective on how your school defines itself through the quality of the materials presented.

Visiting Committee

The period of candidacy culminates in the visit. At the conclusion of the visit, the visiting team sends a recommendation to its appropriate commission for a final decision on whether the school will be accredited. Normally, an association will not schedule a visit to a school that is unprepared for accreditation.

Teams of five to as many as twenty educators, depending on the size of the school, arrive to spend about three intensive days reviewing the school in light of the self-study and the standards. Each team member has specific assignments for observations, interviews, and reports. Most report sections have two or three members assigned by the visiting team chairperson. The report will include a general statement about that area of the self-study, will identify several commendable elements, and will often include recommendations for the school's consideration. Each self-study section includes the school's own analysis of its strengths and of areas for needed improvement. The visiting committee validates the accuracy and completeness of the self-study. Remember, you need a thorough grasp of the self-study in order to prepare articulate responses to the questions team members ask.

You should generally write recommendations as suggestions unless they identify a standard that has not been met. If a school has not fully or appropriately met a standard, the recommendation takes on stronger wording insisting that the school address the matter.

Should your school fail to meet a standard that carries rigid guidelines, the decision on accreditation may be put on hold until the issue is resolved. In other cases, the standards violation is noted as a major recommendation, and the school is given a specific time frame to meet an acceptable compliance level.

The visiting committee conducts an exit interview with selected school leaders to give a general report on its findings. In most cases, the school can infer from that report whether it has done well and will receive accreditation. The committee does not decide whether the school receives accreditation; it recommends action. The regional commission, which reviews the committee's report and the self-study, makes the final determination about accreditation.

Accreditation: Getting Beyond "Fuzzability Thinking"

Any definition of leadership as it applies to results should include some reference to a "led" organization being more mature and hence more effective. Hans Finzel says it simply: "Leadership is *influence*. That's it. A one-word definition. Anyone who *influences* someone else to do something has *led* that person. Another definition might be, *A leader takes people where they would never go on their own*" (1994).

Taking schools to new levels of maturity and effectiveness presents no small challenge. Schools are people-intensive, thriving hubs of activity centered around the chaotic complexity of the teaching and learning process. Every day they demand management and leadership with a whirl of decision making, responding, and monitoring so that the greater organizational needs of vision and direction do not get lost. Ted Engstrom says that purposes show our ultimate hopes and set the direction in which we want to go. But to accomplish our greater purpose, we need to set goals. Engstrom further notes, "Christian organizations have a great tendency to define their purposes and never get around to define what they intend to do." He calls this "fuzzability thinking" (Larson, 1988).

The process of leading a school to accreditation accomplishes a goal on the way to achieving excellence. Accreditation is a mark of quality assurance for an educational institution, and wise leaders, from the earliest days of a school's existence, will point it in that direction. *Accreditation helps us come to grips with the reality that good enough is not good enough.* Schools that achieve accreditation become part of the greater learning community of high quality schools. They move forward in a strategic way because they have disciplined themselves to achieve the affirmation and respect of an independent evaluative agency. Accreditation helps educational institutions establish evidence and a data-supported baseline of quality from which they can proceed to improve, mature, and develop to their fullest potential.

As Dr. Bill Brown, President of Bryan College, has said, "It is not the size or growth rate of an organization that makes it better; *better is better!*"

> I am the Lord your God, who teaches you what is best for you, who directs you in the way you should go. (Isaiah 48:17)

Appendix

North Central Association
Arizona State University
PO Box 873011
Tempe, AZ 85287-3011
800/525-9517
nca@nca.asu.edu

Southern Association of Colleges and
Schools
1866 Southern Lane
Decatur, GA 30033
800/424-5250
elem@mail.sacs.org (elementary)
melgart@mail.sacs.org (secondary)

Northwest Association of Schools and
Colleges
1910 University Drive
Boise, ID 83725-1060
208/426-5727
sclemens@boisestate.edu

Western Association of Schools and
Colleges
533 Airport Boulevard, Suite 200
Burlingame, CA 94010-2009
650/696-1060
mail@acswasc.org

New England Association of Schools
and Colleges
209 Burlington Road
Bedford, MA 01730-1433
781/271-0022
kwillis@neasc.org

Middle States Association of Colleges
and Schools (Elementary)
GSB Building
1 Belmont Avenue, Suite 618
Bala Cynwyd, PA 19004
610/617-1100
info@ces-msa.org.

Middle States Association of Colleges
and Schools (Secondary)
3624 Market Street
Philadelphia, PA 19104-2680
215/662-5603
info@css-msa.org

Commission of International and
Transregional Accreditation (CITA)
University of Colorado
Campus Box 193
PO Box 173364
Denver, CO 80217-3364
866/873-8878
rsinisi@ceo.cudenver.edu

National Study of School Evaluation
(NSSE)
1699 E. Woodfield Road, Suite 406
Schaumburg, IL 60173-4958
800/843-6773
schoolimprovement@nsse.org

Bibliography

Abernathy, W. J. (2000, April). *Accreditation and needs assessment*. St. Louis: Lutheran Church, Department of School Ministry.

Bennis, W., & Nanus, B. (1997). *Why leaders can't lead*. San Francisco: Jossey-Bass.

Bogue, G. (1985). *Enemies of leadership*. Bloomington, IN: PDK Books.

Carver, C. (Ed.). (2001). *The artisan*. Birmingham, AL: Briarwood Christian School.

Finzel, H. (1994) *The top ten mistakes that leaders make*. Wheaton, IL: Victor Books.

Hendrix, O. (2000). *Three dimensions of leadership*. St. Charles, IL: ChurchSmart Resources.

Larson, R. (Ed.). (1988). *The best of Ted Engstrom on personal excellence and leadership*. San Bernadino, CA: Here's Life Publishers.

Pirsig, R. N. (1974). *Zen and the art of motorcycle maintenance*. New York: William Morrow.

Stoops, J. (1998). *CITA and the new education*. Tempe, AZ: International Council of School Accreditation Commissions.

Filling the Empty Self
Understanding the Surrounding Culture

J.P. Moreland, Ph.D.

Chapter Summary

Among those in King David's army were the men of Issachar, who "understood the times and knew what Israel should do." (1 Chronicles 12:32) The call to you as a Christian school leader is the same. Do you understand the times in which we live, and do you know what to do?

A Christian apologist and a strong voice for the Christian school movement, Dr. J. P. Moreland defines the battlefield for every Christian school leader—the minds and hearts of Christian school students. He offers practical suggestions for waging this battle against the marginalization of the Christian worldview in an increasingly secular culture.

About the author

J. P. Moreland, Ph.D.
Professor of Philosophy, Talbot School of Theology, Biola University
La Mirada, CA
22 years of educational leadership experience

Chapter 12

Filling the Empty Self
Understanding the Surrounding Culture

J.P. Moreland, Ph.D.

Every fall Christian school administrators look forward to filling empty classrooms with students, empty teaching positions with faculty, empty athletic facilities with winning teams, and empty coffers with welcome tuition money. Yet a pervasive vacuum can chill our hallways despite high achievement in all these areas of effort. None of them ultimately addresses our mission; none of them reaches our highest goal. Only a fully developed Christian worldview can fill our empty students, so we begin this chapter with that focus.

In 1989 the state of California issued a new Science Framework to provide guidance for the state's public school science classrooms. That document gives advice to teachers about how to handle students who approach them with reservations about the theory of evolution:

> At times some students may insist that certain conclusions of science cannot be true because of certain religious or philosophical beliefs they hold.... It is appropriate for the teacher to express in this regard, "I understand that you may have personal reservations about accepting this scientific evidence, but it is scientific knowledge about which there is no reasonable doubt among scientists in their field, and it is my responsibility to teach it because it is part of our common intellectual heritage. (Hartwig & Nelson, 1992)

A flourishing Christian education movement requires that every Christian educator must approach his or her vocation with more than a surface analysis of what this statement symbolizes for our field. Its real importance lies not in its promotion of evolution over creation, though that is no small matter in its own right. No, the real danger in the Framework's advice resides in the picture of knowledge it presupposes: empirical knowledge gained by the hard sciences is the only knowledge we can have about reality and thus the only knowledge that deserves the backing of public institutions.

The Framework states that nonempirical claims outside the hard sciences, such as those at the core of ethics, political theory, and religion, are not items of knowledge but rather matters of private feeling. Note carefully the words associated with science: "conclusions," "evidence," "knowledge," "no reasonable doubt," and "intellectual heritage." These deeply cognitive terms express the view that science and science alone exercises the intellectual right (and responsibility) to define reality. By contrast, religious claims are described in distinctively noncognitive language: "beliefs" and "personal reservations."

In such a culture, we now live and move and have our being as Christian educators. Among other things, we are in the knowledge business, imparting it to students and providing tools necessary to obtain it. We are not in the "belief business," passing on a mere set of beliefs, a religious "tradition" to our students. So we must understand how our secular culture defines the nature and limits of knowledge. With this in mind, I want to characterize this culture more thoroughly and offer some implications of this characterization for Christian schools.

The Secular Environment Surrounding the Christian School Movement

A Three-Way Worldview Struggle

Currently, a three-way worldview struggle rages in our culture among ethical monotheism (especially Christianity), scientific naturalism, and postmodernism. I cannot undertake here a detailed characterization of these worldviews, but I want to say a word about them and their role in shaping the task of the Christian school (Johnson, 1995, 2000).

First, *scientific naturalism* takes the view that only the physical cosmos that science studies exists. Scientific naturalism has two central components, one metaphysical and one epistemological. Metaphysically, scientific naturalism implies that everything that exists is composed of matter or emerges out of matter when it achieves a suitable complexity. Among other things, this implication amounts to a denial of the soul and the possibility of disembodied existence after death (Moreland & Rae, 2000). Epistemologically, it implies that physical science is the only, or at least a vastly superior, way of gaining knowledge (Moreland, 1989).

The Christian teacher sensitive to worldview issues must meet these two components head on. We must show our students that a number of things that exist are not physical: God, human souls, consciousness, virtues (such as love and kindness), aesthetic beauty, various kinds of normative judgments, the laws of logic, mathematical numbers, theories (yes, theories are mental entities in people's minds!), and so forth. We must also show that knowledge can be gained outside the hard sciences. *Immaterial reality and nonempirical knowledge constitute two key items of focus for the Christian teacher sensitive to worldview struggles.*

Today, a decided pecking order resides between science and the humanities. This has to stop. Science offers one way to gain knowledge. But today people have the idea that it is the only way. Disciplines such as art, theology, history, and literature are viewed as providing mere opinions and not knowledge. We must work hard to elevate the humanities, theology, biblical studies, and other disciplines outside the hard sciences to the level of those sciences in order to promote them as sources of knowledge and truth.

The second worldview is *postmodernism* (Groothuis, 2000). This worldview contains a very complicated set of ideas, and no short characterization of it would be entirely adequate. Still, we may safely say that postmodernism is a form of cultural relativism. According to postmodernism, truth/falsehood, real/unreal, right/wrong, rational/irrational, and good/bad are dichotomies relative to different ethnographic communities. What is true, real, and so forth for one community may not be so for another.

We must stand firmly against postmodernism. Two things anchor Christian teaching in light of the threat of postmodernism: the nature of truth and the objectivity of rationality. First, we need to teach students what truth is. Both common sense and biblical teaching undergird what is called a correspondence theory of truth. Truth does not become reality according to the way one thinks, says, or believes. Instead, truth consists in a relationship of correspondence between a proposition (sentence, statement, belief, hereafter simply proposition) and reality. The proposition "grass is green" is true only if things are really the way the proposition asserts, namely, if grass is actually green. "Unicorns live in Montana" is true only if unicorns actually live in Montana.

The second notion currently under assault by postmodernists is that of objective rationality. In secular contexts, when Christians take a position on something (say the resurrection of Jesus or a pro-life stance regarding the unborn), many claim that they are biased, not objective, and thus disqualified from claiming the support of evidence and reason for their stance. If we accept such a conclusion, it will have the effect of cutting off at the knees any attempt by Christians to support with argumentation anything that follows from a Christian worldview.

What can be done about this issue? We must redouble our efforts at restoring the value of objective reason, rationality, evidence, argumentation, and the like to the Christian community. We must convince our students and parents that Christianity carries the very voice of truth and reason in culture. We should display banners at our schools that celebrate intellectual virtues, such as knowledge, wisdom, truth, and reasoning together, and we should promote the life of the mind whenever possible. Elsewhere, I have provided a rationale and strategy for doing this (Moreland, 1997).

Before leaving the topic of postmodernism, I cannot resist the urge to make one more point. We must help our students avoid the contemporary notion of tolerance associated with postmodernism. To do this, we need to help them distinguish between two different principles of tolerance: the classical and the contemporary principles. According to the *classical sense of the principle of tolerance*, a person holds that his own moral or religious views are true and those of his opponent false. But he still respects his opponent as a person and his right to make a case for his views. Thus, one has a duty to tolerate a different moral/religious view, but not in the sense of thinking that it is correct. In fact, quite the opposite is true. The classical principle teaches that people will continue to value and respect their opponents, to treat them with dignity, and to recognize their right to argue for and propagate their ideas.

Strictly speaking, in the classical view, one tolerates persons, not their ideas. In this sense, even though someone disapproves of another's moral/religious beliefs and practices, she will not inappropriately interfere with them. However, adherents of this view judge opponents' views to be wrong and dedicate themselves to doing everything morally appropriate to counteract those views, for example, using argument and persuasion. It should be clear that the classical sense of tolerance is really an absolutist position inconsistent with postmodern relativism. If one does not consider another position morally or religiously false, what is there to tolerate? Surely, a person is not just tolerating the fact that she doesn't like the view in question, but that she judges it mistaken.

The *contemporary version of tolerance*, popular in the general culture, goes beyond the classical version by claiming that one should not even judge other people's viewpoints as wrong. In this view, absolute truth vanishes, no view may claim superiority over another, and one exhibits intolerance if he judges that his view enjoys truth while an opposing view suffers falsehood. This second notion of tolerance is postmodern and has no place in the life of a disciple of Jesus. However, rejection of the contemporary principle of tolerance does not mean abandonment of tolerance itself. We must assure our students of this fact, and we should teach them about the classical principle of tolerance as a means of providing this assurance.

Secular Culture as a View of the Nature and Limits of Knowledge

Modern American culture is largely secular in this sense: Most people have little or no understanding of how Christians see the world, nor do those who hold a Christian worldview participate significantly in the way we as a society frame and debate issues in the public square. Three major centers of influence in our culture—the universities and public schools, the media, and the government—are largely devoid of serious religious discussion.

The primary characteristic of modern secularism is its view of the nature and limits of knowledge. We must understand this fact because if knowledge gives one power (we give surgeons and not carpenters the right to cut us open precisely because surgeons have the relevant knowledge not possessed by carpenters), then those with the cultural say-so about who does and doesn't have knowledge will be in a position to marginalize and silence groups judged to have mere belief and private opinion.

There simply is no established, widely recognized body of ethical or religious knowledge now operative in the universities and schools of our culture. Indeed, ethical and religious claims are frequently placed into what Francis Schaeffer used to call "the upper story," judged to have little or no intellectual authority, especially compared to the authority given science to define the limits of knowledge and reality in those same institutions. This view raises a pressing question: Is Christianity a knowledge tradition or merely a faith tradition? According to the latter perspective, Christianity, while true, cannot be proven true and must be embraced on the basis of some intellectual state weaker than knowledge.

Secularism and the Marginalization of Christian Claims

At least two reasons suggest why this may well be *the* crucial question for Christian educators to keep in mind as they do their work. For one thing, Christianity claims to be a knowledge tradition, and it places knowledge, not merely truth, at the center of proclamation and discipleship. The Old and New Testaments, including the teachings of Jesus, claim not merely that Christianity is true, but that a variety of its moral and religious assertions can be known to be true (Luke 1:4, John 10:4, Romans 1:19).

Second, as I mentioned above, knowledge provides the basis of responsible action in society. Dentists, not lawyers, have the authority to place their hands in our mouths because they have the necessary knowledge to act responsibly. Christian educators contribute inadvertently to the marginalization of Christianity if they do little to deflect the view that theological and ethical assertions are merely parts of a tradition, or ways of seeing that fall short of knowledge, or merely a source for adding a "theological perspective" to an otherwise unperturbed secular topic. They add to the problem precisely because they fail to rebut the contemporary tendency to rob Christianity of the very thing that gives it the authority necessary to prevent that marginalization, its legitimate claim to give us moral and religious knowledge. *Both in and out of the church, Jesus has been lost as an intellectual authority, and Christian educators should carry out their vocation in light of this fact. We have a duty to present Jesus Christ and the Word of God as a source not only of salvation and meaning, but of authoritative knowledge about all areas of which Jesus and His Word speak.*

The Absolutization of Desire and the Empty Self

The pervasive denial of truth and of rationality outside the hard sciences has left people without hope that they can discover true, rationally defensible forms of wisdom as guides to a flourishing life. As a result, people turn to emotion and the satisfaction of desire as decisive factors in adopting a worldview. This affective approach to life, now embodied in art and culture generally, has created conditions for the emergence of a new personality type that psychologists claim can be found in epidemic proportions in American society. Never before in the history of Western culture has this personality type been seen so pervasively and profoundly; indeed, it is a post-sixties phenomenon—*the empty self.*

The empty self is narcissistic, inordinately individualistic, self-absorbed, infantile, passive, and motivated by instant gratification. The empty self experiences a loss of personal significance and worth, as well as chronic emotional hunger and emptiness. The empty self satiates itself with consumer goods, calories, experiences, politicians, romantic partners, and empathetic therapists. The empty self does not value learning for its own sake, refuses to defer gratification under the demands of discipline, and prefers visual stimulation to abstract thought. In a Christian school, a classroom of empty selves can reinforce the view that learning exists to make students happy, to satisfy their emotional hunger, and to fulfill their own plans for success.

Moreover, with the secular relativization of truth and reason outside the hard sciences, secularism has contributed to *the absolutization of desire satisfaction.* With truth and reason dethroned as guides for life, something had to take their place. The heir to the throne is absolute self-gratification. Secularism helps prop up this value in the culture by its denial of truth and reason in matters of worldview, along with its promulgation of a naive and destructive notion of tolerance.

Finally, the secular relativization of truth and reason outside the hard sciences gives birth to *a growing loss of hope for objective meaning in life.* This emptiness emerges in the face of a cold, heartless, mechanistic universe in which the only relief outside Christianity consists of temporary flirtations with postmodernist irrationality. Hence we see a deep hunger in society for spirituality. Unfortunately, without the rails of biblical truth, the contemporary spiritual train is engineered by a nation of empty selves guided only by the unbridled satisfaction of desire. Current preoccupation with promiscuous sex symptomizes the failure of this sort of "spirituality" to address the human condition.

The Loss of a "Uni-versity" and the Fragmentation of the Curriculum

Given the abandonment of monotheism, the ground weakens for believing in the unity of truth. This is one reason why our uni-versities are turning into multi-versities. The fragmentation of secular education at all levels, along with its inability to define its purpose or gather together a coherent curriculum, indicates what happens when we set monotheism aside. In a monotheistic worldview, God possesses a unified, rational mind, and academic disciplines seek to "think God's thoughts after Him." Thus, wherever truth is found, it comes from God and should harmonize with truth claims in other areas of study. As St. Augustine wisely advised, "We must show our Scriptures not to be in conflict with whatever [our critics] can demonstrate about the nature of things from reliable sources" (McMullin, 1981). Augustine claimed this because he knew that while Scripture was the guiding authority in intellectual exploration, Christianity implied a unity of truth.

With the emergence of secularism, we find it increasingly difficult to formulate a unified school curriculum. Indeed, many now judge it intolerant and politically incorrect to claim that certain authors or items of literature in some area of study are better than others. Consequently, educators find it unclear just exactly what a high school student should know upon graduation. The very attempt to answer this question cuts against the grain of extreme versions of multiculturalism. At this critical hour, Christian educators have something increasingly rare and distinctive to offer because *integration stands at the heart of Christian education.* Because of our monotheistic worldview, we still believe students should learn to integrate studies from one area with insights from another. If Christians seize the day in the next decade or so, it will be our schools and our home schooling that stand virtually alone in providing a synergistic, integrated education for our students.

Implications for Christian Education

In the diagnosis just presented, I have been unable to resist from time to time the temptation to provide some practical application. However, in the final section of the chapter, I shall unpack an educational mandate as we seek to impact our secular culture for Jesus Christ.

Revising Christian Education's Self-Understanding

In several ways, these general cultural shifts continue to impact Christian education. We find the first way in the evangelical community's *expectations for Christian schools*. Basically, many see a Christian school as a fortress where the social/moral influences of the world are kept out. These influences are largely paracurricular, for example, entertainment, sexual attitudes, and so forth. Most agree that Christian schools should emphasize personal holiness, but few expect them to excel as academic centers, precisely because they are Christian.

To be sure, parents clearly want their children to receive a "good education," but often, they have no idea what that means. Their perspective on the subject usually depicts the purpose of education as job preparation—or college preparation, which in turn provides job preparation. Very few have any practical grasp of the notion of integrating a Christian worldview into every course of study. Moreover, Bible classes and their cousins are too often understood in "spiritual" and decidedly nonacademic terms. A Christian high school teacher recently told me that when he gave a student a D grade in a Bible class, he was greeted with incredulity by the student's parents. After all, they said, this is a *Bible* class, and academic standards are inappropriate for this area of "learning." Too many evangelicals do not prize loving God with all their minds, nor do they envision the spiritual journey in terms of a thoughtful, informed approach to life.

In this way, low academic expectations of schooling mirror the general culture, but the church is supposed to flood the world with light and season it with salt, not be squeezed into its mold. The time is ripe for Christian schools to seize the moment, to work on defining their agendas to include development of the Christian mind in their boards, administrators, teachers, and students. They must *press hard to integrate a Christian worldview into all areas of study, rather than allowing Bible classes and chapel to feel like add-ons to an otherwise secular curriculum.* Careful thought forms a central part of life in the Kingdom of God, and it stands at the very core of the spiritual life.

Second, Christian schools need *to work harder at the relationship between faith and reason.* More specifically, we must find creative ways to communicate that knowledge extends beyond what can be known through science and the five senses. We can demonstrate that Christianity expresses a knowledge tradition every bit as much as chemistry or literature does. We can affirm that acquiring knowledge of God, the Bible, and theology is important and takes work, just like other areas of study. Of course, this view implies a greater emphasis in our schools on apologetics (see chapter 13), and it also signals that we can no longer disregard the integration of doctrine and theology into a coherent Christian worldview in all areas of study. Moreover, every Christian school should develop a "hit list" of false, harmful ideas circulating as part of contemporary "folk wisdom," expose them in various classes, and demonstrate through argument and education that they are irrational, false, and degrading. That list should target the ideas our students absorb through magazines, music, television, and movies.

Third, and a bit more controversial, *we must communicate to our students a sense of intellectual balance.* I mean this in a twofold sense. For one thing, not all areas of doctrine and intellectual assent are equally important. Thus, while a school may have a detailed doctrinal statement that specifies commitment to a number of propositions, it should teach students that disagreement exists among Christians of goodwill. Some areas of assent—for example, the great themes in the classic Christian creeds that constitute mere Christianity—are of more importance than other areas, even those specified in a school's doctrinal statement. I am not suggesting that a school should not affirm all the details of its doctrinal statement. I am suggesting that we must graduate students who know how to get along with believers who do not affirm all those details. We must teach our students how to judge which doctrines are more important than others.

The second sense of balance involves our intellectual certainty in having correctly grasped the truth in various areas of Christian commitment. As a Christian, I believe many things about which I am not as confident as I am about other things. We fail our students if we communicate to them that all Christian teachings are equal in certainty and importance.

These points about balance are delicate, and it is unlikely that we will all interpret them in the same manner. But we must think this issue through with greater depth than ever before. To cite one example, I think that in the creation/evolution controversy, issues about the age of the earth carry secondary importance compared with issues involved in critiquing naturalistic evolution. Thus, Young Earth (e.g., Henry Morris) and Old Earth Progressive Creationists (e.g., Hugh Ross) have far more in common with each other than either has with Naturalistic or Theistic Evolutionists, and the things that divide them are less important than the things they share (Moreland & Reynolds, 1999).

So while it is appropriate and important for schools to have specific doctrinal statements (e.g., requiring a Young Earth position on the part of faculty), those schools should not present Young or Progressive Creationism in the same light as they do Theistic or Naturalistic Evolution. If, in the interests of Christian civility and impact, Christians cannot find meaningful ways to rally around what they share with other Christians, what message are they sending to students? While not denying doctrinal differences, mature Christians must manifest the two senses of balance in their relationship with other members of the body of Christ. If they fail in this, what hope remains for our students to integrate biblical teaching appropriately? I say appropriately, meaning with reasonable ideas from secular culture for certain important goals, all the while without compromise.

Finally, Christian teachers *need to develop a richer understanding of their calling and task*. Sadly, for some time now, educators have often not been viewed as intellectuals. Too often, education is depicted as a field that emphasizes methodology to the exclusion of intellectual prowess. Frequently, teachers see themselves as experts in method, as caretakers of children, and as information disseminators. But many of those same teachers do not see themselves as competent authorities in their content areas of teaching.

We need to work at fostering an atmosphere in which teachers come to view as essential to their calling the development of intellectual competence and authority in their areas of teaching. No longer can we leave such a self-understanding to university level teaching. Christian teachers at all grade levels are called to be intellectuals in the relevant world of ideas and not simply experts at educational method. In my view, an overemphasis on method too often compensates for a lack of intellectual confidence in one's area of teaching. If I am right about this, then we need to help our teachers grow intellectually as well as improve methodologically.

Given the loss of the value of the mind in the Christian community, we have a public relations job. We must persuade our boards, parents, and supporting churches that intellectual excellence is central to the cause of Christ and that Christian schools form the main part of the body of Christ that provides intellectual excellence for the gospel cause.

Integration and Holistic Approaches to Curriculum

The rival worldviews of scientific naturalism and postmodernism do not have the intellectual resources to justify belief in the unity of truth and knowledge throughout the academic disciplines. As these worldviews continue to gain prominence, we will see increasing fragmentation in education. By contrast, integration and a holistic view of truth and knowledge rest at the core of Christianity. In the current scene, *we alone offer a justified hope for a unified, integrated education*.

How do Christian teachers decide what is the best investment of their energies in the integrative task? With so many areas of study, what criteria can help us prioritize our efforts? Is there a taxonomy of issues that expresses some priorities that Christian scholars ought to adopt? I'm afraid I have a lot more thinking to do on this before I am prepared to offer anything approximating an adequate answer to these questions. Any taxonomy here would likely express the interests and biases of the taxonomist, and I am no exception to this rule. Obviously, one's own sense of personal calling, and one's own curiosities will and should play an important role here.

However, I think the following three criteria fall close to the mark. First, integration should be focused on those areas of study *that seem to be intrinsically more central or foundational to the Christian theistic enter-*

prise. The metaphysical, epistemological, and axiological commitments that constitute mere Christianity should be preserved. Second, integration should be focused on areas *that are currently under heavy attack*. The objectivity of truth, the existence of moral and religious knowledge, the presence of miracles and divine providence in history, the reality of the soul and life after death, and the bankruptcy of evolution fall under this second criterion. A third and perhaps less important criterion is this: integration should be focused on those areas of study *in which such activity is under-represented, relatively speaking*. Sociology, history, political science, and the arts suffer a lack of Christian influence, and we honor God by mobilizing students to penetrate these fields for the cause of Christ.

It is up to Christian teachers in each discipline to decide how these criteria inform their intellectual work. However, I think points one and two converge to yield an integrative mandate for contemporary Christian teachers, especially those who work on the interface between science and Christian faith. To repeat a point mentioned in the first section of this chapter, Christian educators must face a very important cultural fact when they undertake the task of integration: there simply is no established, widely recognized body of ethical or religious knowledge now operative in the institutions of knowledge in our culture, for example, the universities. Ethical and religious claims are frequently placed into what Francis Schaeffer used to call the "upper story," and they are judged to have little or no rational authority, especially compared with the authority given science to define the limits of knowledge and reality in those same institutions.

An important part of a believer's vocation is his major in college or his main form of work as a career. If we are to be integrated, holistic Christians who make an impact on the world, we need to learn how to be Christian doctors, schoolteachers, lawyers, businesspersons, and so forth. However, if a student waits until college to begin to think about academic subjects in this way, it may be too late.

One of the chief advantages of going to a Christian school prior to college is that the student will already have a chance to study various academic subjects from a distinctively Christian point of view and to consider the reasons a Christian might choose a vocation related to those subjects. Of course, this opportunity means that Christian schools must teach all subjects with two things in mind: (1) How can this subject matter be presented from a Christian perspective? (2) How can this course be presented in such a way that it motivates students to consider the subject as a possible calling from God? We dare not allow our students to approach the selection of future employment as secular folks do. Our students must be taught to seek a vocation, not a mere job.

Spirituality, the Soul, and Bodily Disciplines

The Christian school must provide the rails of biblical truth and practice to guide its students in their quest to satisfy their hunger for authentic spirituality. This hunger is very deep today. Visit any secular bookstore and look at the proliferation of works on the topic. Unfortunately, today's "spirituality" is virtually contentless. Still, spiritual hunger abounds, and we cannot satisfy it with business as usual. Among other things, the Christian school must recapture the Christian emphasis on the body and on spiritual disciplines/practices in its attempt to form Christ in its students.

Strictly speaking, the body is not simply a physical object; that is, one cannot capture the full reality of a body if one limits one's descriptions to the categories of chemistry, physics, and neurophysiology. The body is also irreducibly human, actually an ensouled physical structure. Part of what makes it a body is the soul that diffuses, informs, animates, and is fully present at each of the body's parts (just as God relates to space in general). Take the soul away from a body, and strictly speaking it is no longer a human body, though of course it still retains its status of *having been* a human body.

Dallas Willard has drawn out a number of important implications for spiritual formation from the soul's relationship to the body (Willard, 1988, 1998, 1999). In précis form, I paraphrase a few. Character consists in the sum total of one's habits. A habit is an ingrained tendency to act, think, feel, and behave in certain ways without having to will to do so. Habits form part of the structure of the soul, specifically, the soul as embodied. The body is where the soul "stores" habits; it is the body as an ensouled human entity that contains habits among its members. Thus, we are enjoined by Paul and others to present our members, that is, specific body parts, to God as instruments of righteousness, and the various spiritual disciplines are means of accomplishing this injunction. The body/soul connection is very deep, and the body is actually the repository of our habits that constitute our character and shape the natural inclinations of the operations of the mind, will, sensations, desires, and other factors of the soul. Thus, the spiritual exercising of the body can train it to form habits and therefore character, which changes the soul's structure and thereby shapes the spiritual life of the person.

By way of application, I believe the Christian school should consult the writings of Dallas Willard (cited above) as a template for developing strategies of spiritual formation. I am not suggesting they are exhaustive, but in my opinion, no school would go wrong in attempting to put shoe leather on the insights Willard expresses in these works. In my view, *a faculty committee on spiritual formation should be appointed at each Christian school, and as part of their commission, members should read these three works and develop a strategy for weaving them into the structure of the school.*

Faculty Development

Finally, given the worldview struggle now raging in our secular culture, we cannot afford to define our mission in terms of our students alone. Our Christian schools do not exist simply to teach, train, or in other ways develop students. Indeed, this is one important target group we exist to serve. But there is an important group that I believe should be equally targeted: our faculty. Think of our mission in this way: If we exist to mobilize and equip an army of people to serve Christ in the war of ideas and in the struggle of the kingdom of God against the kingdom of darkness, then we must be sure we nurture and empower our main resource—our soldiers. The main resource of any Christian school is its faculty, and they must be viewed not merely as means to an end (teaching students) but as ends in themselves (see chapters 7 and 8).

We need to think through faculty development in more detail. Continuing education for them is crucial, and I mean education in the world of ideas relevant to their teaching and not simply in educational methodology. Faculty study groups should be encouraged. We should look for certain members on our faculties who have a special gift and motivation toward study and intellectual development. We should reduce their teaching loads and provide them with the vision and resources to become intellectual spokespersons for our schools and for the broader cause of Christ.

These teachers (and others as well) should be challenged and aided in teaching in churches, training adults how to know what they believe and why they believe it. They should be empowered to become local experts in some area—creation/evolution, Christianity and government, the family— and encouraged to write letters to the editors of local papers, appear on talk radio, and in general, be winsome, intellectual ambassadors for the cause of Christ.

Think of it! What would happen if each of our Christian schools had three to four teachers set apart and groomed for this sort of ministry? Not only would our impact be multiplied, but we would not need to advertise for students. Word would get out that such and such Christian school has teachers that really know their stuff and who are winsome, articulate ambassadors for Christ. Only if we work harder at equipping and unleashing the gifts of our faculty will this job get done.

In sum, I have tried to provide a sketch of the contemporary culture in which we live and move and have our educational being. I have also sought to provide some practical application of this sketch to our task as Christian educators. Since it is true that in Christ are hidden all the treasures of wisdom and knowledge (Colossians 2:3), and since spiritual warfare is at its core a struggle of ideas and thought (2 Corinthians 10:3–5), Christian schools are centers of Christian knowledge and spirituality. As such, they are colleagues of war for the body of Christ. I, for one, cannot think of a higher calling.

Bibliography

Groothuis, D. (2000). *Truth decay*. Downers Grove, IL: InterVarsity Press.

Hartwig, M., & Nelson, A. P. (1992). *Invitation to conflict*. Colorado Springs: Access Research Network.

Johnson, P. E. (1995). *Reason in the balance*. Downers Grove, IL: InterVarsity Press.

Johnson, P. E. (2000). *The wedge of truth*. Downers Grove, IL: InterVarsity Press.

McMullin, E. (1981). How should cosmology relate to theology? In Arthur R. Peacocke (Ed.), *Science and theology in the twentieth century*. Notre Dame, IN: University of Notre Dame Press.

Moreland, J. P. (1989). *Christianity and the nature of science*. Grand Rapids, MI: Baker Books.

Moreland, J. P. (1997). *Love your God with all your mind*. Colorado Springs: NavPress.

Moreland, J. P., & Rae, S. (2000). *Body and soul*. Downers Grove, IL: InterVarsity Press.

Moreland, J. P., & Reynolds, J. M. (Eds.). (1999). *Three views of creation and evolution*. Grand Rapids, MI: Zondervan.

Willard, D. (1988). *The spirit of the disciplines*. San Francisco: Harper & Row.

Willard, D. (1998). *The divine conspiracy*. San Francisco: Harper & Row.

Willard, D. (1999). *Hearing God*. Downers Grove, IL: InterVarsity Press.

Any Dream Won't Do!
Preparing Defenders of the Faith

Kenneth O. Gangel, Ph.D.

Chapter Summary

In a culture of increasing disregard for absolute truth, and among a generation almost entirely guided by relative values, how do you prepare defenders of the faith? What are the essential components that a Christian school serious about this task must address? What strategies can you implement to nurture a climate in your school that will cultivate such defenders?

Dr. Gangel defines the parameters for an effective apologetic model for your school—a purposeful one that develops in students the crucial attitudes and engages them in the actions that will equip them to become faith defenders. Clever marketing and public relations plans offer poor substitutes for the education delivered by schools that are committed to shaping minds and hearts for the sake of God's kingdom.

About the author

Kenneth O. Gangel, Ph.D.
Distinguished Professor Emeritus, Dallas Seminary
Dallas, TX
41 years of educational leadership experience

Chapter 13

Any Dream Won't Do!
Preparing Defenders of the Faith

Kenneth O. Gangel, Ph.D.

In the brilliant Andrew Lloyd-Webber musical *Joseph and the Amazing Technicolor Dreamcoat,* lyricist Tim Rice gives the title character a frolicking final song with clever words. Reflecting on all that has happened to him, Joseph sings:

> May I return to the beginning;
> The light is dimming, and the dream is too.
> The world and I, we are still waiting,
> Still hesitating
> Any dream will do.

Great romantic poetry; bad theology. Christians are commonly haunted by the strange idea that our Western culture is completely secular. To the contrary, modern society obsesses over the supernatural in one form or another, demons and angels having the most popularity. That preoccupation makes training the next generation a crucial focus of Christian schools. In this chapter, we'll explore some of the components of that task in simple language for practical understanding.

Biblical Foundations

As I prepare these paragraphs, Invesco is running a television commercial featuring NBA superstar Bill Russell explaining how he became professional basketball's greatest rebounder: "I got most of my rebounds before he took the shot," says Russell, describing his opponents. Russell's point (and Invesco's as well) targets effective preparation—knowing how to play the game and understanding one's adversaries.

Scripture

In basketball films, players can look to those rebounds, but in contending for the faith, we must identify the source of authority—and for evangelicals, that means the Bible. In the postmodern scene, all the familiar players—reason, tradition, and revelation—have marched off the stage. The rejection of universal truth and absolute moral principles has broken the ideals that formerly linked people of different backgrounds, leaving tribal loyalties that serve only to divide us. Apologetics, which can capture the hearts and minds of twenty-first–century people, must anchor our students in God's message of eternal and absolute truth. Have another look at the words of David:

> The law of the Lord is perfect, reviving the soul. The statutes of the Lord are trustworthy, making wise the simple. The precepts of the Lord are right, giving joy to the heart. The commands of the Lord are radiant, giving light to the eyes. The fear of the Lord is pure, enduring forever. The ordinances of the Lord are sure and altogether righteous. They are more precious than gold, than much pure gold; they are sweeter than honey, than honey from the comb. By them is your servant warned; in keeping them there is great reward. (Psalm 19:7–11)

In our day, it appears that only new philosophies and new methodologies capture the contemporary mind. C. S. Lewis once called this the "chronological fallacy," the concept that ideas are wrong just because they are old. Evangelicals measure truth by neither age nor the energy level of those eager to expound it. When we talk about training another generation of apologists, we begin with an appeal to divine revelation, the written Word and the incarnate Word. *If there is a God, and if He has spoken in history, the most important aspect in the nurturing process is to discover what He has said and what we must do about it.*

In our schools, any approach to apologetics that does not find firm footing in biblical study can easily fall prey to a frayed rationalism that overvalues the mind of humankind and devalues the Word of God. Colson reminds us: "We must stand firm in our convictions. Many evangelicals seem so bent on being acceptable to the culture that they avoid any practice that might put off the unsaved" (2000).

Theology

According to Anselm of Canterbury, the role of theology is to declare, deepen, explain, and express the truth of God's Word. When we teach students to defend and explain Christian faith, we utilize many aspects of the discipline of social science as tools—psychology, counseling, and sociology to name a few. But these tools help us work only on the theological building we are raising on our biblical base; they must never become the main focus. Veracity and vision lie in the center of our commitment to revealed truth and its formation of theological principles.

And as there is a learning of theology, there is also a theology of learning, an understanding of truth and humanity that enables us to apply biblical answers to crucial questions. Christian teachers affirm that all truth is God's truth, by which we simply mean that all genuine truth can ultimately be traced back to God as its source. And since the God of revelation is also the God of creation, we can see the true relationship between natural and special revelation only through a commitment to absolute truth.

Hermeneutics

In our construction metaphor, if the Bible is the *foundation* and theology is the *house*, hermeneutics may represent the *windows*. To be sure, in our classes we approach apologetics from different hermeneutical stances, and though the end result may differ, one slant can hardly be called "less Christian" than the other. But we cannot allow a sloppy treatment of our interpretation of Scripture to diminish the way we think about apologetics. The centrality of Christ in the Bible offers a bull's-eye for our hermeneutical target. Here are the words of Michael Horton:

> Christ is the key to knowing God. Apart from Him there would be no world, no human speech, no relationship with God. In fact, apart from the Son, there would be no God at all, since the only God who really exists is the Trinity: one in essence, three in person. This is why Scripture describes God by revealing Christ in promise and fulfillment, from Genesis to Revelation. We know God by seeing Him in action, and the whole biblical story is about His action in Christ, foreshadowed in promise and accomplished in fulfillment. (1998)

Philosophy

Surely my metaphor weakens the further I try to push it, but humor me for the moment and think of philosophy as the *roof* on our house. If we take away theology, we have no framing on which to place the roof. If we take away hermeneutics, we can't see in or out, so the house becomes a closet rather than a home. If we take away the Bible, everything collapses in rubble. But a house with no roof is not viable either. Equipping our students carries with it the awesome responsibility of helping them develop a worldview that leads to responsible life choices. *The concept of worldview assumes they can think long-range thoughts rather than being confined by the need for instantaneous responses.*

When we build our theological house on the biblical foundation already emphasized, we activate this kind of thinking by integrating natural and special revelation into human learning and experience. Integrated truth is a major issue in the concept of a worldview, but so is holism, the biblical unity of life. Thinking Christians reject a divided existence that calls some activities sacred and other secular. In *The Contemporary Christian*, John Stott offers good advice:

> The God many of us worship is altogether too religious. We seem to imagine that He is interested only in religious books and buildings and services. But no, He is interested in us, in our home, family, and friends, in our work and hobbies, in our citizenship and community. So God's sovereignty extends over both halves and over all sections of our lives. We must not marginalize God, or try to squeeze Him out of the nonreligious section of our life. We must remember that our vocation (i.e., God's calling) includes these things. It is in these that we are to serve and glorify God. (1992)

When we teach and train students in biblical living and witness, we demonstrate how a theologically informed education requires flesh and spirit at all times and in all places. Learning unrelated to life fares no better than faith without works. Students experience truth formally or informally, and on the basis of their understanding of special revelation, they ascertain with God's help how truth fits into life.

Basic Essentials

Other chapters in this book treat cultural and philosophical issues with greater detail. Nevertheless, here I want to deal with four pillars on which our theological house must rest. In my view, they represent the *sine qua non* of a faith system that will enable faculty and students of all ages to understand and defend truth in these modern times.

Creation

What we defend is not "creationism" but the clear biblical account of how all life came into existence. Evangelicals disagree on some of the hermeneutical details of the early chapters of Genesis, but no evangelical should ever fail to distinguish between the biblical account and Darwinism.

Rarely do I recommend an article in *National Geographic*, especially an issue with a picture of a pig on the cover! But the October 1999 issue featured a stunning study entitled "Unveiling the Universe," a description of some of the world's great telescopes and their findings. Such pursuits, of course, lead to the question of origins and order in the universe, a subject on which *National Geographic* stands firmly in the evolutionist camp. But consider this sample from the article:

> How did the universe go from simple and smooth to lumpy and complex? Why is it so perfectly balanced gravitationally that it neither flew apart nor crunched back together before the first star of the galaxy could form? (This degree of balance has been likened to that of a pencil standing upright on its point. Any tipping at all and it would immediately fall all the way over in one direction or another.) And why does the universe look so much the same over vast distances? (1999)

Why indeed! With such evidence before them, however, the authors and editors of *National Geographic* never think to turn to the God of the Bible. They have long since ruled out faith as an option for thinking people. Yet our students must know that thinking people have historically often been people of faith. The Apostles' Creed was put together by people of faith and learning, a public confession of truth collected from several centuries of the early church. It earns its name because it is what the formulators thought the Apostles believed, and it begins with the words, "I believe in God the Father Almighty, Maker of heaven and earth."

Before the Civil War, academic understanding of truth and reality grounded people in a powerful faith in the divine order sustained by an all-powerful God. In 1859 Darwin's *The Origin of Species* began the process of disunity in learning. As Zachary Karabell puts it: "Once the Prime Mover became secondary, disciplinary specialization flourished.... Without theology to anchor society, leaders of higher education put forth the claim that the study of science and the humanities would lead America and mankind in the right direction" (2000).

We don't know who wrote Hebrews, but the author had a strong sense of the role of creation in Christian theology and emphasized right at the beginning that Jesus the Son was involved in creation: "In the past God spoke to our forefathers through the prophets at many times and in various ways, but in these last days he has spoken to us by his Son, whom he appointed heir of all things, and through whom he made the universe" (Hebrews 1:1, 2).

A biblical focus on creation shows us that God is the very source of life itself, the one who bothers to make Bermuda butterflies and yet sent His son to die on the cross for our sins. This message of a personal, loving, caring, sacrificial Creator and Sustainer rests at the heart of the gospel, yet is ignored or confused by so many.

The Person and Work of Christ

Jesus is the human name for God, as common among the Jews as Scott or Michael or Todd might be today in North America. "Christ" transliterates the Greek word "Christos," the counterpart to the Hebrew word "Messiah." In other words, Jesus is the Messiah. The whole Old Testament prefigured the coming of the Son of God, and annually the entire world still celebrates this event. Every Christmas, millions in scores of languages sing the theology of Charles Wesley:

> Christ by highest heaven adored!
> Christ the everlasting Lord!
> Late in time, behold Him come—offspring of the Virgin's womb.
> Veiled in flesh, the Godhead see; Hail the incarnate deity,
> Pleased as man with men to dwell, Jesus our Emmanuel.

It seems a gigantic leap from the early chapters of Genesis to the early chapters of Matthew, but Christian school students must see how the story of redemption connects at all points throughout the Bible. No person at any age can make much progress in learning apologetics without a clear grasp of the person and work of Jesus Christ.

While the miracles and parables of Jesus recorded in the Synoptic Gospels are intensely valuable in helping us understand Him, the Gospel of John aims directly at the message of Eternal Light for the world, and it moves quickly from His birth to His death. Ten of the book's twenty-one chapters describe the last week of the Lord's life. The clear message of sub-stitutionary atonement (Jesus died for me) focuses the heart of the gospel and identifies the exclusive route to heaven.

Proofs for the existence of God and arguments for the possibility of mira-cles are important. But in a day when religion tends to be about human experience and when people talk and sing about what they feel as they think about God and then think about themselves, we must return growing Christians to their homes and churches with the facts of history and the meaning of those facts. Once again Wesley helps us say what we mean by substitutionary atonement:

> And can it be that I should gain an interest in the Savior's blood?
> Died He for me, who caused His pain? For me, who Him to death pursued?
> Amazing love! How can it be that thou, my God shouldst die for me?

Clearly an essential part of our understanding of Christ's person and work centers in the Resurrection, in many ways the centerpiece of the gospel. The fact of the Resurrection is important; Christians do not believe (as Rudolph Bultmann argued from the belly of liberal German theology) that the Resurrection means Jesus has risen in our hearts. Proof of the Resurrection is not the issue, though there is a significant body of evidence to support it as all effective Christian schools teach. But people are not saved by facts or by proof, but rather by faith. Through the Resurrection, believers receive justification, which is acceptance by God because of Jesus' finished work (1 Corinthians 15:1–4).

The Nature of Truth

Many areas of philosophy are important in learning apologetics, but none more so than epistemology. I treat this subject ever so lightly here, but educators should not find in this brief paragraph any diminishing of the crucial role this third basic essential plays in the way we teach faith's proclamation and defense. So much of what passes for theology today takes its cue from sociological pragmatism, ignoring or perverting authoritative biblical sources. In many schools (and even churches), learning falls into a superficial pragmatism in which crucial questions about the nature of God, the nature of humanity, and the relationship between them are handled with shallowness or neutrality. *Christian schools wanting to prepare defenders of the faith will anchor absolute truth in Scripture.*

Christian schools make an assumption here, but no more so than any other system of thought. Once we place the source of truth in Scripture, the comparison of all learning must surrender to that focus. It is true that biblical faith is properly experimental and inescapably subjective, but it anchors in logic and history. In my view, it is the one interpretation of reality that can be rationally validated, a body of belief that requires the disciplined use and the full employment of our minds.

As we prepare another generation of apologists, we train them for honest interaction with persons of different ideologies. We help students understand that genuine tolerance acknowledges legitimate claims to truth without insisting on acceptance of antisocial and even bizarre behavior. A genuinely biblical worldview invites interaction that, in itself, attests freedom and calls all humankind to pursue the quest for truth.

A holistic worldview does not just happen; effective communicators deliberately design it through a theological philosophy that brings culture and truth into close union without fearing that culture will destroy truth. Intellectual and spiritual development appears to require at least three steps: *knowing the Scriptures intimately, studying the culture diligently, and analyzing events and issues theologically.*

The Bible

Sadly, biblical ignorance is almost a hallmark of our society despite the proliferation of Bibles. And the attitude, though perhaps worse in this century than the last, is hardly a phenomenon of recent decades. Fifty years ago, President Eisenhower offered an astonishing statement: "Our government makes no sense unless it is founded on a deeply felt religious faith—and I don't care what it is." That is hardly the message of the New Testament, nor of Christian schools. The Bible never suggests that *any* religious faith is better than no religious faith—any dream won't do! Historically, orthodox Christian faith has been built only on a strong commitment to Scripture, and the learning, nurturing patterns of any evangelical school must rest exclusively on biblically defensible truth.

Modern Christians seem to have a difficult time resisting a dependence upon government for spiritual momentum. We get excited about Washington prayer breakfasts and amendments to put prayer back into public schools. But historically the people of God have never forced their faith through legislation and have never found support in human government. The early Christians would have thought it ludicrous to look to Rome or even to the Jerusalem hierarchy for affirmation. Our own children and our students must learn (I intentionally repeat myself) that they do not determine the truth of the Bible by their experience. *Learning to relate truth to life becomes a process of allowing Scripture and biblical principles to shape our attitudes and behavior.*

Evangelical Christians believe that the Bible, in its original manuscripts, was completely without error. Insofar as modern translations capture the text of the original documents, they are reliable. When we use words like "inspiration," "inerrancy," and "infallibility," we are not talking about the King James Version or the NIV but rather the original texts. The proper development of our students requires that they know not only what the Bible says but also why Christians consider it authoritative.

Distinctive Objectives

In effective learning experiences, technique is never the central issue. That slot is reserved for a clear understanding of objectives and a definitive strategy by which to achieve them. Any school intent on preparing people who understand and explain the faith must know precisely what learning outcomes they wish to produce. Most churches focus on content; some on rote memorization. Many modern congregations, as I have noted previously, make much of the role of human experience in worship and learning. None of those approaches is wrong, and all must be combined in some way, but Christian schools can articulate the task with greater precision. We want developing defenders of the faith to:

See the Big Biblical Story

Christian schools preparing students in a spiritual and theological climate must constantly swim upstream against a heavy prevailing tide of naturalistic humanism. Education finds itself increasingly influenced by the federal government and boxed in by powerful lobbies such as the National

Education Association, both of which advance a misguided globalism that reconstructs national histories. If we add innumerable pornographic sites on the Internet, video games that effectively train children for violence, destructive television programming that defies theistic values, then we find ourselves and our students numbed against spiritual sensitivity.

Evangelical educators understand that they cannot create self-esteem by dumbing down educational standards and they cannot develop an awareness of cultural diversity by regarding all lifestyles as equally valid, even those that violate biblical principles. Consider the words of Thomas Oden:

> Each succeeding generation must come to grips with the original apostolic witness. Easy substitutes and glossy reinterpretations will not do. When one generation of Christian discipline fails, it is much more difficult for the next generation. But the church must understand itself to be an intergenerational process, because it exists in time. There is no nonhistorical shortcut to fulfilling the church's mission, no easy all-at-once way to accomplish the task of the church on behalf of every generation. (1992)

Increasingly, both in apologetics and evangelism we have seen a new focus on the full message of the Bible rather than proof texts or sound bites. Have a look at what folks in the missiological arena are saying about this focus:

> I will argue ... that it is Scripture, and not its "message," that is finally transcultural.... Although it will be surely related in some way to Christ and his work, what is transcultural is not some core truth, but Scripture—the full biblical context of Christ's work. It is this that must be allowed to strike its own spark in the light of the needs of particular cultures. (Dyrness, 1990)
>
> To change a people group's worldview so that Christ becomes central requires the hearing and/or seeing of stories from Scripture. Unlike some myths and stories, Bible stories find themselves rooted in history and the Supernatural.... It is these powerful stories ... that the Holy Spirit uses to transform the worldview of people and communities. (Steffen, 1996)
>
> The Bible as a whole document tells a story, and, properly used, that story can serve as a meta-narrative that shapes our grasp of the entire Christian faith. In my view it is increasingly important to spell this out to Christians and to non-Christians alike—to Christians, to ground them in Scripture, and to non-Christians, as part of our proclamation of the Gospel. The ignorance of basic Scripture is so disturbing in our day that Christian preaching that does not seek to remedy the lack is simply irresponsible. (Carson, 1996)

Identify the Cultural Issues

In our country, children now spend or influence the spending of 500 billion dollars a year. Even marketers accustomed to the crass economic behavior of a materialistic society are startled by the impact six- to twelve-year-olds have on how their parents spend money. Yet both parents and children must be in our sights when we talk about training the next generation. We live in a society enchanted by money, entertainment, athletics, and gambling; and in that alien environment, Christian schools make the case for a biblical approach to cultural issues. What issues must we address? Once we have built that biblical, theological, hermeneutical, and philosophical house, in what kind of neighborhood will we be living?

A recent article in *Christianity Today* by Daniel Taylor is a classic, an absolute "must read" for Christian school leaders. He argues that what we used to call "situation ethics" has now been codified as a social law of tolerance. Taylor quotes a line from his son's sociology text on the subject of homosexual practice: "Everything is right somewhere and nothing is right everywhere." Then he observes:

> Thus relativism absolutizes pluralism. That is, it takes the clearly observable fact that we have a multitude of views and values and practices in the world—pluralism—and draws the illegitimate conclusion that there is no justifiable way of choosing among them. Truth is merely opinion, goodness only what the majority says it is. (1999)

With our commitment to the authority of Scripture and our insistence on the exclusivity of the gospel, evangelical schools have become sitting ducks in a society determined to despise intolerance. A marginal fraction of people claiming the name of Christ engage in abortion clinic bombings, mass cultic suicides, and fanciful prophecies of the return of Jesus, and these actions reflect on Christians everywhere. Let's understand the neighborhood—the moral majority is history, and the highly hyped seventy million evangelicals in America is a myth that never had any substance. On this block we are a minority, and people must know exactly who lives in the house and why we built it the way we did. Throughout the current decade and probably for several to come, our schools will face constant battles over issues like homosexuality, racial hostility, social violence, and consistent, perhaps irreversible family breakdown.

Make no mistake about it, there has been a cultural revolution—and we have lost. People well within the evangelical camp listen to music, watch television programs, and go to movies that would have horrified their godly grandparents. In this century, students come to schools and churches out of a culture far more tolerant of evil. Elementary school children watch chaos and violence on television for hours, walking around with intellectual hard drives filled with ideas that should alert those called to lead them. And most of the cultural issues we face stem from family breakdown. Here's a paragraph from Kirby Anderson's book *Moral Dilemmas*:

> Just a few decades ago most children in America (80 percent) grew up in intact, two-parent families. Today children who do so are a minority. Illegitimacy, divorce, and other lifestyle choices have radically altered the American family, and thus have altered the social landscape ... broken homes and broken hearts account for the incumbent difficulties America faces as a culture. The moral foundation of society erodes as children learn the savage values of the street rather than the civilized values of culture. And government inevitably expands to intervene in family and social crisis brought about by the breakdown of the family. (1998)

Let's not kid ourselves into thinking that government attacks (and victories) on tobacco companies and gun makers represent a step forward for American morality. Those crusades are motivated in their entirety by economics and politics. When a first-grader shoots another first-grader or when young teens poison their bodies by puffing outside a mall, the problem lies not in the manufacturers of evil products but in miserable parenting.

Integrate Truth and Life

I keep returning to this theme because I believe it to be the heart and core of our mission. In our schools, rearranging the furniture and changing the logos will solve none of the problems we talked about in this chapter. Indeed, the dangerous temptation facing Christian educators in the twenty-first century is the radical restructuring of programs and services to accommodate the external sociological preferences of "Boomers," "Xers," and "Millenngeners" rather than fighting our way back to solid biblicism (Colossians 2:8). Christian schools should be centers of serious thinking. Our constituents must know that their children attend schools where minds are used to the greatest possible extent for the glory of Christ (2 Corinthians 10:5).

Creativity, individuality, and experimentation are all useful in the process, but in the final analysis, any dream won't do. *Integration of faith and life comes about when Spirit-filled people understand the cultural issues around them and decide how to respond on the basis of their knowledge of Scripture and devotion to Christian principles.* That's what we teach in this nurturing "safe house" we have so carefully built. James Brian Smith puts it this way:

> Adolescents both want and need mirrors.... But the mirrors must be good. They need the eyes and ears of trusted people who can help them develop a proper identity. Like the carnival mirrors that are

bent out of shape, thus reflecting a distorted image, the surrounding world projects a distorted image to adolescents. The church has the ability *to restore a true and accurate self-image*. Distortion can hold many in bondage; the truth can set them free. (1994)

Effective Strategies

Repeatedly throughout these paragraphs, I have argued that technique is considerably less important than the creation of a climate of learning and a clarification of issues and objectives. Consequently, I give lesser space to what many might think should receive greater exposure in this chapter. Experienced practitioners in Christian education have been moving steadily away from a focus on learning *strategies* and toward an insistence on learning *outcomes*. To be sure, strategies either hinder or enhance outcomes, but such discussion can also degenerate into methodological autism. So I close this chapter with a brief mention of several approaches that I believe can produce the results I have described, that can help us build and maintain that apologetic house and live effectively in this postmodern neighborhood.

Irenic Attitude

The landscape of evangelical apologetics has been often marred by polemicism. In defining "polemic" as a noun, Webster calls it "an aggressive attack on or refutation of the opinions or principles of another." Yet that definition is hardly the way one would describe the ministry of New Testament spokesmen for the gospel. Perhaps Paul's most effective apologetic engagement (not measured in terms of results but rather cultural adroitness) occurred in Athens where irenicism marked the entire debate (Acts 17). Teaching our students to beat down their opponents with clever arguments may well help them win the point, but it rarely results in their attracting observers to the meek and humble Lord we profess to serve. Perhaps the most important thing we teach in our schools is an attitude toward truth, toward God, and toward others.

Interrogative Atmosphere

The process of apologetics has often been pictured as an aggressive foray into the domain of godlessness and heresy, rather like an intellectual crusade. Yet we need to consider what is certainly a key verse for Christian apologetics, 1 Peter 3:15: "But in your hearts set apart Christ as Lord. Always be prepared to give an answer to everyone who asks you to give the reason for the hope that you have. But do this with gentleness and respect." This verse implies that God sets up opportunities for Christians to speak the truth, and our students must learn "to give an answer to everyone who asks" and to "do this with gentleness and respect." Indeed, this Scripture describes an attitude, and one we have already discussed; but it also suggests a learning strategy. We teach students to understand questions, respond to questions, and even create questions that steer conversation to an open analysis of truth. Some teachers try to teach this skill through constant bombardment of powerful lecture notes. Instead, it seems that an atmosphere of open discussion much better prepares people to do what this chapter describes.

Involved Students

We've already seen that the nurturing of faith defenders should be *irenic rather than polemic* and *relational rather than confrontational*. Perhaps we should add *involved rather than distant*. To be sure, a teacher effectively creating an interrogative atmosphere will help develop involved students. But we achieve neither of those worthy goals by careless preparation. When the house is built, we invite students in to be a part of what's happening in the neighborhood.

As always, the key to strategy is leadership. Too many modern pastors, presidents, and principals have bought into an autocratic model of leadership that is old covenant in theology, political in style, and condemned in even the current secular literature. The fact that the autocratic model sometimes works cannot overcome the reality of its incontrovertible opposition to the New Testament.

Serious Christian educators must soon recognize that the marketing model with all its spit and polish cannot propel our schools through the marshes of moral miasma in which our spiritual boats ride. We have a historic legacy to defend a legacy that defines who we are and what we do. Christian thinkers best understand their modern role when they see themselves as pockets of resistance in a self-destructive civilization. We operate from an internal sustaining force that draws its wisdom and power from the presence of the Holy Spirit in conjunction with the authority of the Word of God. Such a posture is at the same time liberating and restrictive, carrying with it the exclusivity of the gospel. Clearly, any dream won't do.

Bibliography

Anderson, J. K. (1998). *Moral dilemmas*. Nashville: Word.

Boa, K., & Moody, L. (1994). *I'm glad you asked*. Wheaton, IL: Victor Books.

Boyd, G. A., & Boyd, E. K. (1994). *Letters from a skeptic*. Wheaton, IL: Victor Books.

Carson, D. A. (1996). *The gagging of God*. Grand Rapids, MI: Zondervan.

Colson, C. W. (2000, March). The ugly side of tolerance. *Christianity Today*.

Dyrness, W. A. (1990). *Learning about theology from the Third World*. Grand Rapids, MI: Zondervan.

Geisler, N., & Brooks, R. (1990). *When skeptics ask*. Wheaton, IL: Victor Books.

Geisler, N., & Howe, T. (1992). *When critics ask*. Wheaton, IL: Victor Books.

Horton, M. (1998). *We believe*. Nashville: Word.

Karabell, Z. (2000, April). Same as it never was. *University Business*.

Lewis, G. R. (1976). *Testing Christianity's truth claims*. Chicago: Moody Press.

Oden, T. C. (1992). I'm not whoring after the spirit of the age. In O. Guinness & J. Seel (Eds.), *No God but God*. Chicago: Moody Press.

Rice, Tim. (1982). Any dream will do. [Recorded by B. Hutton]. On *Joseph and the amazing technicolor dreamcoat* [CD]. New York: Chrysalis Records.

Sawyer, K. (1999, October). Unveiling the universe. *National Geographic*.

Schaeffer, F. A. (1976). *How should we then live?* Old Tappan, NJ: Fleming H. Revel.

Smith, J. B. (1994). Spiritual formation of adolescents. In K. Gangel & J. C. Wilhoit (Eds.), *The Christian educator's handbook on spiritual formation*. Grand Rapids, MI: Baker.

Steffen, T. A. (1996). *Reconnecting God's story to ministry*. LaHabra, CA: Center for Organizational and Ministry Development.

Stott, J. R. W. (1992). *The contemporary Christian*. Downers Grove, IL: InterVarsity Press.

Taylor, D. (1999, January 11). Are you tolerant? *Christianity Today*.

Raising the Bar
Assessing School Excellence

D. Bruce Lockerbie, D.H.L.

Chapter Summary

Is your school one that strives for excellence? And in that pursuit, how will you know whether or not you are making progress? Do your benchmarks include public relations talking points such as achievement tests scores, win-loss records in athletics, or certain postsecondary destinations of graduates? And who determines the standards you measure your school against?

Dr. Lockerbie raises the bar for all Christian schools and challenges them to a lifelong commitment to excellence through internal and external assessments. Your school can rightfully claim that it is striving for excellence only after a thorough and painfully honest evaluation of every part of its program in light of its mission, goals, and philosophy of education.

About the author

D. Bruce Lockerbie, D.H.L.
Chairman, Paideia, Incorporated
Stony Brook, NY
45 years of educational leadership experience

Chapter 14

Raising the Bar
Assessing School Excellence

D. Bruce Lockerbie, D.H.L.

In ancient Greece, every visitor to the shrine of the pagan god Apollo at Delphi was met by the command, "Know thyself." Part of the act of attaining that self-knowledge came through the discipline of physical exercise in the gymnasium and competition in the stadium close by the temple. Whether wrestling against an opponent, attempting to throw the discus farther than an opponent, or sprinting toward the finish line faster than an opponent, the ideal devotee of Apollo was committed to demonstrating the extent of his inner awareness by striving to make the most of his physical abilities.

The Greeks regarded physical prowess and the advance toward physical perfection as attributes akin to spiritual development; their goal was *excellence*. For the Greeks, physical excellence represented a correlative spiritual excellence, and as a token of this achievement, they gave a laurel wreath from a tree sacred to Apollo. A first-century observer of popular culture, Paul of Tarsus, wrote to Christian believers in Corinth:

> Do you not know that in a race all the runners run, but only one gets the prize? Run in such a way as to get the prize. Everyone who competes in the games goes into strict training. They do it to get a crown that will not last; but we do it to get a crown that will last forever. (1 Corinthians 9:24, 25)

The Virtue of the Examined Life

Ever practical, the apostle Paul addressed his readers in the most direct terms, saying in effect, "What's the point of entering the race if you don't intend to win or at least do your best?" He reminded the Corinthians that the arduous regimen of an athlete can never be for its own sake but to win the prize. In other words, if *arete*, meaning "excellence," is not your goal, why bother?—especially when the eternal prize exceeds the temporal laurel wreath.

Besides attaining excellence in physical fitness and athletics, the Greeks thought they could elevate themselves spiritually through introspection and self-appraisal. In fact, Plato quotes Socrates in saying that "the unexamined life is not worth living." Educators more than two millennia later would agree—although few would place so great an emphasis on the athletic analogy. In our age of shoulder-shrugging dismissal, when the catchall sneer "whatever" expresses disdain for any serious analysis, many lives are unexamined—and so perhaps "not worth living."

Applying These Principles to Christian Schools

This attitude of apathy pervades many institutions, including some Christian schools. This chapter will paraphrase the philosophers by claiming that *the unexamined school is not worth leading or attending*. While this aphorism might seem obvious to the point of insult, some educators or their board members, especially parent/board members, still resist testing their school's true measure, preferring their own subjective and self-congratulatory estimations of their school's worth. Or they resort to the marketplace argument, assuming that full enrollment and even a waiting list for admissions must signify sufficient excellence, thereby obviating any need for objective and possibly unfavorable opinion contrary to their own.

In time, students may come to realize the need for regular evaluations to determine their progress in learning; we call those instruments of torture *quizzes, tests,* or *examinations.* So too, every school must face this reality. Christian school leaders, including board members, must learn to recognize the importance of internal evaluation and external assessment, and the value of comparison between realized achievement and objective standards—both within their own schools and beyond. To achieve excellence, schools must acquire a greater level of sophistication and tougher hides. Some Christian schools have found inspiration and encouragement toward a higher standard by adopting for themselves a document drafted in 1993 called "A Covenant for Excellence" (Lockerbie, 1994).

What Is Excellence?

As instructed by the apostle Paul, professing Christians are to look for and contemplate "whatever is true, ... noble, ... right, ... pure, ... lovely, ...

admirable, ... [and] excellent or praiseworthy" (Philippians 4:8). Does it not follow, then, that we must be able to differentiate what is *true* from what is *false*, or what is *right* from what is patently *wrong*, or what is *admirable* from what is *disgraceful*? Must we not be able to distinguish what elements make "anything ... *excellent*" rather than *mediocre* or *inferior*? And how can we overcome the tendency to measure excellence only through the limitations of our own experience?

Much has been written about excellence and its qualities of truth, beauty, goodness, durability, universality, and power to inspire. Perhaps, however, not enough has been said about the ephemeral nature of excellence and the fact that today's achievement, however laudable it appears at the moment, merely sets a new standard against which to measure tomorrow's attainment. Thus the definition of excellence must always be fluid, adaptable to higher expectations.

For instance, the common custom in many families is to post a child's preschool or kindergarten scrawlings on the refrigerator door. For a time, the child-artist is proud to have her work on display. But as she grows older and more skilled, she may also grow more critical of her own work. So she asks her mother and father to be less lavish in their praise of her projects as if all of them were equally excellent.

In the jargon of corporate America's fascination with excellence, a healthy dissatisfaction with the ordinary or even the extraordinary is known as "raising the bar." It comes from another sports analogy. A half-century ago, the Olympic champion in the pole vault was Reverend Bob Richards, who won the gold medal in both 1952 and 1956. No one would question that Richards was *excellent* in his day and with the equipment available to him. But although he was the only Olympic champion to repeat in his event, his winning heights were more than five feet lower than today's best male vaulters and lower than even today's best female vaulters. The bar has indeed been raised to a new level of excellence.

Absolute and Relative

In such apparent flux of standards, how can we get a grasp on the meaning of "excellence"? One of the clearest explanations of the word has been expressed by Harold M. Best—a proper name to associate with such a declaration!—former dean of the Conservatory of Music at Wheaton College in Illinois. He intended his original text for other musicians and artists, but he has permitted its use and application to schools and their leaders:

> What is excellence, anyway? ... It is both absolute and relative; absolute, because it is the norm of stewardship and cannot be avoided or compromised; relative, because it is set in the context of striving, wrestling, hungering, thirsting, pressing on from point to point and achievement to achievement. (Lockerbie, 2000)

Here we have a biblically sensitive description of "excellence," which includes descriptions of how it both stays the same and changes. Excellence is absolute because God's mandates are absolute. Because God is holy, He summons us to holiness; because God is just, He demands that we act justly. In the same manner, God expects excellence of those He has entrusted with the *oikonomia*, or "stewardship" of His kingdom. God will settle for nothing less than our best effort in service to Him. In its unremitting sense, therefore, excellence "cannot be avoided or compromised."

Excellence as a Measurement of Grace

Harold Best does not say so, but his words imply that excellence as an absolute cannot be achieved. None of us can rise to God's holiness or justice or excellence. But then Best accounts for God's grace, reminding us that excellence is also relative because of our human condition.

We are not automatons or machines, frozen in some perpetual state of maximal output of energy; we are mere mortals, subject to our redeemed yet sinful nature, constantly "pressing on from point to point and achievement to achievement." We have our ups and downs, our good days and bad days. But we can never afford a *smug* day, a day on which we declare ourselves to have arrived at excellence. As Best writes:

> Moreover, we are unequally gifted and cannot equally achieve. Consequently, some artists [for example, schools and their leadership] are better than others. But all artists [for example, schools and their leadership] can be better than they once were. This is excelling. (Lockerbie, 2000)

Excellence as a Measurement of Growth

Harold Best teaches us that "striving, wrestling, hungering, thirsting" after excellence helps us mature, a process the New Testament emphasizes: growth from birth to maturity. Only the anomaly of stunted growth causes an adult to retain the form of a child. God expects us to grow toward maturity and, as we do, toward excellence. Thus the Christian school administrator, board member, classroom teacher, choral director, or soccer coach who wants to honor God must be willing to (1) humble himself or herself and become like a little child, (2) learn what gifts and talents God has entrusted for stewardship, (3) refine and use those gifts and talents to God's glory, and (4) never be ashamed to admit that there is more to learn and more to achieve.

Excellence as a Measurement of Humility

Even the apostle Paul confessed to his Philippian readers that his growth was incomplete:

Not that I have already obtained all this, or have already been made perfect, but I press on to take hold of that for which Christ Jesus took hold of me. Brothers, I do not consider myself yet to have taken hold of it. But one thing I do: Forgetting what is behind and straining toward what is ahead, I press on toward the goal to win the prize for which God has called me heavenward in Christ Jesus. (Philippians 3:12–14)

So too must Christian school leaders acknowledge what remains to be accomplished. Yet at the same time, they must *press on* toward the excellence found in Jesus Christ and *press on* toward God's ultimate prize, His words, "Well done, good and faithful servant" (Matthew 25:21).

Internal Evaluation: Mission, Goal, Philosophy

Knowing the Mission

A school of integrity will examine and assess its claims against its actual performance. Only by subjecting a school's programs and professional personnel to the rigors of internal evaluation and external assessment can its leaders know how far the school has progressed toward achieving its *mission*, its reason for being, and its purpose as an academic institution of its particular grade levels. In other words, the school must know why it exists and whom it seeks to serve. Finally, the school must know what it wants to accomplish in its students.

Mission as Cornerstone

A previous chapter on achieving accreditation resounds with the warning that every accrediting agency, including the Association of Christian Schools International, bases its recommendation to accredit a candidate school on one foundation stone: *To what degree does this school fulfill its stated mission?* The school's mission is the yardstick for measuring its performance. Thus, whether facing internal evaluation or external assessment, a school's first step toward confirming its excellence must be the board's drafting or revising the school's mission statement. Nothing else can be accomplished, and no reasonable judgment, criticism, or commendation can be issued until a mission statement has been written, approved, disseminated throughout the school, and declared the official standard by which board decisions and administrative action are be weighed.

As has been argued in such books as *From Candy Sales to Committed Donors: A Guide to Financing Christian Schools*, a school's mission statement is essential to its asking for and receiving financial support in the form of voluntary gifts for an annual campaign, a capital campaign, or an endowment fund. But the mission statement also serves as a beacon for board and administrative decision making, strategic planning, curriculum formation, design of new facilities, or avoidance of distracting proposals. A school's mission statement forms the very essence of its existence and provides the framework for any internal evaluation.

Identifying the Goal

"A rose is a rose is a rose," Gertrude Stein is alleged to have told her Paris salon. Similarly, a Christian *school* is a *school* is a *school*. In some instances, the main purpose of a Christian school becomes confused in the minds of some leaders (whether board members or administrators) with that of a year-long youth retreat, a haven for at-risk teenagers, or an adolescent seminary.

Of course, we rejoice when a Christian school serves as the *locus* in which a child comes to faith in Jesus Christ or a teenager commits her life to the Lordship of Jesus Christ. Beyond the emphasis on character education, well explained by Kevin Ryan as "the three Vs" of *views, values,* or *virtues* (1999) or by William J. Bennett as "moral education" (1993), Christian schools have as their ultimate goal creating an environment in which students may become faithful disciples of Jesus Christ, developing the Christian character traits defined as "the fruit of the Spirit" (Galatians 5:22). But such a transforming experience ought to be the result of fulfilling the primary purpose through the influence of strong and respected academic teachers, talented artists and musicians, and competent and inspiring coaches and mentors—not because schools concentrate on their altar calls.

What Makes a School "Christian"?

We need to measure Christian schools in light of what they should be: places where people—dedicated to their Christian vocation and qualified to instruct—influence students. In such environments, the rigorous study of the Bible provides insight into divine wisdom, disclosing what Frank E. Gaebelein called "the unity of all truth under God" (1996). In such schools, as they are taught from a biblical world and life view, students are blessed by the discernment of the Holy Spirit that is apparent in the lives of those who teach and learn.

These schools may or may not be academic institutions where the majority of graduates prepare to enroll in selective colleges and universities. Instead, they may be content to turn out literate young adults fully equipped to enter the workforce, the military, or the home. But whatever their highest grade level or their graduates' aspirations, Christian schools must meet their obligation of providing an academic education graced by a knowledge of God's Word and of Jesus Christ as Lord.

Specifying the Philosophy

Christian schools that know their *mission* and identify as their *goal* the offering of a strong academic education through the lens of a biblical worldview, must also specify *how* they presume to fulfill their mission and meet their goal. They answer this *how* of education by adopting a distinctive philosophy of education.

Learning from the Reformed Theological Tradition

Among Christian schools, those with the most evident philosophy, both in principle and in practice, belong to the Reformed theological heritage of John Calvin, John Knox, and the later Dutch theologians Abraham Kuyper, Cornelius Van Til, and the founders of the National Union of Christian Schools, now called Christian Schools International. N. H. Beversluis provides this synopsis in a posthumous volume compiled by his widow:

> Already in 1848 a church council (in Holland, Michigan) had urged the establishment of Christian schools to be "the cradle for the church." But Christian schooling did not flourish until after 1880 when a new kind of immigrant from The Netherlands promoted the notion of rearing the young in separate schools.... This profound change represented the views of the great Dutch scholar and statesman Abraham Kuyper. The cultural-philosophical movement he led declared that each major domain of human activity should be accountable directly to God; that the school, like every other "sphere," should be sovereign in its own right, existing in a reciprocal relation with other spheres but subordinate only to Christ. (2001)

As for the distinctives of Reformed theology and its concomitant philosophy, Beversluis writes:

> This Reformed tradition has valued a way of thinking and a way of living; a way of interpreting history and a way of reading the Bible; and a way of accepting the Christian's vocation in the world under the real and present lordship of Jesus Christ. By *Reformed* is meant a way of understanding and obeying God's three great commands, which were given at the beginning in the garden and reaffirmed through Christ's restoration of "all things." These are the commands to love God above all, in personal piety; to love one another in human community; and, under the impulse and power of those loves, to do the world's work in cultural affirmation and transformation. (2001)

So schools in the Reformed tradition honor "the cultural mandate" and "sphere sovereignty" in ways as mundane as their students' dress codes. Strictly Reformed schools will rarely impose a dress code on their students, believing that parents—not schools—should decide how their children dress.

The Canons of Dordt

Such schools have a heritage that dates from the 1619 *Canons of Dordt* (Lockerbie, 1994), which urged:

> In order that the Christian youth may be diligently instructed in the principles of religion, and be trained in piety, three modes of catechizing should be employed.
>
> I. In the House, by Parents.
>
> II. In the Schools, by Schoolmasters.
>
> III. In the Churches, by Ministers, Elders, and Catechists, especially appointed for the purpose.

Then the canons stipulated the responsibilities of each adult authority. Parents, given primary responsibility, are accountable to the Church's leadership to "impress and illustrate the truths contained in [the Scriptures] in a familiar manner, adapted to the tenderness of youth" (Lockerbie, 1994). Otherwise, "Parents who profess religion, and are negligent in this work, shall be faithfully admonished by the ministers; and, if the case requires it, they shall be censured by the Consistory [the Church's governing body], that they may be brought to the discharge of their duty" (Lockerbie, 1994). Can we imagine such disciplinary action by today's typical pastor and board of elders?

By What Method?

But *how* were children to be instructed—by what philosophy of education? According to the *Canons of Dordt*, the philosophy of Reformed theology called for a reliance on didactic instruction, memorization, and application: "The schoolmasters shall take care not only that the scholars commit these Catechisms to memory, but that they shall suitably understand the doctrines contained in them" (Lockerbie, 1994). Memory work, long since disdained by modern educationists, held the most significant place in Reformed schooling. Not only did the *Canons of Dordt* dictate that children memorize the Catechism (available in short form for the youngest children), but the children also had to be able "to give an account of the sermons they hear[d]" and "commit to memory" selected passages of Scripture. Much more can be said about a Reformed philosophy of Christian schooling; documented information is available from Christian Schools International in Grand Rapids, Michigan.

What About Evangelical Christian Schools?

We note that many evangelical Christian schools—unlike Reformed schools—barely consider *philosophy*. We hear about mission statements, vision statements, and strategic plans, but what about *philosophies of edu-*

cation? Instead of an institutional philosophy to guide curriculum delivery, too many evangelical schools allow their administrator's personal philosophy alone to determine *how* they educate their students. For example, lacking a coherent philosophy of education, a board hires a new head-of-school whose philosophy is classical. The ancient trivium becomes the basis for instruction, and every teacher takes a crash course in Latin. But two years later, a new administrator is appointed; she is student centered, insisting that every teacher adopt the Socratic method of teaching. But all too soon, another new head-of-school arrives and installs yet another philosophy ... and so it goes, while the faculty members reel from having to adjust to a different philosophy with every new leader.

To evaluate themselves, schools must have an institutional philosophy against which to measure their performance. Such a philosophy needs to be developed by the board, probably with the assistance of an experienced educator who knows the full range of Christian school philosophies. Thereafter, the board can hire administrators who already assert that philosophy and agree on the way to implement it.

Internal Evaluation by Self-Study

The cardinal principle of internal evaluation is self-study. The accreditation process demands a rigorous self-study for the visiting committee to use in their review. But schools striving for excellence will not wait for the accreditation calendar to impose demands; they will make time annually to examine their policies, personnel, and programs in the following ways:

1. The board will assign the task of considering the contents of its policy handbook to a standing committee. Some policies will no longer apply and can be deleted; some will be outdated and in need of revision, and some will be inadequate or altogether missing. This committee will make its recommendations to the full board.

2. Another standing committee of the board will address financial and benefit issues related to personnel. But the board will not evaluate the administrative, academic, or coaching performance of any employee other than the head-of-school. He or she is the board's sole employee and subject to a periodic performance review conducted by the executive committee of the board. If the board is in the habit of hiring and firing teachers or judging the quality of their work, that board has moved from governance-by-policy to governance-by-interference-and-intimidation.

3. The head-of-school and any designated subordinate, such as an academic dean, curriculum supervisor, or grade-level principal, will evaluate the faculty according to professional and personal goals established by each faculty member at the outset of the academic year. These evaluations will include planned and spontaneous

classroom visitations, follow-up discussions and recommendations, mandatory in-services, attendance at professional conferences, and graduate schooling.

4. An *ad hoc* committee of administrators and general or department-based faculty will annually review parts of the school's program. They may examine biblical integration throughout the curriculum, or selection of textbooks and other learning aids; they may consider curriculum mapping, computer-assisted instruction, calendar and daily schedule issues, or methods of improved communication with parents; they may study the implications of adding a foreign language or a competitive sport, criteria for honors classes or participation in the Advanced Placement Program, or policies on absences for college interviews. These and a myriad of other topics are subject to review and then recommendation to the head-of-school for action as chief executive and educational officer of the school.

External Assessment: Audits and Consulting Reports

While schools seeking excellence will conduct their own internal evaluations, they will also seek the help of external experts in achieving their goals:

Professional Consultants

The use of professional consultants by Christian schools has grown as school boards and administrators have become familiar with benefits of wise and experienced counsel. Consultants come in all shapes and sizes. Some are lone rangers, while others claim affiliation with a firm; some know Christian schooling well, but others do not. So the board or head-of-school must determine in advance how well a consultant can satisfy the school's expectations. References from other Christian schools, which should be available upon request, are helpful in reaching a decision.

Schools retain a consultant for two purposes, to make *observations* and, when asked, to offer *opinions*. In addition, as an objective third party, a consultant can usually obtain honest constituent opinions, often withheld from a school insider.

A consulting firm may be invited to conduct an audit (a close professional analysis) of the development office and its mode of raising gift support, asked to survey a school's methods of marketing for admissions, retained to review the counseling program, named to facilitate creating a strategic plan, hired to mentor the relationships between the governing board and head-of-school, or appointed to conduct a performance review of the head-of-school on behalf of the board (Lockerbie, 1999).

A reputable consulting firm will specify the work to be completed within a certain time and the product of that work, whether an oral or written summary or a fully documented report. It will also enumerate the cost of services, including fees and expenses.

Accreditation by a Recognized Agency

The word "accreditation" has its root in the Latin word "credo," meaning "I believe." Banks issue a *credit* card to someone in the belief that the cardholder will pay what she owes in a timely manner. We deem a *credible* witness in a courtroom believable because the evidence he gives comports with the facts of the case. "Credo" also applies to the school that receives *accreditation*, which means that a body of peers in education affirms that one can believe the school when it claims to offer a valid education according to its mission, goals, and philosophy.

Accredited Christian Schools

We can thank God that Christian schools have emerged from the paranoia of the early 1970s, when rather than acknowledge that any external entity—especially the state—might have any legitimate interest in or authority over their existence, pastors and administrators chained themselves to the schoolhouse door. Today, Christian schools aiming for excellence are eager to be recognized, not only within such friendly organizations as the Association of Christian Schools International and other federations of like-minded schools, but also by secular regional accrediting associations. Thus ACSI accredits its members jointly with the New England, Middle States, Southern, North Central, Northwest, and Western associations of schools and colleges.

Chapter 11, "Achieving Accreditation," presents in detail the steps to follow. The next few paragraphs offer a complementary summary, which is based on the experience of preparing for several accrediting visits and participating on accrediting visiting teams.

Requirements for initial accreditation vary from one agency to another; in general, however, a school must apply for candidate status and meet stipulations regarding financial accountability, governance, site and facilities, personnel, curriculum, learning resources, and other conditions signaling a sound and stable school. Upon meeting these standards, the school may apply to the accrediting agency for a preliminary visit. During this visit, a representative of the agency discusses any remaining conditions to be met and forecasts the timing of a formal visit by an accrediting committee of peers. Usually the committee visits in a year or more.

Organizing for the Self-Study

The self-study, required by each agency, takes place before the formal visit. If a school has been conducting its own internal evaluation by means of its annual self-study, it will not find this requirement daunting. A few tips on the self-study process follow:

1. Be *positive* about the whole process of the self-study. Yes, it requires an enormous amount of work, and it costs both time and money. But its purpose is to enhance the whole school by identifying elements that are strengths and weaknesses in the opinion of your school's peers. Thus, the steering committee appointed to oversee the self-study during the preparatory year must consist of persons who joyfully advocate the process and can influence others to do the same.

2. Encourage *fresh perspectives* by appointing to the steering committee some people who did not serve on the last steering committee or whose maturity can help the committee avoid defensiveness about particular programs.

3. Seek *diversity* of age, experience, official responsibility, or other distinctions to ensure that the steering committee can get a view of the school from all perspectives.

4. Remember that the steering committee's oversight of the self-study requires honesty, achieved only by critiquing the school *objectively and scrupulously*.

5. Appoint as chair or cochairs of the steering committee a person or persons who can *organize* a schedule of meetings and *maintain sufficient momentum* for the self-study.

6. Authorize the chair/cochairs to require that your board, administration, and faculty *promptly and completely fulfill* all reasonable tasks required for the self-study.

7. *Appoint or, if necessary, hire an efficient editor* to assemble and prepare the massive paperwork. Composing the final document for submission to the accrediting agency is not a part-time job.

8. *Involve the full school*, including board members, administration, faculty, and support staff, in a final presentation prior to submitting the self-study report to the accrediting agency. Everyone in your school will thus be assured that, to the greatest extent possible, the steering committee has tried to report a consistent and coherent overview of the school.

However you proceed, the self-study should create a high level of morale among your administrative and teaching teams.

Other Means of External Assessment

This chapter ends with a list of external assessment options that a school intending to be excellent must note:

• A regular but not overbearing schedule of standardized tests, preferably not comparing the results only with public schools or ACSI member schools but also with local, regional, and national independent schools. People often judge a school by its test scores, particularly in the lowest grades, when reading ability is especially important to parents, and in the highest grades, when SAT or ACT scores are significant in college admissions.

- For secondary schools, participation in the Advanced Placement Program of the College Board or International Baccalaureate in Geneva, Switzerland. These programs provide enhancement to a school's curriculum, afford a challenge to teachers and qualified students, and make available possible college advanced placement for the most successful candidates. No secondary school claiming excellence can afford to ignore the Advanced Placement Program, which is easier to offer.
- A highly personalized college admissions counseling program (or in the case of elementary or middle schools, counseling regarding admission to the next level of schooling) to provide graduates with the best opportunity to be accepted by and enroll in a college or university well suited to their needs and gifts. Parents pay tuition to a school not only for what it offers now but also for what it prepares and qualifies its students to achieve upon graduation. Parents expect a school to provide such counsel.
- A final controversial item is in order. Some Christian schools pride themselves on the fact that every member of their faculty is state certified. This claim may be an instance of "damning with faint praise." It is reported that college students with the least academic ability enroll in education courses, that the common denominator among public school teachers is a state certificate verifying that the holder has passed such courses, and that large numbers of state-certified teachers fail national qualifying examinations whose level is not as demanding as an advanced placement exam. If these reports are believed by people who are choosing a school, then claiming that its teachers have state certification alone does not speak well for a school. The only exception may be in a state so controlling of nonpublic schools that it demands state certification, a signal that educational bureaucrats may be in cahoots with the state university's school of education to guarantee tuition payments by compulsion.

Conclusion

The cycle of internal evaluation and external assessment continue without ceasing, never allowing a school, its administrator, or its teachers to take a vacation from self-examination. When a school seeks to raise the bar, it faces one of its most difficult challenges—but one that will be worth the effort as the school answers God's call to excellence.

Bibliography

Bennett, W. J. (1993). *The book of virtues.* New York: Simon & Schuster.

Beversluis, N. H. (2001). Let children come: A durable vision for Christian schooling. Grand Rapids, MI: Christian Schools International.

Gaebelein, F. E. (1995). *Christian education in a democracy.* Colorado Springs: Association of Christian Schools International.

Gaebelein, F. E. (1996). *The pattern of God's truth: Problems of integration in Christian education.* Colorado Springs: Association of Christian Schools International.

Lockerbie, D. B. (1994). *A passion for learning: The history of Christian thought on education.* Chicago: Moody Press.

Lockerbie, D. B. (1999). *From candy sales to committed donors: A guide to financing Christian schools.* Stony Brook, NY: PAIDEIA Press.

Lockerbie, D. B. (2000). *The timeless moment: Creativity and the Christian faith.* Stony Brook, NY: PAIDEIA Press.

Ryan, K., & Bohlin, K. E. (1999). *Building character in schools.* San Francisco: Jossey-Bass.

Schultz, G. (1998). *Kingdom education: God's plan for educating future generations.* Nashville: LifeWay Press.

Stop and Smell the Coffee
Thinking and Planning Strategically

Ken Smitherman, LL.D.

Chapter Summary

"Target audience," "expected outcomes," and "core values"—strategic planning requires exploring these concepts. Whether your school is large or small (or anywhere in between), the importance of strategic planning cannot be overstated. Everyone in your school must understand its significance to the school's mission and vision.

Prayerful and careful strategic planning—mission driven and vision focused—will help you to "keep the main thing the main thing" and avoid the rabbit trails that expend energy and resources needlessly. Strategic plans will help you stay in touch with your reason for existence as well as guide you in charting the future. In easy-to-understand terms, Dr. Smitherman explains what is necessary for your school to begin developing such a plan and to stop making decisions based on expediency.

About the author
Ken Smitherman, LL.D.
President, ACSI
Colorado Springs, CO
35 years of educational leadership experience

Chapter 15

Stop and Smell the Coffee
Thinking and Planning Strategically

Ken Smitherman, LL.D.

Coffee was the biggest thing going in Seattle. There was a kiosk on wheels on nearly every corner—at least it looked that way. And the daily paper presented the glory stories of latte and espresso entrepreneurs who had set up shop in strategic locations and were amassing annual net incomes in excess of $100,000.

Six-figure numbers usually catch the attention of Christian school administrators, particularly when the numbers are tied to matters of income. My mind began to conjure up ways that I could legitimize my love for latte into an income-generating opportunity that would enhance school programs.

It did not take long to determine that the latte business could propel the school's student missions program to new heights. The business manager and I developed and presented our business plan aggressively to our chief financial officer. With all the right approvals, we placed our order for a custom-made business on wheels. The health permits were secured, and we arranged for the clean-up station. Then we installed additional outside electrical service, and about $12,000 later, we opened for business. Now, $12,000 is no small amount to any Christian school, but to keep things in perspective, our school had an annual operating budget at that time of about $6 million. But regardless of the size of your school and its operating budget, you can apply nearly every illustration in this chapter—forget the number of zeroes because the principles remain the same.

Our plans included significant use of volunteer labor that would send our profitability soaring. Well, we could dream on—even if our motives were quite pure and straightforward. We rapidly discovered that overnight our school business manager became a restaurant owner-operator. The tasks ranged from controlling inventory to managing human resources to scrubbing the espresso machine.

To bring a rather long illustration to conclusion, we determined that we had better cut our losses and sell out. At less than fifty cents on the dollar, we sighed and wiped our collective brow. Fortunately, I have been able to look at such dollar losses as "tuition," for in such situations I often find genuine lifelong learning.

So, what went wrong? We were in the coffee capital of the world. The motivation and intent were strong. And the equipment functioned exceptionally well.

What went wrong? We had departed from our mission. Our school had strayed from the business for which we were in business. We had diverted crucial leadership staff to run a coffee enterprise because we liked the smell and taste of coffee.

God had called us to educate students for His glory, but we had chased a rabbit trail because we lacked appropriate strategy. More basic than that, we had not built a foundation for strategic planning that would provide both a guide and parameters for planning so that we would stay mission driven and vision focused.

What Is Strategic Planning?

Strategic planning is an intentional design for accomplishing what God has called us to do. It requires thinking through several crucial areas, then moving ahead deliberately and strategically with God's direction.

The Internet Nonprofit Center views strategic planning as a management tool alone. The Center exists to help organizations improve by focusing their energy, ensuring that their members work toward common goals, and assessing and adjusting their direction in response to a changing environment. Strategic planning assures that organizations can move toward accomplishing what they have intended to accomplish.

Often, people use the terms "strategic planning" and "long-range planning" interchangeably. Although they are related, the difference is significant. Long-range planning in its simplest form refers to developing a plan for accomplishing a goal or set of goals over a predetermined number of years.

In contrast, in strategic planning, an organization focuses on achieving its vision by carrying out its mission. Strategic planning recognizes that everything takes place in a dynamic environment, so if we as Christian school leaders want to achieve our mission, we must recognize the impact of a changing environment on our strategies and plans.

Who Is Responsible for Planning?

Different leaders answer this question in different ways. Frequently we have seen an institution's board as the entity responsible for strategic planning. Recently, however, boards have been urged to devote their efforts to their real task of governance rather than to administration and micromanagement. For example, John Carver, a leading expert on boardsmanship for nonprofits, says:

> Good governance calls for the board role in long-range planning to consist chiefly in establishing the *reason* for planning. Planning is done to increase the probability of getting somewhere from here. Enunciation of that "somewhere" is the board's highest contribution. In a manner of speaking, boards participate most effectively in the planning process by standing just outside it. Boards can make an invaluable contribution to planning; however except for planning the improvement of governance itself, *boards should not do the actual long-range planning.* (1997)

In a school focused on accomplishing its mission and seeing its vision realized, the administrative team should be responsible for strategic planning. They should present the completed plan to the board of trustees as a proposal for accomplishing the business of the school. If the term "administrative team" is a stretch for a small Christian school, a planning team can include other educators in the school. Remember that the overall scope of the school's program must be appropriately represented. In a very small school, this team could (and probably should) be the entire faculty. For this type of planning, the team should include no fewer than three and no more than twelve people.

A planning retreat to launch this endeavor works well since it provides an opportunity to pull away from all the other issues on campus. Two days can be an ideal amount of time to develop the foundation for strategic planning. This retreat should precede the annual budget planning and preparation time. Academic planning always precedes financial planning.

The interactions of a group and the relationships of individuals within the group are key elements in effective planning. As Dayton and Engstrom note:

> There was a time when common wisdom said that great ideas and inventions came only from individuals. If that was ever true, it is no longer so. Despite all of the jokes about committees, it is through joint endeavor that human progress is made in the Western World. This means that we must find some ways to bring people together to do corporate thinking, inventing, uncovering

the future, or whatever term we might use to describe planning—the process of trying to find ways of reaching a given goal.

The people involved in the group planning process will be able to work together to the degree that they hold a common view. On the other side is the fact that if a group is too homogeneous, there is a danger of its becoming ingrown and coming up with the same old solutions, even though the problems have changed. Irving L. Janis, in his book *Victims of Groupthink*, points out that when a group is too cohesive, or too willing to bow to the whims of its leadership, it can often make very poor decisions. What is needed is "a member of the loyal opposition" to keep the group in line. (1979)

Understanding the Terms

Planning strategically simply will not happen unless we build the plan on a foundation. Five key terms, when fully developed, are basic to such a foundation:

1. *Target Audience*: the audience we accept the responsibility to serve.

   First, our schools must determine whom they serve. In some instances, there may be more than one target audience, but in Christian schools, students clearly constitute the primary target audience. When identifying the target audience, the planners should include information on ages and/or grade levels, numbers of people served, their location, and any other criteria distinctive to their school.
   At appropriate stages of planning, we can identify other target audiences. These might include parents, nonstudent children in the community, or others.

2. *Expected Outcomes*: the measurable change or transformation that will occur in the people the school serves.

   The term "outcomes" has acquired negative connotations, particularly among some in the conservative Christian community. It is linked to the often disdained concept of outcomes-based education. I would like to reclaim the concept, however, noting that Christian schooling *must* be outcomes based. Our schools should focus on achieving predetermined outcomes, or in this case *expected outcomes*. We must clearly identify and delineate what we expect our students will be like if we effectively achieve our mission.

3. *Vision*: what the people in the target audience will be like if we effectively serve them.

   At this point, we sense a strong similarity between expected outcomes and vision. In this case, vision is a summarized composite statement of our expected outcomes. In other words, our expected outcomes result from a controlled explosion of our vision into its separate parts.

4. *Mission*: what the school will offer or provide to its target audience as a means for the vision to be realized.

It is not uncommon to see "vision" and "mission" used incorrectly as interchangeable terms. We need clarity, and a journey can serve as a helpful analogy. The place we want to go is the vision. How we get there is the mission, and if we do arrive, we accomplish the mission and realize the vision. The itinerary is the strategic plan—the map, traveler's checks, suitcases, and passengers who are bundled together ready to travel.

5. *Core Values*: a set of values or principles that guide the practice of the school in fulfilling its mission.

In a recent study of blue-ribbon companies in corporate America, James Collins and Jerry Porras noted that a common characteristic of visionary, highly recognized, and profitable companies was their nearly cultlike adherence to a set of core values.

> Core values are the organization's essential and enduring tenets, not to be compromised for financial gain or short-term expediency.... Thomas J. Watson, Jr., former IBM chief executive, commented on the role of core values (what he calls beliefs) in his 1963 booklet *A Business and Its Beliefs*: "I firmly believe that any organization, in order to survive and achieve success, must have a sound set of beliefs on which it premises all its policies and actions. Next, I believe that the most important single factor in corporate success is faithful adherence to those beliefs.... *Beliefs must always come before policies, practices, and goals. The latter must always be altered if they are seen to violate fundamental beliefs*." [emphasis ours] (1997)

Core values offer a powerful and crucial ingredient for success. This fact is no less true in Christian schools than elsewhere, and we see that even more poignantly when the authors note, "In a visionary company, the core values need no rational or external justification. Nor do they sway with the trends and fads of the day. Nor even do they shift in response to changing market conditions" (Collins & Porras, 1997).

Core values cannot be bought off at any price. They form the essence of the school. They are like a solid-rock foundation; they will withstand storms, time, and even seemingly fickle constituencies.

A Lesson from the Book of Nehemiah

Although I doubt that Nehemiah brought his administrative team together for a strategic planning retreat, I have no question that he was a strategic thinker and planner of the highest magnitude. A brief look back at his plan shows that clearly. Let's examine each of the five components of his strategy:

Vision

His vision was that the exiled people of Israel might be reunited: "[B]ut if you return to me and obey my commands, then even if your exiled people are at the farthest horizon, I will gather them from there and bring them to the place I have chosen as a dwelling for my Name" (Nehemiah 1:9). Nehemiah had caught God's vision—he knew where he must go and what he must accomplish.

Mission

Nehemiah's mission was to rebuild Jerusalem: "[S]end me to the city in Judah where my fathers are buried so that I can rebuild it" (Nehemiah 2:5). Rebuilding the city was what he offered to his primary target audience, God's people, as the mission that would enable them to fulfill the vision.

Target Audiences and Expected Outcomes

- The Israelites, the target audience, will have a place to come home to (Nehemiah 1:9).
- King Artaxerxes, a secondary target audience, will grant Nehemiah permission to rebuild the city (Nehemiah 2:5).
- The governors of Trans-Euphrates, a secondary target audience, will provide safe conduct through their land for the journey (Nehemiah 2:7).
- Asaph, the keeper of the king's forest and a secondary target audience, will provide the timber to make beams (Nehemiah 2:8).

The primary target audience identifies for whom we accomplish the vision. There may be secondary target audiences, and if so, they are essential to the strategic plan. We identify them because of their importance and role in accomplishing the vision.

Core Values

- Recognition and acknowledgement of God's sovereignty and power
- Recognition that God provides the needed success
- Recognition of God as the great Protector
- Commitment to obey what God puts in our hearts

These core values drove every aspect of Nehemiah's work. They would remain true regardless of any external conditions or stresses. Although we could identify other core values, these formed the essence of Nehemiah's service to God.

The above account is a biblical example of strategic planning. The entire process remained vision focused and mission driven. The text clearly identifies who does what for whom and what outcomes Nehemiah expected. Even though the account does not include an institutional or organizational entity, the principles are clear and, in the final analysis, effective. Nehemiah accomplished what God called him to do. He thought through the crucial issues, and then he moved ahead deliberately and strategically with God's direction and clear blessing. This kind of thinking will make a difference in Christian schooling.

Nehemiah modeled effective leadership, an essential ingredient in the planning process. Our leadership must result in appropriate influence on all who serve and are served within our Christian schools. Bob Biehl recounts:

> On the first anniversary of the creation of the citizens' group Common Cause, founder John W. Gardner wrote a summary of the rules this group had learned for influencing decision makers and accomplishing change. Among them were these:
>
> • Limit the number of targets, and hit them hard.
> • Put a professional cutting edge on citizen enthusiasm.
> • Form alliances.
> • "Tell the story."
>
> By following these and other fundamental rules, Common Cause in its first year grew to include 250,000 members (its first-year target was only 25,000). (1989)

Nehemiah applied these four rules to the greatest advantage. Every Christian school needs to invest significant energy in matters of influence. We need influence in right measure with the planning team, the board of trustees, the parent constituency, the donors, the churches with whom the school has a relationship, and the community at large. Good planning never ignores any targets that require influence.

Nehemiah demonstrated professionalism in the high level of orderliness he maintained when he implemented his plan. In addition, the plan harnessed the enthusiasm of the participants in ways that made maximum use of their resources and energies.

Alliances formed in the right quarters can help us achieve what we cannot do alone. Nehemiah illustrated obtaining expertise and resources that he alone could not produce—acquiring timber from the king's forest for building. We have uncounted potential alliances and collaborative efforts that can strengthen our schools' objectives, enhancing everything from curriculum to facilities.

"Telling the story" may be one of the most underachieved ways to impact and influence others. We must articulate the message in understandable ways, create a desire for action, and reflect a passion for the cause. Only through clear communication of the message can we gain the needed support to move the plan ahead.

What Makes a Plan Strategic?

A strategy is a plan or means that has been devised thoughtfully to achieve something at a higher level—a level that has been considered, contemplated, and targeted for achievement. The care and preparation that go into the plan give it strategic quality. First, we carefully develop a strategic planning foundation on the basis of the five points: target audience(s), expected outcomes, vision, mission, and core values. Now we can design initiatives and action plans that keep our institutions true to their reason for existence.

Remember the espresso stand? We had good intentions, but our plan was inappropriately linked to the vision and mission of the school. Implementing our plan would actually require us to pull key resources, both human and financial, from their original purposes.

The Foundation Document of the Strategic Plan

Let's take a look at what the foundation document of the strategic plan might look like for *Anywhere Christian Academy*:

Vision

It is the vision of Anywhere Christian Academy that our graduates have a Christian worldview that permeates all of life, are prepared for university level studies, and will:

Spiritually: have a personal relationship with Christ that exhibits the desire and ability to apply and practice biblical principles of Christian living as they serve God and others in the home, church, workplace, and community.

Intellectually: be able to think critically, communicate clearly, and use mathematics, science, and computers effectively; find, examine, and evaluate information; and appreciate literature and the fine arts.

In Citizenship: understand and implement skills of effective citizenship and democratic ideals; discern changes and differences in world cultures, histories, and governments of other peoples; and respond to God's leading in mission outreach.

In Life Skills: respect others and relate appropriately to them, practicing principles of integrity, commitment, and biblical morality; be able to solve problems, make decisions, appreciate work, and practice being good stewards of their physical health, resources, and opportunities.

Mission

Anywhere Christian Academy's mission is to educate students for the glory of God. We accept students capable of achieving at or above grade level while exerting a reasonable effort in a traditional school setting. Our program prepares students for higher education while developing and implementing a Christian worldview that permeates all of life.

Clearly, few will commit the above mission statement to memory or will want to print it on a coffee cup with the school logo. Therefore, we need to design a "coffee-cup version." The result:

Anywhere Christian Academy ... educating students for the glory of God

Target Audience(s)

Students:

- Whose parents desire a Christian education for them
- Who are capable of higher education preparatory courses
- Who are in any grade from preschool through twelve
- Who, if they are determined by review to have learning disabilities, can have their educational needs met by the school

Geography and Capacity:

- Generally serving those within a twenty-mile radius of the campus
- Availability for 80 to 100 students per grade, kindergarten through twelve
- Availability for 200 preschoolers

We define our target audience so that the staff and the school constituency clearly understand whom we serve. This definition limits our enrollment possibilities, but whom we choose to serve determines how we will staff our schools and plan our curricula.

Expected Outcomes

With Christ as the center of truth and as God's model for His people, the expected outcomes at Anywhere Christian Academy are to develop graduates who:

- Reflect an understanding of and a desire for a commitment to God through a personal relationship with Christ.
- Have knowledge of God's Word and apply it in daily life.
- Participate actively in a church community by serving God and other people.
- Know how to find, examine, evaluate, and use information.
- Have knowledge of significant people and events in the history of the Christian church.
- Have an appreciation for fine arts.
- Understand, value, and practice the skills of effective citizenship.

- Understand the cultures, histories, and governments of other peoples and places, and consider what is appropriate for them in missions outreach.
- Respect and relate appropriately to the people with whom they work, play, and live.
- Use leisure time wisely.
- Have the skills to solve problems and make decisions.

When approved, the list of expected outcomes becomes a crucial document for a school. It is the framework on which a school's curriculum must be developed. Simply picking up an order form for Christian school textbooks and "ordering the curriculum" will not do.

Curriculum, staffing, and facilities must work in harmony to achieve the expected outcomes. If we want students to know God's Word and apply it in daily life, we must select or design the appropriate teaching materials, and hire teachers who model the application of God's Word in their lives. If we require students to find, examine, evaluate, and use information, the library or media center is a crucial area both in space and content.

If we want our students to develop an appreciation for the fine arts, our schools must make a commitment to teaching everything from poetry to pottery. Clearly, expected student outcomes determine how we allocate financial, human, and physical resources.

Core Values

- All learning experiences aim to move students toward their full spiritual and intellectual potential.
- Scripture is taught as the revealed truth of God.
- Every element of the curriculum radiates God's Word and its implications for living.
- All trustees, administrators, faculty, and staff know Jesus Christ as personal Savior and Lord.

These kinds of core values need no justification beyond their biblical basis. They do not sway with trends and fads, nor do they shift with changing market conditions.

Assessing Our Schools

In preparing for a road trip, we can use a map only if we know our starting point. So it is with planning. Knowing our present status is vital to planning the future.

The SWOT analysis is a highly effective tool in determining where our schools are at the present. Many have used this instrument to define their schools' *strengths, weaknesses, opportunities*, and *threats*.

Strengths are positive aspects internal to a school. A strength may be the *excellent elementary library.* Weaknesses are negative aspects internal to the school, for example, the *lack of a qualified and effective chemistry teacher.*

Opportunities and threats are external to a school. Opportunities may include an *influx of families with school-age children in the school's service area,* while threats may include the *possibility of governmental intervention in the school's curriculum.*

A SWOT analysis, developed by different segments of the constituency, provides a variety of perspectives, such as those of the administrative team, the board, the faculty, and a representative parent group. In certain cases, a high school student council or other appropriate student leadership group may also develop an analysis.

The SWOT analysis should not be simply a list of everyone's thoughts but rather a consensus on each item by each constituent group. The same facilitator should lead each analysis and thereby provide consistency in terminology.

Upon studying the various SWOT analyses carefully and combining them appropriately, a picture will emerge showing *strengths, weaknesses, opportunities,* and *threats.*

This explanation is not meant to devalue or to oversimplify a complex concept, but the challenge before the leadership of our schools is really quite clear:

- Capitalize on the strengths.
- Eliminate the weaknesses.
- Seize the opportunities.
- Neutralize the threats.

With this challenge in mind, wise administrators prioritize the issues they plan to address. Then they develop an appropriate plan to address each issue strategically within a feasible time, most likely more than one year.

Developing the Strategic Initiative

Developing a formal strategic initiative or implementation plan, a commonly overlooked step in strategic planning, requires diligent adherence to the following criteria:

1. *Goal:* We state the goal clearly but simply. The possibilities for the goal can range from a construction project to the development and implementation of a new curriculum. The point is to begin addressing the prioritized list systematically.
2. *Rationale:* What is the reason for this initiative? We must state the reason clearly so that everyone understands both God's direction and the leadership's thinking behind the goal.
3. *Target Audience and Expected Outcomes:* In combination, these must

come only from the foundation document we previously developed. Here the rubber meets the road as we seek to stay vision focused and mission driven. We must pursue only those initiatives that focus on the audience we are committed to serving. We must commit to achieving the predetermined outcomes that provide ongoing focus for the school, identifying at least one of these. If that is not possible, the goal does not deserve further time or energy. We should pursue only those initiatives that move us closer to the realization of our vision.

4. *Major Thrusts*: We identify in a bulleted format the major points that we plan to achieve by accomplishing this initiative. We summarize the high points by giving an overview of the schedule.

5. *Action Plan*: We identify the details in a step-by-step format, including the time needed for each step.

6. *Costs*: We determine the projected costs for the initiative by major items as in a normal budgeting process. The diligence we put to this task will provide invaluable information for both annual and longer-term financial planning.

7. *Responsibility*: There may be more than one office or person responsible for various phases of the initiative. Clearly defining these duties will result in a higher level of empowerment and accountability.

This strategic initiative or implementation plan needs to address only these seven issues. We can include other supporting documents and materials as addenda if we determine that such support would be valuable. Depending on the school's governance structure, we may have now completed a proposal appropriate for a board presentation. With issues that require only administrative approval, we have developed the plan, which provides budgeting, planning, and scheduling data. The steps are clear; now it becomes simply a matter of following the blueprint.

Conquering the Proverbial Rabbit Trail

Most schools often have staff or board members who present "great ideas"—but sometimes those great ideas do not always match where the school *is* or *ought to be going*. This strategic planning process offers a professional and positive approach to dealing with both great and not-so-great ideas.

When we hear such a presentation, we may say, "That is really an interesting idea. Would you be willing to submit it to me in a written form that follows our strategic initiative format? As you know, we now use this process to help us stay on course and do the very best job that God has called us to."

Then we clearly explain the process and provide a copy of the foundation document so people can understand how to identify the target audience and expected outcomes. This method will generally put to rest inappropriate ideas while providing an excellent forum for the truly great ideas. We must offer this approach as a professional method of presenting ideas rather than as some kind of "put it in writing" dismissal.

I believe God enables us to do the work He has called us to. Thinking and planning strategically maximizes limited resources, including time, money, and people. These principles for strategic planning can make a difference, enabling our schools to stay their course—not only surviving through a myriad of challenges but also capitalizing on a myriad of opportunities.

Bibliography

Biehl, B. (1989). *Increasing your leadership confidence.* Sisters, OR: Questar.

Carver, J. (1997). *Boards that make a difference.* San Francisco: Jossey-Bass.

Collins, J. C., & Porras, J. I. (1997). *Built to last.* New York: HarperBusiness.

Dayton, E. R., & Engstrom, T. W. (1979). *Strategy for leadership.* Old Tappan, NJ: Fleming H. Revell.

Support Center, San Francisco, CA (1994–1995).
<http://www.supportcenter.org/sf/genie.htm> Reprinted with permission. All Rights Reserved.

Turning Vision into Reality
Managing School Budgets

David L. Roth, Ed.D.

Chapter Summary

Like leaders in every Christian school, you and your board wrestle with seemingly endless financial issues such as tuition increases, faculty compensation, tuition assistance, and capital improvements. Unfortunately, for too many schools, the budget-planning process consists of either hoping that each issue will be resolved or guessing what will be needed to accomplish at least something.

Dr. Roth offers a clear alternative. He outlines in precise terms the basics of the budget-planning process as well as the essential components of a school budget. Applying the truth of the Bible, he identifies principles and practices that should characterize your school's budgeting process and help you address those nagging financial issues.

About the author
David L. Roth, Ed.D.
Headmaster, Wheaton Academy
West Chicago, IL
35 years of educational leadership experience

Chapter 16

Turning Vision into Reality
Managing School Budgets

David L. Roth, Ed.D.

It quickly became apparent that Wheaton Academy had hired the right business manager—at least relative to budgeting—when he said to me, the headmaster, "What is your vision for this school?" The new business manager was serious, but not patronizing. Before he began the annual budgeting process, he wanted to know the vision of the administration and the board of trustees and their strategic plan to reach that vision. *Academic planning must precede financial planning.* We can't express our vision and goals clearly enough and often enough. I was more than happy to review with him our future as a school.

> Your school is both a ministry and a business. Good business planning frees the school to pursue its ministry unhindered by financial frustrations. Financial planning and management are a central part of the school's ministry. Your treasurer, business manager, and bookkeeper are all a vital part of your ministry team. They provide the support network out of which Christian education can occur. (Miller, 1998)

Money and Mission

A strong sense of mission, clear goals, and strategic long-range planning form the basis for good financial planning. A budget is a plan that allocates a school's resources toward activating its purpose, that is, its mission and goals. It is a snapshot of a school's educational plan for a fiscal year (Anthony, 2001). Well-known Christian financial planner Ron Blue says, "Financial planning is the predetermined use of financial resources in order to accomplish certain goals and objectives" (1997).

Budget Planning

The budget makes it possible to manage a school's finances. Properly built and managed, the budget facilitates reaching goals, and it safeguards against confusion and serious problems with the IRS. Few problems in a Christian school evoke low staff morale and frustrate parents more quickly than poor planning. Evidence of poor planning may be seen in poorly maintained washrooms, unkempt grounds, underpaid teachers, or a myriad of other undesirable situations. Poor planning usually relates to poor budgeting.

Veteran Christian school administrator Robert Siemens gives a good overview of the budget and its importance:

> The school budget is a simple concept with profound implications for educational administration. The budget can serve as an instrument of fiscal policy. It is also an instrument of fiscal control. The budget deserves recognition as the heart of fiscal management. (Lowrie, 1984)

Today Christian schools like to include the word "excellence" in describing their programs. We are bombarded by phrases like academic excellence, athletic excellence, and excellence in the fine arts. But our schools must also develop financial excellence.

Financial Credibility

Disproportionately large annual deficits, or unmeasurable long-term debts and serious cash flow problems undermine constituents' confidence. These conditions negatively impact donors' willingness to give and our ability to recruit good families and students. As a result, long-term stability and viability of the school may be at stake. Effective fiscal planning and management build *consumer confidence* in our schools. Too many Christian schools suffer from a lack of credibility because of fiscal issues. Their constituents seem to say, "I can't hear all those good things you claim about Christian education because what you do fiscally speaks so loudly."

A startling number of businesses operate without a budget, trusting memory or luck to sort out expenses and income throughout the year (J. K. Lasser Institute, 1994). Given the number of Christian schools that struggle financially and the many that simply go out of business, I suspect that administrators and board members of many Christian schools do not know how to prepare or manage a budget properly.

Scripture admonishes us to "let all things be done decently and in order" (1 Corinthians 14:40, KJV). Surely part of that rubric requires that Christian school leaders understand the biblical principles of money management. God has called us to be salt and light (Matthew 5:13–16). As we grow and improve our schools, we need to remind ourselves that "[u]nless the Lord builds the house, its builders labor in vain" (Psalm 127:1). Money management in Christian schools needs to be firmly founded on biblical principles.

California Pastor John MacArthur, in his tape series *Mastery of Materialism*, says that many of Christ's parables deal with money. "The New Testament says more about money than heaven and hell combined—five times more about money than prayer; and while there are 500 plus verses on both prayer and faith, there are over 2,000 verses dealing with money and possessions" (Blue, 1997). The Bible has much to say about money management.

There are four basic biblical principles, according to Blue, that summarize the Bible's teaching regarding money and money management.

Basic Biblical Principles

God Owns It All

When we presuppose that God owns it all, the managing of money, in this case the managing of the school budget, takes on a very distinct thrust. Now the emphasis is on stewardship, not ownership. As a Christian school administrator, I must look at funds received and funds spent from a stewardship or responsibilities perspective. I may manage much, but I own nothing. God owns it all!

Recently an Academy parent and contributor sent me a handwritten note summarizing a conversation we had on money and stewardship. The note said, "He's the creator of *all*. Anything we have here is His. We're just 'stewards' of His riches!" This parent reminded me that as Christian school leaders, we must be responsible stewards of our schools' God-given resources and use them wisely for the purposes for which they have been given. Among the questions we should regularly ask are the following: How well do we impart this concept to others in our school? Are the faculty and staff wasteful? Do we make every effort to keep on budget and get full funding for the budget?

We Are in a Growth Process

The second biblical principle of money management cited by Blue is that we are in a growth process. God uses money and our management of money to grow and mature us in the faith. Sometimes we in Christian ministry look at money issues as a test, and indeed they are. We face a constant test of our faith regarding God's provision. The test also includes our faithfulness in handling what God has entrusted to us (Blue, 1997).

The Amount Is Not Important

We live in a power-hungry, materialistic culture where bigger is better and more is revered. A successful businessman once said to me, "David, I could never run a Christian school as well as you, but I know how to make money." In observing this man's stewardship of his wealth and listening to his heart attitude, I could see that God had entrusted him with much, and yet he seemed to remain good and faithful as was the servant described in Matthew's parable of the talents, whose lord said, "Well done, good and faithful servant; you have been faithful over a few things, I will make you ruler over many things. Enter into the joy of your lord" (Matthew 25:23, NKJV).

One of the regular contributors to our school, a mother of a former student, is also a single parent who lives very simply. She periodically contributes ten dollars. The first time I opened her gift envelope, I prayed, "Lord, how do you expect us to balance a multimillion dollar budget with gifts this size?" Then I was reminded of what Jesus said while standing in the temple and watching worshippers put money into the temple treasury. The rich men poured in their bags of gold. A poor widow put in two small copper coins. Jesus said, "[T]his poor widow has put in more than all the others" (Luke 21:2, 3).

I went out to a coin shop and bought an actual widow's mite made in 103 B.C. I keep it on my desk as a reminder that the size of the gift doesn't matter; only the giver's attitude counts. Little in God's hands becomes much. Likewise, the enrollment of our Christian schools or the size of our budgets does not matter. God cares about how we manage what He has entrusted to us.

Faith Requires Action

God repeatedly pours out His blessings on our Christian schools in terms of needed resources. All of us as Christian school leaders and money managers should be proactive, not passive, in managing the resources God provides. In the parable of the talents, Jesus had harsh words for the servant who received one talent and did nothing with it. His lord called him a "wicked and lazy servant" and ordered the talent to be taken from him and given to another (Matthew 25:24–30). God cares how we handle what we have.

Some Christian school board members and some administrators like action for action's sake. When I use Blue's phrase "faith requires action," I presuppose that action is predicated on good planning. Christian school leaders involved in strategic planning and budget preparation need to remember that a wise person counts the cost before building a house, and in the council of many one finds wisdom.

In preparation for a recent school board retreat on planning strategically for the next decade, I came across some wise words in Proverbs 16:

- "All a man's ways seem innocent to him, but motives are weighed by the Lord."
- "Commit to the Lord whatever you do, and your plans will succeed."
- "In his heart a man plans his course, but the Lord determines his steps."

Whether we oversee a large system with several schools or a small Christian school of fewer than 100 students, we must acknowledge and be accountable to the *Owner* of all our school's resources. We must complement our faith with action that befits a good steward.

One of the classics among materials helpful to Christian school administrators and board members is a small book entitled *Serving God on the Christian School Board*, written by the late Roy Lowrie Jr. and revised a few years ago by his son R. Leon Lowrie. The chapter on board committees includes a list of typical board committees and their suggested responsibilities. The fourteen responsibilities of the business or finance committee directly or indirectly impact an administrator's ability to create and manage a school budget:

- Recommend business policies and procedures to the board.
- See that the school's business operations are effective and efficient.
- Work with the administrator and the board in budgeting and in budget control.
- Make recommendations to the board concerning tuition, registration fees, and other charges.
- Collect delinquent tuition accounts.
- Keep all financial statements and reports current, understandable, and orderly.
- See that all financial records are audited annually, with accompanying recommendations for the improvement of the school's business practices.
- Establish judicious procedures for handling incoming funds, investing surpluses wisely for short periods.
- Set up sound procedures for ordering supplies and for the payment of bills.
- Negotiate the best financing available for capital expenditures or for short-term loans.
- Arrange adequate insurance, including faculty-staff liability, at the best rates.
- Be certain that legal requirements are fulfilled for tax exemptions and for foundation proposals.
- Maintain a five-year projection of the school's finances to keep the

board alert to future financial demands.

- See that all the school's legal documents are listed in the master book of minutes and are kept in a safety deposit box. (Lowrie, 1998)

Over the years I have used the above items as a checklist to make sure that as the administrative head of the school, I handled fiduciary responsibilities properly.

In short, we must take appropriate precautions in order to administer properly the money given to our Christian schools (2 Corinthians 8:18–22; 1 Corinthians 16:2, 3). Perhaps we can infer from texts like these that one person shouldn't handle all the incoming and outgoing money. Another related precaution common to Christian schools requires two signatures on checks of over $500 or some other designated amount.

Structure of the Budget

A solid budget projects anticipated income and expenses. In Christian schools, income generally comes from tuition and fees, special fund-raisers, capital campaigns, and earnings from investments or endowments.

Expenses usually fall into two areas, operational and capital expenses. Typically, we classify operational expenses as program expenses, those costs directly related to delivering the product—instruction, administrative expenses, managerial support for the school, and property and facility expenses. Powerful budgeting begins with well-defined policies. Consider some policies that can add strength and meaning to your budget:

- Financial aid is set to ten percent of gross tuition receipts.
- Salaries are preapproved by the board.
- Tuition rates are carefully studied and preapproved by the board.
- Capitalized versus expensed items are carefully defined so one can't hide expenses on the balance sheet.
- Key ratios, such as both deficit and administrative overhead, are defined as a percent of revenue. Then you can quickly determine when the financial picture begins to deteriorate. (John Thomas, personal communication)

Long-range planning takes policies like these and turns them into key assumptions. These assumptions form the backbone of a long-range financial forecast. If properly integrated, the long-range plan provides guidance for each one-year budget and becomes the budget for the budget, so to speak. We can see how this kind of financial planning can easily set the stage for substantive multiple-year financial planning.

Early in my efforts to raise money for the Academy, I attended a meeting with the chief executive officer of a large Chicago area corporation. After we engaged in some small talk, this friend and supporter of the school asked me to tell him about the three-year and five-year financial plans for the

Academy. I couldn't answer him because we had no viable three-, five-, or ten-year financial plans. We just lived from annual budget to annual budget.

That experience, along with the persistence of several trustees on our board, became the catalyst for our school to hammer out an annually updated five-year financial plan, which has proved over the last ten years to be the cornerstone of our financial planning.

The revenue assumptions used in our five-year plan include projections related to enrollment, tuition rate, fee rate, financial aid, multiple-child discounts, employee tuition discounts, attrition, receivable write-down, bookstore and cafeteria income, and other income. The expense-related assumptions include faculty compensation, administrative and maintenance compensation, operating expenses, occupancy costs, and mortgage expenses.

One of the most difficult areas to manage is budget flexibility. The budget *must be kept*, but within certain flexible guidelines. Ultimately though, the grand total *must not be violated!* Here confidence in and respect for your CFO (chief financial officer) becomes critical (John Thomas, personal communication).

Respect for the CFO makes possible the effective accomplishment of the school's mission within the boundaries of its resources, because even a one-year budget is only a projection. Managing actual as opposed to projected budgets becomes the "art work" of the CFO. If he or she does well, the mission will be accomplished, the budget balanced, and cash flow adequate. However, that scenario does not mean that areas dictated by mission will never go slightly over budget.

Managing a capital campaign or major building project is slightly different from managing daily operations. Cash flow becomes a distinct process requiring forecasting, tracking, and careful attention. Other areas impact expenditures versus budget as well:

- Purchasing policies
- Managerial discretion (Can the headmaster violate the budget?)
- Vendor relationships
- Departmental structure and purchasing authority

Capital expenses relate to buildings, equipment, and technology systems. These one-time costs have an ongoing value to the school (Anthony, 2001). Administrators in Christian schools must understand the distinct components of the budget and their delicate interplay.

The Budgeting Process

The budgetary process requires decision making initiated by the school administration. Before the process can begin, the school must have its philosophy, mission, and vision for the future clearly in place. Beyond that, the administrator—with input from faculty, staff, and trustees—

should prepare an educational plan for the year, along with an accounting of anticipated costs.

Who Is Responsible?

The school budget becomes the educational plan expressed in terms of desired expenditures and anticipated income. In smaller schools the administrator alone may prepare, present, and defend the budget. Such an administrator serves part-time not only as the CEO but also the CFO. In somewhat larger schools, the business manager serves as point person in the budgeting process. The business manager or the administrator elicits input from teachers, staff, and often department heads. The administrator and the finance committee of the board also provide input. Then the business manager builds the expense side of the budget.

It is tempting for overwhelmed Christian school administrators, especially those of us who like to focus on academic issues, just to add a percentage for inflation to last year's expenses. Zero-based budgeting, which demands that we justify every dollar and each account, begins with zero and builds on actual needs and projections for the forthcoming year. This approach offers a financially healthier way to budget (Miller, 1998).

Christian schools need to project conservatively for expected revenue from tuition, fees, interest, investment income, and gifts. Failing to meet revenue projections can be as traumatic to schools as allowing expenses to go over budget.

How Do We Balance the Budget?

We consider a budget balanced when income and expenses match. I know of a Christian school that after a number of years of financial ups and downs gained increased credibility among parents, alumni, and the local Christian community as a whole just by being able to report each year that they had balanced the budget with a little surplus. That report also increased donor confidence. Giving goes up when a Christian school's *financial house* is in order.

In all our efforts to manage and control the budget, let us not forget our biblical responsibility to provide financial aid to single parents and families with limited income that truly want Christian education for their children. We should help people according to their resources and needs (Leviticus 25:14–17, Deuteronomy 24:17).

When Does Budget Planning Take Place?

But, you may ask, when should all this work on the budget be completed? Let me suggest a time for preparing the budget, presenting it, and getting it formally approved.

October/November: Project enrollment and determine anticipated staff size for the forthcoming year. Be realistic in your enrollment projections and in the teacher-to-student class ratios.

December/January: Determine compensation costs and establish tuition and fee levels. At this point, department heads and faculty can provide valuable input. The school administrator, the school business manager, and the finance committee of the board then need to design a recommended budget for the forthcoming year.

February/March: In our school, the business manager presents the proposed budget. In some schools, the administrator may handle that. In others, either the chairman of the finance committee or the board treasurer may do the honors. Whoever presents the budget should be prepared to justify each item. By then approving the budget, the board allows the administrator to proceed with reenrollment of students and rehiring of staff. In some schools, the budget must also be approved by voting members of the governing body composed of parents and others interested in the school.

September/October: After the fall term has begun, determine the actual enrollment, accompanying revenue, and staff salary expenses. Since tuition is the primary source of income and salaries are the primary expense, you can now revise the budget with these established figures to ensure a positive cash flow and a balanced budget by the end of the year.

Compensation

Salaries and fringe benefits are important variables in the budgeting process. Compensation may comprise up to seventy-five percent of the costs on the expense side of the ledgers, a major factor to be reckoned with when creating a budget. Expect annual tension between appropriate teacher compensation and affordable student tuition. Every administrator deals with this challenge.

Purchasing Policies

Effective budget control includes appropriate requisitioning and purchasing of school materials and supplies. Gone are the days when a Christian school teacher can, on a whim, make a purchase and then ask for compensation when the money spent is not in that teacher's preapproved budget. Well-run schools require a written request or requisition to the administrator or department head. An approved requisition should result in a purchase order, which authorizes the purchase. The purchase order then becomes a contract between the school and the vendor.

Tuition and Fees

Tuition and fee schedules cut to the heart of the school's philosophy and vision. Raising tuition too high may create the impression of a rich kids' school, excluding students from less affluent families. Not raising tuition to appropriate levels can result in poor compensation for teachers, inadequately funded programs, and deteriorating facilities. Tuition should be based on the history or experience of the school and its vision for the future.

> No matter is more closely related to morale in the Christian school than the salary structure and fringe benefits. The Christian school has a clear responsibility to compensate its employees properly in a biblical manner (Luke 10:7, 1 Corinthians 9:6–14, Galatians 6:6, Colossians 4:1). (Lowrie, 1984)

Most Christian schools cannot afford salaries equal to those of the local public schools. However, Christian schools are doing a better job today of sensitizing parents and supporters, reminding them that attracting and retaining great teachers requires aggressive and creative patterns of compensation.

We can build a climate of mutual respect and confidence among teachers and staff when the administration and board creatively consider special needs and special merit while making decisions about rewarding their faculty members. Through carefully selected tangible tokens of appreciation and creative compensation based on extra projects, extra work, or outstanding effectiveness in the classroom, you can build a faculty of great teachers.

Bookkeeping, Accounting, and Financial Reporting

Integrated software and the ever increasing power of the personal computer make bookkeeping and accounting easier than in the past. Thus we can accomplish financial reporting in a more timely and complete manner. Software and systems that allow the establishment of a common database make it possible to track and interact with students and families from recruitment through graduation. Using the same database, other software can be expanded to run the bookstore and cafeteria operations, and the library and student attendance programs. Even alumni and development offices can work from a common database and reduce the chance of duplication or error.

Responsible school administrators monitor budget accounts. We may delegate the details of that responsibility to others, but we must provide the financial data reports to the board treasurer, the finance committee, and the board as a whole. We compare income and expenses with those of previous years and decide how unused funds should be noted and used. We prepare the annual report for the board and the school's constituency so that we can determine such matters as what goals have been met and which programs need review, change, or extension in order to achieve their objectives.

The Audit

Every Christian school should have an annual general audit. The school should be audited in accordance with generally accepted accounting principles. The audit provides an opinion by the audit firm of the soundness and accuracy of the school's financial statements. Scripture admonishes us to avoid every appearance of evil (1 Thessalonians 5:22). Parents who pay tuition and donors who invest in the school want to trust its financial operations. A Christian school leader must verify, for anyone who asks, that all financial transactions are legal, accurate, and reported in accordance with accepted accounting principles.

Property and Facilities

When asking a major donor for a gift to use toward a new building project, I received this response: "What are your plans to maintain the building?" His concern was that we might build a new building and then in ten or fifteen years it would fall into such disrepair that we would have to raise money for another new building. Maintenance means keeping the school's property, facilities, and equipment in the best possible condition of completeness, functionality, and efficiency. Such housekeeping or custodial duties provide students and teachers with facilities that are clean and conducive to teaching and learning. Careful planning and budgeting allow the people involved in property and facilities to support the mission of the school. I admire a sister Christian school that invites its support staff, including its property and facilities people, to march at graduation with the school's faculty.

Board members hesitate to commit adequate funds to maintenance because the negative impact of neglecting this area is not immediately seen. Nevertheless, a policy that demands excellence in maintenance and support functions must have full board support. Otherwise you will "liquidate" your facilities one year at a time until the costs to fix them are huge. The quickest way to increase turnover in your support staff is to complain about lack of excellence but fail to support them with adequate resources.

Insurance

Good administrators select and maintain school insurance. We live in a litigious society. Insurance premiums have increased dramatically in the last few years. Property insurance, liability insurance, and personnel welfare insurance (health, accident, and life) are important and need regular review to ensure appropriate coverage and to assess their impact on the budget.

Managing a school budget well provides a platform from which to talk about excellence in other areas of the school's program. More importantly, good management of the school budget gives school leaders the wherewithal to create a vision and to implement it. Sound money management in the Christian school provides one of the greatest catalysts to transform vision into an educational plan that can greatly impact many students' lives, not only for now but for generations to come.

I believe you have a vision for your school. That vision will determine your school's budget. How you handle your school's budget will, to a large extent, determine whether your school's vision becomes reality.

Bibliography

Anthony, M. J. (Ed.). (2001). *Evangelical dictionary of Christian education.* Grand Rapids, MI: Baker Academie.

Blue, R. (1997). *Master your money.* Nashville: Thomas Nelson.

Haycock, R. C. (1993). *Encyclopedia of Bible truths for school subjects.* Colorado Springs: Association of Christian Schools International.

J. K. Lasser Institute. (1994). *How to run a small business.* New York: McGraw-Hill.

Lowrie, R. W. Jr. (Ed.). (1984). *Administration of the Christian school.* Colorado Springs: Association of Christian Schools International.

Lowrie, R. W. Jr. (1998). *Serving God on the Christian school board.* (2nd ed.). Colorado Springs: Association of Christian Schools International.

Miller, R. M. (Ed.). (1998). *How to start a Christian school.* Colorado Springs: Association of Christian Schools International.

Robert D. Herman and Associates. (1994). *The Jossey-Bass handbook of nonprofit leadership and management.* San Francisco: Jossey-Bass.

Welsch, G. A., Hilton, R. W., & Gordon, P. N. (1998). *Budgeting, profit planning and control.* Englewood Cliffs, NJ: Prentice Hall.

Nehemiah and the Golden Rule

Finding Friends and Funds

Stephen Dill, Ed.D.

Chapter Summary

If your experience is similar to that of most school administrators, you find that tuition dollars are just not enough to support your program, so you depend on the financial and volunteer support of constituent groups. But how do you establish an effective development program that can provide the funds needed beyond tuition revenue and can also support expansion of your school's overall program?

Dr. Dill, with more than twenty years of experience in school development, outlines the essential components for an effective program that every Christian school can put into practice. The process is not complicated, nor is it designed to be a quick-fix solution. Proper school development requires a commitment from your school in terms of both time and resource allocation.

About the author
Stephen Dill, Ed.D.
Assistant Headmaster, Delaware County Christian School
Newtown Square, PA
30 years of educational leadership experience

Chapter 17

Nehemiah and the Golden Rule
Finding Friends and Funds

Stephen Dill, Ed.D.

When God gave Nehemiah a vision for a new task, rebuilding the wall of Jerusalem, Nehemiah did not hesitate to seek out the needed resources to implement that vision. As God shaped this vision in his heart for rebuilding the wall, Nehemiah began to see achievement that "the experts" said was impossible. Leaders paint a picture of possibility and encourage others to participate in developing that picture.

Nehemiah shared his vision with the king of Persia and asked him for a major gift. He prayed for God's help before he made the request, and acknowledged that God's hand of blessing brought the results. When he arrived in Jerusalem, Nehemiah shared his vision with the leaders of Jerusalem. God gave him success in raising friends and funds for the task given to him. Successfully finding friends and funds is a challenging and rewarding component of Christian school leadership.

Christian schools, like all nonprofit organizations, depend on supportive constituencies. Although specific audiences and levels of support vary considerably among schools, strengthening and expanding that support is not an optional leadership task. In essence, we communicate an urgent mission and a compelling vision utilizing a variety of methods. The process takes the form of a triangle that represents levels of commitment to the school. Leaders increase the degree of commitment among existing supporters while expanding the number of people who have some degree of interest in the school. In essence, we seek to move people up the triangle to higher levels of commitment and involvement while expanding the base of the triangle with new supporters.

We commonly call this process of building support *development* or *advancement*. Many educational institutions employ a director of development or a vice president for advancement who assumes responsibility for development. These staffing patterns assume that institutional activities of strategic significance need adequate staffing and that the development function has major long-range significance for schools. Consider a simple definition: *development is a leadership process that articulates the vision and goals of the school and secures the necessary resources to implement those goals through a planned program of prayer, marketing, and fundraising.*

The remainder of this chapter seeks to explain the development concept and explore strategies and staffing that often bring development success to educational institutions. There are, however, several prerequisites that must be in place before a successful development program can be launched.

Prerequisites for Development

At the heart of every successful organization, you will find an *inner core of committed leaders*. Schools that implement their mission and vision have capable leaders (plural) on the board and among the administration and the faculty. The "benevolent dictatorship" style of leadership can be effective on a short-term basis, but effective schools build leadership teams at all levels. Leadership is a prerequisite for development; chapters 2 through 4 of this text address these leadership issues in more depth.

A second prerequisite for a successful development program is the presence of an *effective educational program* in the school. Although development professionals may think that their task lies at the core of the school, development remains peripheral to the school's basic purpose. Developing curriculum, training and retaining faculty, achieving accreditation, and developing our students as faith defenders are core issues covered in other chapters. *As we accomplish the core mission, many "development" functions can take place without active school management.* Goodwill, additional students, and financial support become natural by-products when parents, grandparents, and friends see the impact of Christian education in the lives of students. It is notable that outstanding development programs will have little effect if we neglect the core mission.

Third, a successful development program requires *prayer*. In the early years of our movement, some viewed development as a worldly activity unnecessary for truly Christian schools. Leaders stated that they trusted God, not development directors, and prayer would be their primary fundraising method. This approach, often based on accounts of George Mueller's approach to caring for orphans in nineteenth-century England, is hardly the *only* fund-raising method that is biblical. However, as the Christian school movement has matured and the numbers of students and dollars have significantly increased, the pendulum has swung in the other direction. Today some act as if friends and funds derive solely from effective development programs.

The Bible often mentions the link between faith and works, human effort and divine provision. The exact nature of the relationship is a mystery, but there can be no doubt that we are to place our total trust in God and yet work diligently in His vineyard. Paul the Apostle expresses this truth: "We proclaim him, admonishing and teaching everyone with all wisdom, so that we may present everyone perfect in Christ. To this end I labor, struggling with all his energy, which so powerfully works in me" (Colossians 1:28, 29).

It seems that we court error when we emphasize human effort alone or divine provision alone. In my initial interview to move into a development responsibility more than twenty years ago, an older and wiser board member gave me this advice: I should pray as if I were not working at all and work as if I were not praying at all. Nehemiah demonstrated the proper role of prayer in leadership with his prayer for his people and his brief prayer before asking the king for support (Nehemiah 1:5–11, 2:4).

God provides friends, funds, and students for our Christian schools. We emphasize prayer for God's grace in the relationships with parents, faculty, administration, the development committee, and the board. But that emphasis on prayer must not excuse us from working diligently to communicate our mission and vision and to invite others to invest in our ministry.

Strategic Planning

Although chapter 15 addresses this topic in detail, an effective development process begins here. Supporters of any ministry want to know about the mission, vision, and plans for that ministry. The cry for mission-driven programs and marketing reflects the importance of clearly articulating the mission of the school. Not many years ago, donors would support ministries because of their loyalty to those ministries. Donors today focus more on mission, vision, goals, and results. They want to know how their dollars will accomplish strategic plans.

Mission defines why the school exists. It is broad and general. In his book *The Power of Vision*, George Barna provides a helpful distinction between mission and vision. He writes that "mission is essentially a philosophic statement that undergirds the heart of your ministry." Likely, many Christian schools could share the same mission, since mission is a "definition of ministry. It is not geared to uniqueness or distinctives or directions" (1992).

Barna also observes that vision provides a more detailed painting of the future. "Vision is specific, detailed, customized, distinctive and unique" to a ministry. "It allows a leader to say no to opportunities, it provides direction, it empowers people for service, and it facilitates productivity.... The vision statement puts feet on the mission. While the mission statement is philosophic in nature, the vision statement is strategic in nature" (1992).

Clear and compelling mission and vision statements offer powerful foundational tools for effective development programs. Strategic planning takes those statements and draws a specific design on them. A complete strategic plan gives specificity to goals, strategies, programs, facilities, and finances. Major donors look for organizations with stretching yet feasible strategic plans.

Marketing, Public Relations, and the Golden Rule

In the development cycle, "friend raising" precedes fund-raising. The friend-raising process begins simply with the identification of various publics that make up the current and potential audiences for the school. Every school serves not one, but many "publics," and the list will vary in different situations. The publics for church-sponsored schools include parents who attend the church, church members who do not have children in the school, and school parents who do not attend the sponsoring church. We can think of constituencies in terms of concentric circles of importance. At the center of the circle we see the internal audiences—board, faculty, and staff. The very next circle includes parents and students, followed by a circle representing institutional "relatives"—alumni, parents of alumni, and grandparents of current students. The outer circles include the Christian community and the geographic community. Attention and resources initially target inner circles and then move outward.

Public relations and *marketing* are not synonymous terms. Historically, schools have embraced public relations and failed to understand marketing. In a classic textbook *School Public Relations*, Leslie W. Kindred defined public relations as "a process of communication between the school and the community for the purpose of increasing citizen understanding of educational needs and practices and encouraging intelligent citizen interest and cooperation in the work of improving the school" (1957). Although this definition depicts a two-way flow of information between the school and community, the term "public relations" often carries a connotation of one-way communication from the school to various external audiences. In the recommended two-way communication, Christian school leaders must educate parents about the philosophy of Christian school education. An effective public relations program assists in meeting this challenge.

Understanding Marketing

Marketing implies a very different approach with an emphasis on listening to what the "customer" wants, more of a mind-set than an activity. A marketing mind-set values the benefits of the school program for students and parents, though it also includes the belief that everything we do can be improved. It includes passion about the issues that concern people as well as response to their concerns.

Although some believers think marketing has no place in Christian organizations, we consider a marketing orientation very important in seeking friends and funds for schools. Jesus Himself gave us the Golden Rule, which has also been referred to as the Golden Rule of Marketing: "Treat people the same way you want them to treat you" (Matthew 7:12, NASB). A marketing orientation portrays an attitude of servanthood, modeled for us in the ultimate sense by our Lord and Master, Jesus Christ. Obviously we do not shape doctrinal statements on the basis of market surveys. But a commitment to marketing means we work diligently at listening to the opinions of the families we serve. We can listen informally and formally. Some Christian schools do extensive and systematic surveys of alumni, faculty and staff, school parents, and nonschool Christian parents.

The Marketing Plan

Your marketing plan flows out of your strategic plan. The marketing plan identifies objectives, target audiences, strategies, and means of measurement. While most schools have enrollment goals, few break down those goals to specific objectives. Consider a few examples of specific marketing objectives:

- Increase the number of inquiries for admission from (a region, a church, for certain grade levels, etc.) by fifteen percent.
- Survey fifteen preschool directors about their perception of your school, and provide informational materials and a personal open house invitation to them and their school families.
- Listen to perceptions of each of the pastors of the ten largest churches represented in your school family and provide them with informational materials.
- Increase student enrollment to twenty percent for (ethnic, denominational, church families, nonchurch families, etc.).
- Develop printed materials that will enhance your basic informational packet for prospective parents.
- Provide published alumni news twice a year; increase alumni reunion attendance by ten percent.

Marketing Strategies for Internal Audiences

If we display love and service for people, we will see positive results in our internal audiences. This demonstration begins as the school administration works diligently to communicate effectively in three directions: with the board, with the faculty and staff, and with the parents. We must view parents as partners, not critics. Every school must cope with difficult parents, but the negative minority must not color our view of all parents. If parents are partners, they deserve timely and accurate information about their children's progress or problems. They deserve to have phone calls returned and letters answered promptly. Callers should gain quick access to a warm and friendly human voice that welcomes their questions.

Parents should receive a written news/prayer letter with school calendar updates on a regular (monthly) basis. This strategy may seem obvious, but we can waste complex and expensive advertising and direct-mail campaign efforts if we do not give priority to internal audiences. The very best marketing is unsolicited endorsement from the mouths of satisfied customers.

A Sampling of Marketing Strategies for External Audiences

The fundamental building block for friend raising is the *mailing list*. Someone in the office must consider as a responsibility of great importance the care for and expansion of the database. Inexpensive software programs make this task easy, although you will be better served if your development software integrates with other applications such as adequate receipts, thank you letters, mailing labels, donor relationships, and giving histories. The system should also store email addresses and facilitate sending email messages to groups since many of today's parents and young alumni are more likely to read and respond to email than printed letters.

We can use direct conversation to communicate with internal audiences, and printed materials to express the school's mission and accomplishments to external audiences. Although electronic methods of communication are likely to become primary in the future, printed materials continue to offer the best link between the school and its institutional relatives (alumni, former parents, grandparents, prospective parents, interested friends, and donors). Every school should utilize a *professionally designed newsletter* with good pictures, uncluttered layout, and mission-appropriate news. It's better to produce only two or three per school year than to send unprofessional versions more frequently.

Prospective school parents make up a very significant audience (admissions and recruitment issues are discussed in depth in chapter 9). Essentials include an attractive *package of materials* sent promptly upon request, a professional website that includes detailed information about the school, and personal follow-up inviting prospects for a campus visit. In most Christian schools, campus visits result in a high yield of applications.

Multimedia tools that appeal to both sight and hearing can be powerful communication tools. For example, you can produce an excellent videotape or compact disc that communicates the right messages about your school.

Once you make the initial investment, producing multiple copies is inexpensive. Information packets for today's prospective school parents can include a video or CD at reasonable cost.

Attention from the news media may come at the wrong time for the wrong reasons, and you must be prepared to handle those occasions. But cultivating *relationships with the news media* can bring opportunities to communicate your school's mission and programs to a wider audience. At local newspapers, staff members decide what to include, and they should have a connection with someone from your school. Although breaking into major metropolitan media can be very difficult, local papers generally have community acceptance and are willing to carry most of the local news they receive. When school news appears in the local paper, internal morale gains strength, and external audiences pay attention.

Successful Fund-Raising

The definition of development given at the beginning of this chapter includes fund-raising as one component of the cycle. However, the general public often views development as fund-raising. The term "fund-raising" sometimes refers to candy sales and auctions. In this chapter, it describes *voluntary gifts given in support of the mission and vision of a particular institution*. Needs of Christian schools continually increase as the schools move toward excellence yet seek to maintain affordability. Trustees place heavy pressure on development officers to produce results, which means to bring in more money. Several years ago I received a "help" letter from a newly appointed director of development. He wrote:

> Our needs here are many and great. We received $209,000 this year from tuition, but we budgeted in the neighborhood of $450,000. We have sold property this year to clear the year in the black, *but next year we cannot sell it again. So, I have to figure out ways to raise money*. We have tentatively scheduled a car wash and an auction. Beyond this, I am really begging for ideas to generate the funds we will need to keep the school going this coming year. [italics added for emphasis]

Many people picture crisis fund-raising, as illustrated in this example, when they think about development. But that picture is inaccurate. Christian school development extends opportunities to supporters to make significant and sometimes urgent investments in a ministry of critical importance. We should focus on the participation of people in a worthwhile mission—not on trying to raise large sums of money at the last minute to meet our budgets.

Types of Gifts

There are three main categories of gift support that schools seek. *Annual gifts* augment tuition and fees by supporting current operating expenses. These gifts may be undesignated or designated for scholarships, enhancements to curriculum or facilities, or other current operational needs. *Capital gifts* provide major additions to a school—usually property or new facilities—and endowment funds. The third category we call planned or *deferred gifts*. These gifts that are planned through wills or trusts can provide income or security for family members while they are alive and eventually result in a significant gift to the school. A mature development program pays constant attention to all three categories.

Major Gifts

The familiar eighty/twenty rule, which states that twenty percent of the people do eighty percent of the work in any organization, can be applied to fund-raising efforts. Typically, ninety percent or more of the funds that are raised come from ten percent or less of the people. We dare not limit our sovereign God by fund-raising formulas; He can choose to provide for His work in unique ways. But generally, in large fund-raising campaigns for Christian schools, the eighty/twenty or ninety/ten rule tends to hold true. This fact means that schools must seek large gifts.

Scripture clearly points out the dangers of giving special privileges or recognition because of wealth (James 2). However, it also speaks about the responsibility of those who have significant resources:

> Command those who are rich in this present world not to be arrogant nor to put their hope in wealth, which is so uncertain, but to put their hope in God, who richly provides us with everything for our enjoyment. Command them to do good, to be rich in good deeds, and to be generous and willing to share. In this way they will lay up treasure for themselves as a firm foundation for the coming age, so that they may take hold of the life that is truly life. (1 Timothy 6:17–19)

This passage supports the concept that we should approach people who have material wealth differently. Some may think the best way to raise $250,000 for a new library is to find 250 people who will each give $1,000. This approach represents good math, but poor fund-raising. In reality, most Christian school constituents can't afford to give $1,000, yet some could give far more.

During the stock market growth of the 1990s, many wealthy people became more wealthy. A surprising number of people among Christian school supporters can donate large gifts. Paying attention to the major donor process is an important development responsibility. This process includes identification, cultivation, solicitation, and appreciation of major donors. Schools must also develop all the other levels of support. Many small gifts add up to a large gift. The analogy of a triangle described at the beginning of this chapter suggests that the development challenge involves continuing to add more donors (expanding the base) and moving donors up the triangle to greater levels of commitment. The tip of the triangle represents major donors.

Four Main Issues Impacting Fund-Raising Success

Case: We believe that Christian education is a cause worthy of support. But why do we? And why should people support a particular Christian school? Every school should articulate the answers to these questions. We call the written answer a case statement. The case statement must be a clear and compelling expression of what God is doing at a school and why this particular project represents a very worthwhile investment. An articulate case statement will guide verbal presentations, audiovisual messages, and formal publications. We produce new case statements for a capital campaign, but the school should always have available a relatively recent case for support of the school. In his classic text *Designs for Fund-Raising*, Harold Seymour says that the case "should aim high, provide perspective, arouse a sense of history and continuity, convey a feeling of importance, relevance, and urgency, and have whatever stuff is needed to warm the heart and stir the mind" (1966/1988).

Prospects: Fund-raising success demands an adequate base of prospects while we continue to find more potential donors. The best ideas come from records of the past. A development program should work diligently to manage those records and acknowledge important gifts made by everyone supporting the school. The mailing list should grow through the addition of prospective school parents, potential friends, new alumni and alumni parents, and new donors.

In view of the earlier discussion about major gifts for any school, a key committee should pay attention to the major gift process. This committee will look at past, present, and potential major gift sources for the school. The committee will discuss existing and potential donors as it tries to develop new sources of support for the school.

Leadership: Successful campaigns depend on successful volunteers. Although the staff who work in these efforts are critically important, they cannot achieve development goals without the help of volunteer leadership, and volunteering begins with the trustees. Board members must understand and support the development function through their own financial involvement in the school. Schools should always look for ways to enlist additional volunteer leaders who have significant influence in the community. Generally, the commitment of known leaders encourages the involvement of others.

Staffing: Schools must designate resources to tasks of importance if they want those tasks completed. Christian schools have been reluctant to fund development staff because of other urgent needs. Such shortsighted thinking ignores the fact that a successful development program brings enrollment growth and thereby enables the funding of other worthwhile programs.

Where do Christian schools find willing, capable, and effective development staff members? Some prerequisites are the same as for any other employee, beginning with a personal commitment to Christ. Development staff must also have a bone-deep commitment to the schools they represent. If our representatives don't believe in the program deep down, they will not be very effective. Other important qualities include the abilities to function as a team player, to organize, and to communicate. Helen Colson, in *Philanthropy at Independent Schools*, writes:

> A development director is an advocate, and the most effective advocates are passionate about their cause. A development director is a professional, and the best professionals have high standards, extensive knowledge, and a desire to learn even more. A development director is also a leader and a follower, a teacher and a student. It's a worthwhile challenge—but it's not an easy job. (1996)

Sometimes schools find an experienced development director, but most schools end up looking to their existing constituencies in order to create their development staff. Perhaps an existing faculty member or parent has the personal qualities needed to become an effective development representative for the school. However, development leadership cannot be totally delegated.

School administrators often come to that role through early experience in the classroom. They usually bring experience in curriculum, personnel, and student discipline, but they often lack experience in financial management and development leadership. Top leaders in Christian schools have more in common with Christian college presidents than with public school principals. The top leadership roles in Christian schools and colleges include the ultimate responsibility for financial, academic, and development issues. Most college presidents give more of their time and focus to development issues. Christian school leaders must also model leadership in development by taking every opportunity to communicate the mission and vision of the institution and by becoming involved in the cultivation and solicitation of major donors.

Constituents

Should we employ outside consultants? Those with experience and strong recommendations from other clients can be very helpful in establishing a development office or providing guidance for a major capital campaign. Experienced consultants can give an objective third-party opinion regarding case, prospects, leadership, and staffing. They can also furnish critical expertise in the major donor process.

Fund-raising that honors God is ministry. Building relationships with people lies at the core of development activity, and people give to people. In *The Ministry of Fund Raising*, Whitney Kuniholm (1990) clearly articulates the biblical basis for fund-raising and explains its ministry to donors. Sharing needs and results, calling people to discipleship and obedience in giving, and using personal relationships for counseling and encouragement—they all add up to ministry.

Just as God used Nehemiah's leadership to accomplish His mission, God will use Christian school leaders—men and women who have been called to lead—to accomplish the mission of Christian education. God blessed Nehemiah's efforts to share the vision with leaders, the people of Jerusalem, and major donors. God will also use Christian school leaders who understand the importance of a solid base of friends. He will bless requests for support when we bathe those requests in prayer and honor Him.

Remember, not every effort will bring success. Development is similar to evangelism. None of us can lead someone else to Christ. We can share the gospel, but only the Holy Spirit convicts of sin and nudges the heart. In development work, we share the mission and vision, ask for support, and trust God for the results. Nehemiah persevered in the midst of strong opposition in order to accomplish the goal. God expects us to do the same. "Therefore, my dear brothers, stand firm. Let nothing move you. Always give yourselves fully to the work of the Lord, because you know that your labor in the Lord is not in vain" (1 Corinthians 15:58).

Bibliography

Barna, G. (1988). *Marketing the church*. Colorado Springs: NavPress.

Barna, G. (1992). *The power of vision*. Ventura, CA: Regal Books.

Broce, T. E. (1986). *Fund raising: The guide to raising money from private sources* (2nd ed.). Norman: The University of Oklahoma.

Bryson, J. M. (1988). *Strategic planning for public and non-profit organizations*. San Francisco: Jossey-Bass.

Collins, J. C., & Porras, J. I. (1994). *Built to last: Successful habits of visionary companies*. New York: HarperBusiness.

Colson, H. A. (1996). *Philanthropy at independent schools*. Washington, DC: National Association of Independent Schools.

Conway, D., & Hart Price, C. (Eds.). (1997). *The practice of stewardship in religious fundraising*. San Francisco: Jossey-Bass.

Dove, K. E. (1988). *Conducting a successful capital campaign*. San Francisco: Jossey-Bass.

Drucker, P. F. (1990). *Managing the non-profit organization*. New York: HarperCollins.

Elve, P. (1984). *Financing Christian schools*. Grand Rapids, MI: Christian Schools International.

Englund, G. (1993). *Beyond death and taxes*. Boston: Estate Planning.

Getz, G. A. (1990). *Real prosperity: Biblical principles of material possessions*. Chicago: Moody.

Jeavons, T. H. (1994). *When the bottom line is faithfulness: Management of Christian service organizations*. Bloomington, IN: Indiana University.

Jeavons, T. H., & Burcbah Basinger, R. (2000). *Growing givers' hearts: Treating fundraising as ministry*. San Francisco: Jossey-Bass.

Katzenback, J. R., & Smith, D. K. (1993). *The wisdom of teams: Creating high performance organizations*. New York: HarperBusiness.

Kindred, L. W. (1957). *School public relations*. Englewood Cliffs, NJ: Prentice-Hall.

Kouzes, J. M., & Poshner, B. Z. (1993). *The leadership challenge*. San Francisco: Jossey-Bass.

Kuniholm, W. (1990). *The ministry of fund raising*. Washington, DC: Prison Fellowship Ministries.

Lockerbie, D. B. (1995). *From candy sales to committed donors*. Milwaukee, WI: Christian Stewardship Association.

Lord, J. G. (1983). *The raising of money: Thirty-five essentials every trustee should know*. Cleveland, OH: Third Sector.

Pollard, C. W. (1996). *The soul of the firm*. Grand Rapids, MI: HarperBusiness & Zondervan.

Ries, A., & Trout, J. (2001). *Positioning: The battle for your mind*. New York: McGraw Hill.

Rosso, H. A. (1991). *Achieving excellence in fundraising: A comprehensive guide to principles, strategies and methods*. San Francisco: Jossey-Bass.

Seymour, H. J. (1988). *Designs for fund-raising*. New York: McGraw-Hill. (Original work published 1966)

Stone, S. C. (1993). *Shaping strategy: Independent school planning in the 90's*. Washington, DC: National Association of Independent Schools.

Vincent, M. (1997). *Teaching a Christian view of money: Celebrating God's generosity*. Scottdale, PA: Herald Press.

Williams, K. (1997). *Donor focused strategies for annual giving*. New York: Aspen Publishers.

Navigating the Maze
Coping with Constant Change

Jerry L. Haddock, Ed.D.

Chapter Summary

How do you handle change in your school? Granted, some changes are absolutely unacceptable, particularly those that violate the Scriptures. But you live in a changing world. Are you proactive or reactive to those changes that press in? As the educational leader in your school, do you manage and direct changes, or do they manage you?

Coping with change does not have to be reactionary. Dr. Haddock identifies principles that you as an educational leader can readily put into practice. Preparing for change and responding appropriately characterize mature leadership and foster stability in your school. New opportunities arise when change comes. You can view it as such and take advantage of it for the betterment of your school.

About the author

Jerry L. Haddock, Ed.D.
Director, ASCI Southern California Region
LaHabra, CA
24 years of educational leadership experience

Chapter 18

Navigating the Maze
Coping with Constant Change

Jerry L. Haddock, Ed.D.

In his simple yet amusing parable *Who Moved My Cheese?* Spencer Johnson reveals profound truths about change through four imaginary characters—the mice, *Sniff* and *Scurry*, and the little people, *Hem* and *Haw*. As Johnson leads us through this make-believe maze of life, he effectively portrays parts of all of us in each character. Sometimes we may act like *Sniff*, who sniffs out change early, or *Scurry*, who scurries into action, or *Hem*, who denies and resists change because he fears it will lead to something worse, or *Haw*, who learns to adapt in time when he sees change leading to something *better* (1998)!

As Christian school leaders, we quickly learn one thing about change—it is constant! If we ask any seasoned administrator about what has happened in Christian schooling over the past thirty to forty years, we are sure to hear a litany of changes. Society has changed. Demographics have changed. Technology has changed. The family unit has changed. Jobs have changed. Ways of doing our work have changed. Everything around us exists in a state of upheaval. We might more easily list those areas of life that have *not* changed, even over the last two or three decades.

The number of changes escalates as external forces increase pressure on our society. We shouldn't be surprised. Consider the following hard statistics by the organizational change authorities Pritchett and Pound:

> [T]he human population of our planet didn't reach a billion until the early 1860s.... Within ... 75 years, the head count *doubled* to

two billion…. By 1975, it doubled *again* to four billion…. Today we're closing in on six billion, with U.S. Census statistics predicting a world population of ten billion by the year 2040. (1995)

We've experienced an increase of ten times in world population in 180 years! As the population increases, so do our uses of technology. "It is said that well over eighty percent of the world's technological advances have occurred since 1900 … a rapidly accelerating rate of technological advances are basically guaranteed" (Pritchett & Pound, 1995). As further evidence of rapid advances, a recent report from Berkeley University maintains "there were 130 websites in 1993. By June 2000, the figure had risen to 17,119,262. And over the next twenty-four hours another 4 million new pages will appear on the web" ("The Real Value," 2001).

Consider information. Did you know that "there was more information produced in the thirty years between 1965 and 1995 than was produced in the entire 5,000-year period from 3000 B.C. to 1965"? We are now being told "that the amount of information available in the world is doubling every five years" (Pritchett & Pound, 1995).

Nowhere are these changes more evident than in education. More than ever, Christian schools are inundated with external forces of change. Changing demographics, advancing technology, expanding research on the learning process, and newly discovered knowledge skills demand that today's educational leaders adapt quickly to change.

Structuring for Change

A *Financial Times* poll recently declared Dr. Peter Drucker the individual having the greatest influence on organizational management. In his 1995 book *Managing in a Time of Great Change*, Drucker contends that "in the next 50 years, schools and universities will change more drastically than they have since they assumed their present form more than 300 years ago when they organized themselves around the printed book." Drucker warns, "there is one clear imperative: every organization has to build the management of change into its very structure."

How do we build change management into organizational structure? First, suggests Drucker, effective leaders enable the organization to prepare for abandonment of everything it does. This preparation requires a systematic and periodic review of every service, every procedure, and every policy. The question is simple: If we did not do this already, would we be going into it now, knowing what we now know?

Second, every organization must devote itself to creating the new, including new ideas as well as continuous improvement of everything it does. The Christian school has historically been somewhat sluggish in this area. Far too often Christian school leaders find themselves desperately *reacting* to change rather than *leading* change.

Many Christian school leaders view change as an enemy of spirituality. They see any variation from traditional approaches as a slide toward secularism, as if change were in and of itself evil. One need go no further than the Christian school curriculum to make the case. Too often Christian school leaders view the curriculum as the one element that makes the school *Christian*. Many even view their particular curricular series as sacred, claiming that abandoning it would lead to the demise of the school.

Let me illustrate with an experience I had several years ago while working with a group of Christian schools in a country where such entities were just developing. Among them were several schools strongly devoted to a curriculum written from a solidly Christian worldview, though educationally unsound and flawed. Some in the group had discovered the weaknesses in those materials and wanted to change. Despite their good intentions, the controversy caused a serious division among the leaders because the resisters of change charged that those who adopted a different curriculum, albeit another Christ-centered curriculum, should no longer consider themselves Christian schools. The resisters viewed a move away from the familiar as a compromise in mission.

The above story offers a particularly interesting perspective in light of the fact that most publishers of Christ-centered textbooks used in Christian schools today did not even exist forty years ago. The point is not whether a particular Christian school curriculum is good or bad. Abundant criteria help us determine that. Rather, the lesson emphasizes that many methods and approaches are available to teach God's truth. We must find the best ones. Just as an effective administrator would not select curricular materials solely on the strength of their pedagogy with no regard to philosophical presentation, we would be equally wrong to select a Christ-centered curriculum with sloppy pedagogy. Christian schools excel only when the entire faculty is committed to meeting needs, both spiritual *and* academic. As Christian school pioneer Roy Lowrie often counseled so eloquently, "No child should receive an academic penalty because he or she attends a Christian school." Such a view requires constant assessment and refinement.

Today's world demands new skills and knowledge not even conceivable just a few years ago. Drucker reminds us that "throughout history, the craftsman who had learned a trade after five or seven years of apprenticeship had learned by age eighteen or nineteen everything he would ever need to use during his lifetime." In today's "society of organizations," Drucker continues, "it is safe to assume that anyone with any knowledge will have to acquire new knowledge every four or five years or become obsolete" (1995). Modern organizations have changed the demand for skills and knowledge. Drucker warns that "just when every technical university is geared up to teach physics, organizations need geneticists ... grizzled model makers who have spent years learning their craft are replaced with twenty-five-year-old whiz kids who know computer simulation" (1995).

The fact that our world is rapidly changing has broad implications for Christian schools. Christian school leaders face a dual challenge. *First, leaders must demonstrate competency in gauging the changing horizon in order to determine what they need to do next.* Organizational leaders who react swiftly to societal shifts have a significant advantage in a future where the rules change rapidly.

Consider the Girl Scouts of America as a prime example of an organization that perceived a changing horizon and adapted in time to reap the benefit. Nearly twenty-five years ago, the Girl Scouts realized there was a demographic shift in the United States caused by the fast growth of minority populations. As the leaders of the Girl Scouts looked to the future, they saw both a declining number of scouting-age girls and an even more drastic decline in the number of girls in the areas traditionally served by their organization.

Rather than viewing this change negatively, the leaders responded with renewed optimism. Instead of seeing a problem, they saw opportunity. "How can we restructure to attract more minority girls?" they asked. They carefully designed a new strategy to reach these children. Over fifteen percent of the Girl Scouts now belong to minority populations, a fact that helps explain why the number of Girl Scouts continues to grow in the midst of the decline in the number of scouting-age girls.

As someone perceptively said, "If you think adapting is tough duty, just see how difficult life becomes if you don't." We can imagine the problems of a Christian school that in twenty years refuses to implement technology across the curriculum, modify courses of study to include new knowledge and skills, or change marketing strategies to reach a diverse population. Even an understanding of today's youth culture, with its buster and mosaic generations, alters the approach we take in fostering spiritual formation in our students.

The second major challenge targets the administrator's ability to lead others through the change process. In every organization there are those who adapt to change early, not so early, and late (Rodgers, 1971). The two latter categories, the hesitant and late resisters, can cause school leaders to have sleepless nights. We will deal with resisters later in this chapter, but first we will look at ways Christian schools can implement change.

For the purposes of this chapter, the following section deals with two approaches in initiating change. First, *Change Through Staff Development* suggests a five-step plan for more effective employee training in change implementation. Second, *Change Through Personal Leadership* offers guidance for avoiding pitfalls and gaining the greatest amount of support possible in the change process. Both approaches are useful in coping successfully with change.

Initiating Change

The 3M company manufactures 200 new products every year! It starts with the premise that eighty percent of the products that will be on-line in ten years have not even been heard of yet. The company doesn't wait for change to happen; it creates change! Every day it looks for new opportunities or finds better methods of doing what it currently does. Should we be surprised, then, that 3M has been one of the world's most successful and enduring companies?

Someone once said that change takes place best when everything is going well. In other words, we should change it before it breaks. An anonymous author put it this way: "Do not follow where the path may lead; follow God where there is no path and leave a trail." We as Christian school leaders would do well to lead the way in discovering new paths, trying new ideas, and developing better methods. Pioneering marks good leaders.

Certainly we have learned by now that change, especially educational change, is often an experiment with ideas that show very little evidence for long-term improvement. We have all been caught up in change for its own sake. Our goal is to implement change in our schools that results in long-term improvements that help us provide students with Christ-centered education.

Effective change begins with individuals. When people change, their product or service changes also. In Christian schools, we administrators must change before we can expect teachers or staff members to change. Teachers and staff must change before we can expect significant change in our students. Certainly as Christian leaders, we have a tremendous advantage in bringing about change because we have the Holy Spirit dwelling in us. Through prayer, God gives wisdom, direction, encouragement, and correction. We can rely on the Holy Spirit for guidance.

God has also given us minds for thinking, reasoning, and creating. Our Savior encouraged us to "Love the Lord your God with all your heart and with all your soul and with all your mind" (Matthew 22:37). All Christian school administrators should take this admonition seriously. We must passionately work to make our schools the best possible environment for training and scholarship. We shoulder the responsibility for improving our students and our schools. We strive for excellence, and in doing so, we need to improve constantly, and improving means changing.

When initiating change, administrators need to lean heavily on a strong staff development program. Staff development is the vehicle through which schools can make the greatest strides in positive change. Most staff developers agree that the goal is to bring about change in knowledge, understanding, behaviors, skills, and values or beliefs. And we change in these areas as a full staff, in small groups, or as individuals.

Change Through Staff Development

Staff development is a widely used tool in schools throughout the world. Regrettably, it is misused more often than not. Again, Christian schools have a significant advantage because the Holy Spirit provides strength and wisdom for the heavy responsibility of leading personnel. We administrators need to develop a strong devotional life of prayer and Bible study. As the spiritual and instructional leaders of our schools, we must view staff development as an opportunity to mentor, cast vision, and teach new knowledge and skills. In this process, however, the staff development program must be planned and administered well.

Research consistently demonstrates that staff development has generally failed to bring about significant change in education, largely because of poor implementation. Administrators who have been unsuccessful in bringing about change through the school staff would do well to consider a new approach. Several research studies reveal significant results from change implementation programs that include, but are not limited to, the following five stages (Hall & Hord, 1987):

Stage 1   Articulating a Vision of the Change

In various studies, the variable that correlated most significantly with change implementation was the principal's passion and ability to articulate a vision of what the school could become. The studies revealed that the more the principal supported the teachers and worked with them in their efforts to change, the more the teachers succeeded at doing so.

Stage 2   Plan and Provide Resources

This stage of change implementation is vital and is widely used in schools. During this process, however, most staff development programs flounder. This stage includes presenting theory, or describing a new skill or behavior deemed useful or desirable. The material is presented in a one-way delivery mode to a passive audience. Resources are generally provided to implement the plan. One research study revealed that staff development ending at this level resulted in only ten percent of the participants being able to transfer the new skill to the workplace (Bush, 1984). Yet this description gives the general approach used in most educational settings.

Stage 3   Invest in Training and Development

Despite the well-recorded research about effective staff development, the temptation remains to implement the *Three-Step Fable*, which suggests:

1. give teachers the box of materials,
2. provide a half-day orientation, and
3. bid them Godspeed and good luck! (James, Hord, & Pratt, 1988)

This three-step approach to educational change assumes that teachers can implement the new information and/or skill with little or no additional assistance. However, this approach has proven ineffective. We need to view staff development as a long-term project, not a quick-fix assignment.

Stage 4   Assess or Monitor Progress

Research associate Shirley Hord had this to say about the fourth stage of change implementation:

> It is at this point that change efforts typically fall apart. Leaders and leadership teams are frequently uncomfortable in executing this strategy. However, intervention study results … reported that the frequency of monitoring interventions correlated significantly with a higher degree of implementation. (1994)

Stage 5   Provide Continuous Assistance

Often referred to as coaching, consultation, or follow-up, this component provides assistance on the basis of information gathered in the assessment. Again, the Bush study revealed that when coaching is provided as a component in change implementation, up to ninety-five percent of the participants transferred the skill into classroom practice (1984). Compare this finding to that of stage one, which produced only ten percent results when presented as the sole component of the change process!

Change Through Personal Leadership

Leadership is "the process of persuasion or example by which an individual … induces a group to pursue objectives held by the leader, or shared by the leader and his or her followers" (Gardner, 1990). As stated earlier, change must start with people, not with the organization. Too often we see overly zealous administrators come to a new school and immediately take on the school as a change project. This approach violates two very basic but important rules of school leadership.

First, administrators should make a careful study of the school before initiating major changes. This process requires analyzing the entire school culture by getting to know the people and finding out as much as possible about them. Administrators should also determine the current level of support. What has the school been through? Did previous leaders promise more than they could deliver? These are important questions to ask before charging in with an agenda that the school community may not be ready to accept. Before making significant changes, leaders new to their positions should know their school, know its history, know its strengths, know the areas of vulnerability, know the hurts, and know the disappointments.

During the early years, leaders should be confident of the constituency's support before engaging in major change. Veteran administrators know that it takes approximately three years to gain the full trust and support of the school community. For example, launching into a major building program within the first year or two on the job is not wise. After three years of proven leadership, administrators are in a good position to advance major projects.

On the other hand, research tells us that new leaders don't have much time to begin establishing themselves and thus need visible smaller-scale improvements immediately. They should begin with needed enhancements or tackle crisis-type problems that call for attention.

John Maxwell, well-known pastor and leadership consultant, uses the analogy of winning the confidence of people we serve as putting change in our pockets. When we implement a small idea or innovation that succeeds, we earn a little respect, so we put a little change in our pockets. With our next success, we earn a little more respect and put a little more change in our pockets. After a number of successes, we may have significant change in our pockets. A time will come when it is necessary to spend the change we have accumulated. We need the change to spend when plans do not go the way we intended.

I think of a well-qualified administrator hired as the superintendent of a well-established school. It seemed to be a good decision on the part of the board, and it was evident that the superintendent was highly accomplished. From all indications it was a good match. Just prior to being hired, however, the superintendent had completed an advanced degree and was eager to try out ideas he had heard about in graduate school. Within the first year, he developed and implemented an elaborate merit pay plan for the faculty. As might be expected with such a volatile issue, the new plan resulted in serious backlash. A veteran administrator might have experienced the same challenge, yet the level of resentment would likely have been substantially less. The new leader simply had not allowed enough time to establish the level of trust needed for such drastic change. Despite a strong effort to amend the situation, the damage was irreparable. The superintendent had launched an operational shift too immense for the amount of change he had in his pocket! School leaders must build respect little by little so that when plans backfire or crises appear on the scene, they can stand confident, knowing that they have the support of their constituents.

The second rule of school leadership is that leaders should facilitate change, not legislate it. Many times administrators arrive on the scene with a brimming agenda but without any plan to involve others in the process. This kind of leadership is doomed for failure. A dean of education at the University of Toronto gives this advice: "Principals would do more lasting good for schools if they concentrated on building collaborative cultures, rather than charging forcefully in with heavy agendas for change" (Fullan, 1992). Research shows that school administrators are critical in making change happen (Lieberman & Miller, 1981). If leaders fail to cast a convincing vision about how things can be better or more effective, positive change will elude them.

On the other hand, administrators who fail to build a network of support throughout a school will leave the school no better than they found it. This network is especially important among the school faculty. Positive change requires the cooperative effort of the entire faculty working under the leadership of a capable administration. The leadership is the linchpin in the change effort, but administrators do not have a monopoly on great ideas. Wise educators regularly discuss the school's mission and values, select and nurture staff who share the school's mission and values, work together to develop a *shared vision*, schedule meaningful planning times, and provide support and encouragement as staff implement new ideas.

Change does not happen without resistance, nor would we want it to. Alfred P. Sloan, former head of General Motors, reportedly said at a meeting of one of his top committees, "Gentleman, I take it that we are all in complete agreement on the decision here. If this is so, then I propose we postpone further discussion of this matter until our next meeting to give ourselves time to develop disagreement and perhaps gain some understanding of what the decision is all about" (Drucker, 1966). When making major changes, effective leaders should not make affirmation the goal. Ignoring the opinions of others in the change process may avoid temporary conflict and resistance, but it will certainly lead to rancor and blundering error. Scripture warns that "plans fail for lack of counsel, but with many advisers they succeed" (Proverbs 15:22). Wise leaders heed this admonition throughout the change process. St. Thomas Aquinas so fittingly said, "We love them both, those whose opinions we share and those whose opinions we reject. For both have labored in the search for truth, and both have helped in the finding of it" (Stoesz & Raber, 1994).

Sometimes, however, resistance signals more than a difference of opinion. People resist change for many reasons. Our first duty is to determine a person's motive for resistance and then to skillfully deal with it when necessary.

Dealing with Resistance

While dissent is necessary and even welcome, at some point a decision has to be made and carried out. The greater the involvement and support of those affected by the change, the more likely it is that the new idea will move forward successfully. It is important for administrators to gather support at the ground floor of innovation, rather than after launching the change. Having cast the vision, good leaders garner as much support as possible. The likelihood of success diminishes with each person who determines to defeat the idea. For this reason, leaders must realize that converting resisters into supporters is critical.

We must learn to understand the resisters and their resistance. First, we should try to determine the reason for the resistance. Some resisters may refuse to go along because they didn't think of the idea; some resist because they do not want to put forth the effort to change; some resist because they fear failure; and a few resist because they gain a feeling of power from thwarting a plan. Effective leaders first determine the motive for resistance and then skillfully lay out a plan for converting the resisters into supporters.

An approach to understanding resisters was identified by two prominent change agents several decades ago (Chin & Benne, 1969). The model defined three categories of responses to a new idea or innovation:

Empirical–Rational

Usually people will be rational and adopt a change if we give them enough information. In education this information includes educational research, statistics, recommendations from respected authorities, and practices that have produced results. We need to educate people about the benefits of any proposed change. Once they have enough information, we can usually move them quickly from resistance to support. These people are the *Sniffs* and *Scurrys* in our schools. When they oppose a new idea, we must first ask ourselves, "Have I provided enough information on the benefits of the change?"

Normative–Reeducative

A number of people do not passively accept change but take action to protect, defend, and advance their own goals. Sometimes they are unable to adapt because they cannot set aside personal agendas for goals that benefit others. Often spiritually immature, such people are guided by social and institutional norms. These are the *Hems* of the school, who fear that change will lead to something worse. They may have blurred vision or lack commitment to the school's mission, philosophy, and goals. Although we sometimes become frustrated with these resisters, we have the opportunity to mentor them spiritually and assist them in changing their values and habits through personal reeducation.

Power Coercive

Some people support change only when they feel coerced by people they view as powerful. In this scenario, however, the support is likely to result only in limited change. Here we find the *Haws* of the school. These people will usually comply when they see that continual resistance will lead to something worse, not better.

The power coercive method is used significantly less often than the previous two. Yet at times, we need to implement tough love in our schools. Several years ago a highly respected Christian school superintendent shared the following story, which I abbreviate here:

She was one of the school's most high-profile resisters! This teacher

> prided herself on *bucking the system and thwarting the superinten-*
> *dent's plans.* One day, having reached his pinnacle of frustration, the
> superintendent called the teacher into his office and reprimanded
> her for her bad spirit and negative attitude. The teacher responded,
> "Okay, then I won't be negative anymore!"
>
> "No," the superintendent remarked, "I need more than a pledge not
> to be too negative. If you are going to be on the team, I need your
> full support."
>
> Hesitating for just a moment, the teacher looked the superintend-
> ent in the eyes and said, "Thank you, I respond well to clear instruc-
> tions. You will have my support."

Nearly ten years later the teacher remains as an effective educator in her same assignment.

We need to deal differently with resisters who lash out with harsh criticism and a defiant attitude than with those in the previous two categories. We cannot allow an employee to impede the progress of the institution. Here our mettle is tested.

We cannot tolerate a consistently incorrigible spirit in our schools. Scripture clearly commands us to submit to those in authority over us (1 Samuel 15:23, Romans 13:2). In addition, the writer of Hebrews instructs us to help those in authority over us to enjoy their work. The passage admonishes Christians to "obey your leaders and submit to their authority. They keep watch over you as men who must give account. Obey them so that their work will be a joy, not a burden, for that would be of no advantage to you" (Hebrews 13:17). If students in our schools are to learn the proper view of authority, the school's administration, faculty, and staff must model it. What a testimony for a Christian school to have employees who enable one another to enjoy their work!

Effective educational leaders learn to cope in a constantly changing world. As we perceive change taking place, we can adapt and find new opportunities, or we can stay stuck in the maze. Schools that adapt also improve. Visionary schools see change and adapt before others do. Collins and Porras, in their profound study of companies that have stood the test of time, distinguished visionary companies as "a very special and elite breed." These companies are not just successful and not just enduring, although these characteristics are important. The visionary companies reported in the *Built to Last* study were found to be the "best of the best in their industries, and have been that way for decades" (Collins & Porras, 1994).

Visionary leaders in Christian schools that will make a difference in times to come realize their first priority is to seek the mind of Christ in all they endeavor to do. We have no interest in building schools that simply last, but schools that *last* and *effectively prepare students* to be the leaders of the next generation.

Because we seek His blessing in our schools, it seems appropriate that this chapter conclude with a daring Old Testament prayer that Dr. Bruce Wilkinson, president of Walk Thru the Bible, has so indelibly established upon the hearts and minds of the millions who have benefited from his popular work entitled *The Prayer of Jabez*: "Oh, that you would bless me and enlarge my territory! Let your hand be with me, and keep me from harm so that I will be free from pain" (1 Chronicles 4:10).

Bibliography

Bush, R. N. (1984). Effective staff development. In *Making our schools more effective: Proceedings of three state conferences.* San Francisco: Far West Laboratory.

Chin, R., & Benne, K. D. (1969). General strategies for effecting changes in human systems. In *The planning of change.* Austin, TX: Holt, Rinehart, & Winston.

Collins, J. C., & Porras, J. R. (1994). *Built to last.* New York: HarperCollins.

Drucker, P. F. (1966). *The effective executive.* New York: HarperBusiness.

Drucker, P. F. (1990). *Managing the non-profit organization.* New York: HarperBusiness.

Drucker, P. F. (1995). *Managing in a time of great change.* New York: Truman Talley Books/Dutton.

Drucker, P. F. (1999). *Management challenges for the 21st century.* New York: HarperBusiness.

Fullan, M. G. (1992, February). Visions that blind. *Educational Leadership.*

Gardner, J. W. (1990). *On leadership.* New York: The Free Press.

Hall, G. E., & Hord, S. M. (1987). *Change in schools: Facilitating the process.* Albany: State University of New York.

Hord, S. M. (1994). Staff development and change process: Cut from the same cloth. *Issues...About change (4)2.* Austin, TX: Southwest Educational Development Laboratory.

James, R. K., Hord, S. M., & Pratt, H. (1988). Managing change in the science program. In L. L. Motz & G. M. Madrazo Jr. (Eds.), *Third sourcebook for science supervisors.* Washington, DC: National Science Supervisors Association and National Science Teachers Association.

Johnson, S. (1998). *Who moved my cheese?* New York: G. P. Putnam's Sons.

Lieberman, A., & Miller, L. (1981, April). Synthesis of research on improving schools. *Educational Leadership.*

Pritchett, P., & Pound, R. (1995). *The stress of organizational change.* Dallas, TX: Pritchett & Associates.

Rodgers, E. (1971). *Diffusion of innovations.* New York: The Free Press.

Stoesz, E., & Raber, C. (1994). *Doing good better!* Intercourse, PA: Good Books.

Wilkinson, B. (2000). *The prayer of Jabez.* Sisters, OR: Multnomah.

The real value of information. (2001, August 6). *Financial Times* [website]. Retrieved August 2001 from <http://www.ftdynamo.com/about.cfm?CFID>

It Can't Happen to Me!
Responding to Crisis

Barbara A. Bode, Ph.D.

Chapter Summary

If there is a constant in Christian school leadership, it is to expect the unexpected. Smooth sailing is rare. So what do you do when you face those complicated issues that threaten to consume the better part of your time for the foreseeable future? As a school administrator, you will have these adventures, but how can you be prepared to direct them to a God-honoring conclusion?

Dr. Bode identifies a number of issues that will sound all too real for many. While she does not offer cookie-cutter answers, she highlights the relevant questions to ask as you develop an action plan to address each situation. She also presents principles that are applicable to many different circumstances, always recognizing that God's wisdom and leading are essential as you face the tough issues that will surely come.

About the author

Barbara A. Bode, Ph.D.
Administrator, Tampa Baptist Academy
Tampa, FL
20 years of educational leadership experience

Chapter 19

It Can't Happen to Me!
Responding to Crisis

Barbara A. Bode, Ph.D.

"It can't happen to me." These are famous last words. Perhaps you have been lulled into the notion that you are immune to those unsettling, serious things that happen to other people. In your Christian working environment, you may be unprepared for that unexpected crisis or issue that catapults you into uncharted territory. Believing yourself insulated, you are surprised by a tough situation that explodes into your life.

I write this chapter within two weeks of the worst terrorist act ever against the United States, when New York City and our capital fell under attack. An atrocity of this magnitude caught our country unprepared. Those who developed the Federal Crisis Management Plan never conceived of this kind of assault. Tough issues and tough decisions mobilized the United States out of its complacency. No longer can we say, "It can't happen to us."

We looked to our president and other leaders as we traveled into uncharted territory, and we witnessed amazing leadership as crisis teams moved into action. Within those first crucial hours, people made critical decisions that set the stage for what would follow. President Bush pulled together his team and other world leaders to develop a plan. They lived out Proverbs 15:22: *Plans fail for lack of counsel, but with many advisers they succeed.* Mr. Bush led our country to its knees to pray about the tremendous issues that faced us. He communicated well to our citizens and to the world our unwavering resolve to defeat terrorism.

We witnessed the honing of the leadership skills of our president. Reflecting on his careful approach to leading our country and the world opened our eyes to leadership principles in action. At this writing, we anticipate that the journey to end terrorism will be long.

Your own leadership role holds unknown challenges as well. This chapter presents case studies of tough issues that can happen anytime, anywhere. Following sound leadership principles helps protect you from the many hidden minefields that can exacerbate a difficult situation. Knee-jerk reactions prove inadequate when you have to make tough decisions. Perhaps this chapter will provide thought-provoking insight into possible situations any school administrator can face without warning and will bring to mind other issues that must be given serious consideration. The chapter will examine tough issues in order to help you as a school administrator succeed and bring honor and glory to God in the face of challenges.

Surprise Evacuation

That infamous day, September 11, 2001, held for us in Florida a special challenge we had never planned on. As we watched the atrocities unfold on television, we became acutely aware of the presence in Florida not only of the president, who was near the US Central Command for the Persian Gulf and Europe, but also of the Special Operations Command, whose responsibilities included antiterrorism worldwide. We knew of the strategic role of the Special Operations Command in Desert Storm. Was it a target? Were we therefore in danger? Uncertainty filled the air. Parents began to pick up their children. Should we call the other parents of our 525 preschool through twelfth-grade students? Similar questions could bombard any administrator under different circumstances such as a fire, tornado, or bomb threat.

We had to consider the level of risk. As the pastor and I pondered this issue, a jetliner crashed into the Pentagon. We decided to evacuate and quickly improvised a plan that included evaluating our communication resources: intercom, cell phones, two-way radios, and telephones. How could we best utilize our staff and students in the calling process? How would we delegate and communicate responsibilities? What was the most expeditious way to connect parents with their children? As people left the school, we realized we needed to pray with our staff, to debrief, and to get their input on the best way to deal with students when school reopened. For liability reasons, you as a school leader must follow policy on picking up children. In addition, keeping a phone log is imperative.

At a time of crisis, you must not micromanage; you must simply release the plan and empower your teams to carry it out. In the process of dealing with a crisis, you need to remember that God is in control and trust Him to lead and guide those who help.

To Expel or Not to Expel

The high school guidance counselor tells you that a senior girl says that she is pregnant and the father of the child is the senior pastor's son. In such a situation, you can expect hidden minefields. If you rush in too fast, you can make the problem worse. So you prioritize your actions and anticipate possible scenarios before you act. What if it is true? What if it is true, but the male student denies it? What if it is a false accusation? What if the girl isn't pregnant or sexually active? What if they are both sexually active but she is not pregnant? Getting to the truth can be a long process.

Once you know the truth, what do you find in your policy manual about this issue? Where do you start? Do you call a lawyer to get guidance? When do you let the board chairman know? When the case comes to resolution, what chain of command should you follow to apprise appropriate people of the situation? How will you minister to everyone involved? Do you have support people or a Christian counseling center for the families? Confidentiality is most important throughout, and taking notes will help you navigate through the information.

Getting to the truth poses the initial challenge. Perhaps you can begin by meeting with the female student and the counselor (a witness). At least one adult must be a woman. Reserving judgment and condemnation can open doors of communication. In talking with the student, you discover what her parents know. You persuade the students to talk with their parents. You call the parents in soon and help them deal with the truth. If the student is eighteen, the situation is more complex, but the process of dealing with it will ultimately be the same.

The information you gather and the reactions of those involved in the situation will determine your next course of action. Once you have met with the girl and her parents, you meet with the young man to get his side of the story. Is he involved, and to what extent? You contact his parents and give them the information you have collected. Their reaction also becomes part of the equation. At this point, if you decide that the incident really happened, you follow written policy. At the same time, you consider how to minister to the families in order to meet their immediate needs. Is there alternative education they can choose such as home schooling? Giving direction to parents for educational needs helps them cope with this life-changing event.

To expel or not to expel depends on the information you uncover and your school's policies. Your handbook should state that because he or she is part of the administrative team, the guidance counselor cannot be held to confidentiality rules. In addition, when students approach a teacher with a concern, the teacher must be sure not to tell them that their conversation will be confidential.

Financial Crisis

You have worked hard all summer getting ready for that first day of school. Your teachers are all hired and under contract. The first day is filled with excitement until you discover that fifty students have not shown up. You discover that the week before school started, families were called to fill slots in newly formed state-sponsored charter and magnet schools. They simply forfeited the registration fee and first month's tuition for a free education. What do you do now?

As soon as possible, you assess the damage to the budget and contact the school board chairman. You notify the school board and any church-related leaders. Trimming the budget with your administrative team is a challenge. Are there positions not under contract? Does your contract contain a clause allowing you to release employees during a financial crisis? Should you talk with your staff and ask everyone to take a cut in pay? Do you ask for volunteers to pray about their stepping down?

How might you make up the shortfall? How many and what kinds of fund-raisers will your families tolerate? Can you contact specific benefactors? Do you have a savings account or endowment? If the school is a ministry of a church, can it provide a loan or line of credit? Should you let the school parents know your need without implying that the school is "going under"? Can your development office take the need to the community? The answer is not a simple one, and it will take the involvement of the stakeholders to help with the resolution.

How do you prepare for the future? Can you set goals and have your school's vision for the future renewed? Conducting a SWOT analysis to identify internal *strengths* and *weaknesses* as well as external *opportunities* and *threats* can help fine-tune your mission and vision statements. What can positive public relations achieve in promoting your school? Will raising the nonrefundable registration fee to the amount of one month's tuition deter people from sitting on the fence? As you pray and seek the Lord's guidance for the shortfall, you trust Him for the wisdom to prevent such a financial situation from impacting your budget.

Do You Remember That?

You receive notice that someone has sued regarding an incident that happened three years ago. The suit alleges that the school was negligent during a middle school boys' basketball game when one of your students supposedly slipped on sand on an outdoor court. As he ran backward, he fell and broke his arm. Supervisors called 911 and his parents. He finished the school year but did not register for the following year.

An insurance investigator makes an appointment to see you. You begin to gather information you anticipate he will need, such as the accident report and the team roster. You alert the coach, who is still on your staff. The investigator meets extensively with the coach and takes pictures of the scene. You supply the insurance representative with as much information as you can about contacting the students and adults who were present that afternoon. But no one can find the game book, and no one remembers the names of the referees. As time passes, you find yourself in legal mediation, trying to reach a settlement.

Whenever possible, you ask the investigator and your lawyer what you should have done at the time of the incident. You learn that you should have (1) called the liability insurance company immediately so they could determine if they should send an investigator; (2) before leaving the scene, collected the names, addresses, and phone numbers of as many witnesses as possible; (3) asked witnesses to write down what they saw; (4) inquired about possible videotapes of the game; and (5) taken pictures and made a video of the scene as soon as possible. In crisis situations, you learn all you can, keep a file, and wait.

Life Is Precious

Two young men come to you after lunch, genuinely concerned about another eighth-grade boy. He indicated at lunch that life isn't worth living; he wants to kill himself, and he gave them details on how he will do it. He told them he has a knife. He recently had an outburst of anger in class. His mother works on staff.

As you assess the situation, you examine the risk to other students—and the risk to him. You call him in and talk with him. He may corroborate the other boys' statements and explain further. He seems very angry. You consider the best course of action. Will his parents follow through with a psychological evaluation if you make that a condition for his returning to school? Will that process take too long? Should you call them in and let them know what he said?

As you think about this crisis, you consider the other students. Will he harm them? Will he harm himself? Should you call in a professional? Too much is at stake. You cannot let him out of your sight because of what he may do. You call the police; they arrive, assess the situation, and decide to "Baker Act" him (have him hospitalized). You then call his parents and let the officer explain what has happened and what you and he chose to do in order to protect their son and others. The school's policy manual must include a weapon policy as well as a search-and-seizure policy.

Split-Second Decision

Before school begins, a thousand people fill your auditorium to attend an orientation night for middle school and high school students and their families. You have already met with the elementary students and their families, who are still on campus visiting classrooms. With the administrators on stage and the teachers seated up front for their introductions, you approach the podium.

A high school student runs down one of the aisles and talks to one of the administrators, who subsequently runs out of the building. You begin to pray silently as you carry on with the program. A few minutes later, the administrator runs up to the stage and tells you someone has been stabbed outside the foyer. You decide to announce that someone has been hurt outside and to ask if there is a doctor present. A doctor and a nurse leave the auditorium. At that point, you ask the audience to pray, and you lead them in prayer.

A few minutes later, the administrator runs to the front again and tells you that the ambulance and police have arrived. The father of a student is the victim. The police say you should announce to the audience that they should be careful when they leave the school. The program stops, and all eyes are on the two of you. You realize that you have to follow through with the policeman's admonition.

So many questions race through your mind. Is the school liable if someone else gets hurt? Will you lose students because of this announcement? You conclude that the safety of the families takes priority, and you decide to make the announcement. How will you phrase it? You know that you must keep calm; you dare not cause families to panic. You decide to give as little information as possible but caution the parents to be careful as they leave. You pray all the while for the Lord to give you the appropriate words. The program continues.

As you dismiss the teachers to their classrooms to meet with the parents and students, you head back to the foyer. The man has been taken to the hospital, but the parent who handled the scene informs you that he kept the man from coming into the auditorium and called the ambulance. You walk down the street where the incident allegedly occurred and see no evidence of a struggle. Questions come to mind. You call the police officer with that information and some background data on the man identified by one of your staff members. You note that for liability reasons, you absolutely must follow the directives of police officers. What next?

The next morning you discover that the parent's wound was self-inflicted. You decide you need legal assistance because of the nature of the incident and the student's privacy. (Your attorney will tell you not to give out any specific information about the incident because of the privacy act.)

How do you prevent the father from coming on campus repeatedly to share his version of the incident? Can you get cooperation from his family? Should you call the police to tell them the wound was self-inflicted?

When will you communicate with the staff, and how many details will you share? You identify yourself as the only spokesman for the school and prepare for the media and parents. When a few phone calls come in from parents, you explain the privacy act issue and emphasize that this isolated incident does not endanger the safety of their children and your staff.

In evaluating the situation, you decide to have a staff member with a cell phone at each entrance during all public events. Others are delegated to patrol the parking lots. This proactive approach provides an action plan for each person to follow.

You work with the family of the student and ask that they notify you if the father plans to go to any school events. During those he attends, you have someone carry a cell phone, monitor his behavior, and follow the action plan.

An Unbelievable Accusation

The high school math teacher has been on staff for two years. His charismatic presence is magnetic, and students seek him out at lunch and after school. One day, another teacher comes to you with eyewitness information that the math teacher and one of the students in the high school have been intimate. The math teacher has a wife and child.

Has a crime been committed? How can you find out? Should you contact the police sex crimes detective division for their assistance? You do not know where this journey will lead. The investigators arrive and spend many hours interviewing you and some high school students. You realize that your role is to facilitate their investigation. When you find some students who are willing to share what they know, you invite their parents to be present. The investigation continues and confirms your worst fears. The teacher faces arrest.

You know that the media will contact you for comment, so you call the school's lawyer for direction. He suggests that you grant the interviews and appoint one spokesperson. Then he gives coaching tips about what to say. The lawyer also suggests that you tape any news coverage.

That night the teacher's picture appears all over the news since he has been taken into custody. The chief administrator takes the responsibility for media interviews. The next morning you meet with the staff to give them the basic facts. You pledge them to silence because nothing is final yet. You don't forget that the teacher's wife and daughter need support during this time.

Next, you contact your liability insurance company so it is aware of the situation and can thus follow its protocol. Do you face a potential lawsuit? Possibly, but the insurance company needs to know up front so it can move forward with an investigation. You assume this crisis will require all your time for the next two weeks.

Many Questions, No Answers

You walk in the door for the first day of school. It has been a tough summer consisting of ten-hour days when you had to get faculty lined up, curriculum ready, and facilities reorganized for eighty more students than were enrolled last year. Your adrenaline flows with excitement—until the board chairman walks in and tells you that you are fired; you are to clear out your desk today and not come back. No warning—no contract (you trusted the board)—no severance pay. Within hours, the school has the locks changed, and you are history. By the way, your wife is a prekindergarten teacher, and you have two children enrolled in the school. What now?

Wow, talk about being caught off guard! The main question you want answered is, Why? Will they give you an answer? Probably not. Where do you go from here? Call your pastor? Call a trusted friend? Call a lawyer? Call the regional director? Sorting out options and getting in touch with networks of godly people are your starting points.

On the other hand, should you lash out and call parents to mobilize against the school board's decision? What will that gain for you and the ministry? Honoring Christ and not giving in to feelings of vengeance or bitterness will result in godly direction.

Focusing on the Lord and His Word can provide the beginning point for obtaining His answers. Maybe you will never understand the reason the board fired you. Trusting God to be God should be the focus. God is bigger than any ministry. You rely on Scriptures such as Jeremiah 29:11–13: " 'For I know the plans I have for you,' declares the Lord, 'plans to prosper you and not to harm you, plans to give you hope and a future. Then you will call upon me and come and pray to me, and I will listen to you. You will seek me and find me when you seek me with all your heart.'" Romans 8:28 offers you encouragement as well: "And we know that in all things God works for the good of those who love him, who have been called according to his purpose." Your personal relationship with Jesus Christ will sustain you, and He will show you the way.

On a practical note, it is wise to follow financial planners' advice to hold three to six months' worth of emergency funds in savings. The fact that you work for a Christian ministry does not mean you can be complacent. Being as proactive as possible rather than being reactive will prepare you for the future. Also, make sure your contract addresses unexpected, undeserved termination.

Conclusion

The famous last words "It can't happen to me" apply to you as a leader. You must be spiritually prepared for the unexpected. This chapter touches upon a few crises. It would be prudent to evaluate other possible scenarios such as a student entering the building with a gun, a parent with no parental rights trying to take his child from school, a parent attacking a student, a bus turning over with a school sports team on board, two students being killed in an automobile accident, a student being left behind at a field trip fifty miles away, a teacher dating a student, and a parent assaulting a teacher.

Each crisis holds its own unique challenges, but all crises provide opportunities to depend on God for His wisdom and direction. Strong leadership is crucial in each situation—with God as the primary leader. A team that works together on a daily basis can also work together in a crisis to assess damage and respond appropriately. In spite of your best efforts, there may be times when you make mistakes. *The Leadership Bible* offers these words of wisdom: "Most leaders have learned that there are three ways to deal with mistakes. First, there's the easiest way: learning from others' mistakes; then there's the harder way: learning from our own mistakes; and then there is the tragic way: not learning from either" (Buzzell, 1998).

Good decision making depends on learning from the mistakes of others and your own (see chapter 6). These case studies present challenging situations that require rapid and mature decision making. *The Leadership Bible* offers more direction on decision making:

> Decision making is one of leadership's core competencies. In fact, decision-making ability differentiates between poor and good, and between good and great leaders. Decisions reveal values and intelligence. They require obedience to and dependence upon God. They demand wisdom.... All wisdom comes from God, and using his wisdom to make good decisions is something God wants to help us learn to do. (Buzzell, 1998)

"Commit to the Lord whatever you do, and your plans will succeed" (Proverbs 16:3).

Scripture gives additional insight on good decision making. First Chronicles 12 describes warriors who joined David at Hebron and came armed for battle in order to turn Saul's kingdom over to David: "men of Issachar, who understood the times and knew what Israel should do—200 chiefs, with all their relatives under their command (1 Chronicles 12:32). *The Leadership Bible* refers to this Scripture also:

> This statement underscores two essential components of effective decision making: awareness and decisiveness. Good decisions require adequate information and careful analysis of all of the pertinent facts. Although there is a place for spontaneity, important decisions generally should not be rushed, since they require adequate time for gestation. But once made, such decisions should be decisively communicated and implemented. Like the men of

Issachar, leaders need to understand the times and be well aware of the cultural climate in which they live and work, so they may become transformers rather than conformers. (Buzzell, 1998)

As you reflect on this chapter, you can consider the pitfalls that may lie ahead in your own ministry. Then you can prepare to make good crisis decisions on the basis of God's wisdom—to bring honor and glory to His name.

Bibliography

Arp Independent School District Crisis Management Plan (1999). Retrieved October 8, 2001, from <www.arp.sprnet.org/admin/CRISIS/Default.htm>.

Buzzell, S. (Ed.). (1998). *The leadership Bible: Leadership principles from God's Word.* Grand Rapids, MI: Zondervan Publishing House.

Guetzloe, E. (1997). *Developing a plan for crisis management.* Retrieved October 9, 2001, from <www.wm.edu/TTAC/articles/ articlesChallenging/.htm>.

Model school crisis management plan (1999). Retrieved October 9, 2001, from <www.pen.k12.va.us/VDOE/Instruction/model. pdf>.

It's Your Call

Considering Ministry Beyond

David K. Wilcox, Ph.D.

Chapter Summary

Have you considered ministry beyond—beyond where you are today—in new areas of ministry in your community, region, state, or the world? Does the fact that the call of God is irrevocable (Romans 11:29) mean that your present circumstance is the extent of that call? Might the Lord be prompting you beyond the "comfort zone" of where you are or what you're doing now?

The opening chapter of this book defines the high calling of Christian school education—to fight the culture's intellectual and spiritual battles for young minds and hearts. In this concluding chapter, Dr. Wilcox challenges you to explore the depths of God's mysterious call to new possibilities of ministry and service.

About the author

David K. Wilcox, Ph.D.
Assistant to the Vice President of International Ministries, ACSI
Colorado Springs, CO
17 years of educational leadership experience

Chapter 20

It's Your Call
Considering Ministry Beyond

David K. Wilcox, Ph.D.

In 1997 Ken called ACSI. It was a fateful call. "Can you tell me if ACSI has a member school in Ireland? I have been asking myself why I should do what others can and will do ... when there is so much out there that others cannot or will not do. I sense the Lord leading me to serve Him in support of the church in Europe, perhaps Ireland."

"Ireland? You want to serve as an administrator in a Protestant school in Ireland?" Dr. Philip Renicks responded. "Frankly, I'm not sure whether Protestant, evangelical schools exist in the Republic of Ireland. I know we don't have a member school there. But we have schools in over 100 other countries. How about Hungary? We are trying to help several mission agencies find an administrator to lead a new school for missionaries' children—taking them through the process of accreditation. Didn't you just lead your school through the accreditation process?"

"Don't remind me," Ken replied.

A year later, Ken and his family began serving in Budapest, Hungary.

What do we mean when we say someone has been called to lead, or called to serve as an administrator? The very title of this book demonstrates the complexity of the term "called." Surely it means more than the call of God extended to all mankind and personally voiced by Jesus in John 3:16: "that whoever believes in him shall not perish but have eternal life."

In the postconversion sense, the word "calling" refers to a life direction, a personal mission, perhaps a vocation, or a specific assignment in a definite location. But how specific is it? How permanent? Does it include a clearly delimiting aspect? How about a call to be the assistant principal of your town's Christian elementary school? Once you know the general nature of your call, what should you continue to ask of God's Spirit?

This chapter explores whether some have inappropriately placed a limit on God's call for their lives, a limit He never intended. Do you believe God has restricted your call to lead? This chapter challenges you to:

1. Reflect on the nature of your call to lead
2. Consider the reasons for an expanded vision for ministry
3. Be open to God's promptings and respond to needs that match your skills
4. Know some of the possibilities for expanded ministry and specific next steps

Understanding God's Call

The Spirit of the living God lives in every believer; this we know. We are less sure about how the Spirit works in our lives, what constitutes His leading, and why He seems to point people in such different directions. As a reader of this book, you experienced some motive that has carried you this far in your reading. Was some of that prompting from the Spirit? Why doesn't everyone read a book on Christian school administration?

The Question of Specificity

Clearly, some aspects of the Spirit-initiated call are the same for all of us who follow the living God as revealed in Jesus. Do all believers have a "call"? Yes. We have been called by Him to be His, and He has given all of us a vision of what He considers important. The Lord calls us all to pick up our cross daily, to believe the teachings of the Word of God, and to obey the commission to become disciple makers. We find immeasurable joy in knowing God and deepening our relationship with Him by joining in the sufferings of Jesus and experiencing the power of His resurrection. But are we called into the same specific ministry role as all other believers? Obviously we are not.

We can see in the Scriptures that God's call is person-specific in some respects. First Corinthians 12 clearly teaches that we have different roles in the Body of Christ because of differences in giftedness. James tells us that not many of us should presume to be teachers, and we believe that the Church acted within the will of God when it selected Matthias instead of Barsabbas, even though both were qualified to replace Judas Iscariot.

Examples abound of God's clear call to specific people to accomplish a specific task or serve in a specific role: Abraham, Moses, David, Jeremiah,

Esther, Mary, Jesus, Paul, and the list goes on. Other than Jesus, these were all imperfect people who chose to respond in obedience to divine direction, either auditory or nonauditory. Differences in giftedness and specific revelation from God partially explain why we have different callings.

A Personal Testimony

The last week of 1976 was a turning point in my life, a time of surrender. That night, listening to Billy Graham at Urbana '76, I gave up my own ambitions. I had finished my college education in June 1976, having already seen the Lord redirect my interests from banking to teaching. I had thrived in a ten-week missions experience on an Indian reserve in British Columbia and discovered the joy of cross-cultural ministry. But I held on to my plans of pursuing a lucrative career after devoting one or two years to missions. That night I asked the Lord to use me wherever, however, and for as long as He wanted to. If that meant thirty years in the backwoods of the far side of the earth, so be it.

In retrospect I see the importance of the "blank check" nature of my sense of call. God knows my strengths and weaknesses, He knows the desires of my heart (travel, mountain climbing, teaching), and I gave them to Him to use as He saw fit.

After I served at the Alliance Academy in Quito, Ecuador, for seven years with my wife and children, my mission agency asked if I would be willing to leave what had become a comfortable place of ministry and serve as the headmaster of a school for missionaries' children in the tropics of Malaysia. This decision whether to transfer between mission fields was the hardest one of my life, more difficult than the initial one of going into missions. Uprooting my family and myself, giving up a fruitful ministry, and accepting what would surely result in great financial cost all seemed to weigh against this change.

Only reflection on the nature of my calling from God made the difference and led me to accept the new assignment. Had I been called to a specific set of kids, a specific job, a specific country? In my case, the answer was *no*. My wife and I were called to educate missionaries' children and the children of other expatriate families. The core issue wasn't the place, a specific position, or service to certain people. Rather, it centered in a call to utilize our skills to the glory of God wherever He led. God used those in authority over me to offer new opportunity for ministry beyond. God greatly blessed our obedient response, both our family and, I believe, the schools involved.

Unprecedented Opportunity

Reflect on your understanding of God's call on your life. Have you laid before the King your skills, your situation in life, and the desires of your heart? If you do, He will show you great and mighty things you cannot imagine. If your heart desires to know Him and to be a part of His work in this world, the sky is the limit for ministry beyond.

As a Christian school administrator, you must lead by demonstrating a commitment to the equipping of the saints—and that may well mean more than just the saints in your immediate surroundings. As you develop skill in your current position, realize that God may be preparing you for other avenues of ministry beyond what you see now. The opportunities may include serving, supporting, training, and offering consultation to other schools and administrators, including those in urban or impoverished settings, or indeed, in international settings.

Considering Ministry Beyond

Obeying God

In the fall of 1986, I had the privilege of visiting the home villages of the Warani (Auca) Indians in the jungles of eastern Ecuador. During that visit and then again in January 1987, I talked with Rachel Saint, missionary to the Warani for many years following the martyrdom of her brother Nate and his four missionary colleagues. Her living conditions in the jungle, still primitive and rustic after thirty years, left her isolated from civilization and drenched in tropical heat. At one point I asked what I considered a simple question: "Have you found fulfillment in your ministry with the Warani?"

Though then in her late seventies or early eighties, Ms. Saint didn't let that question slip by with a simple, "Of course, sonny." Instead, she turned her eyes toward me with intensity and with a look that said, "I hope you hear me well, young boy." She responded, "I didn't come here looking for fulfillment. I came out of obedience."

Ouch! Here I was, a veteran of five years on the mission field, a leader of one of the largest international Christian schools in the world. Yet I had just been taken to the proverbial woodshed in a loving way by a missionary who responded to the call of God in a way that most of us would consider sacrificial beyond belief. She wanted me to clearly understand that she had answered God's call neither to find happiness nor to feel fulfilled, but to obey the command of her Lord and Savior to spread the good news of Jesus Christ.

Placing God's priorities before our own will make us willing to accept any path He presents. Placing our personal goals, desires, and values above our Lord's is sin. God's call requires obedience, wherever that may lead.

Modeling Responsiveness

Another reason we should consider opportunities to apply our administrative skills in settings beyond is that leaders need to model responsiveness. School administrators fit nicely into that group of church leaders that

Peter addresses in the final chapter of his first epistle. Here Peter calls upon church leaders to shepherd the flock of God, admonishing them in the same way Jesus admonished him in John 21. Peter challenges each of us who are called of God to influence and care for students, thereby serving as shepherds of the flock.

> To the elders among you, I appeal as a fellow elder, a witness of Christ's sufferings and one who also will share in the glory to be revealed: Be shepherds of God's flock that is under your care, serving as overseers—not because you must, but because you are willing, as God wants you to be; not greedy for money, but eager to serve; not lording it over those entrusted to you, but being examples to the flock. (1 Peter 5:1–4)

What is a shepherd's job? Shepherds tend their sheep. By spiritual analogy, this shepherding applies to a defending and discipling process. Shepherds don't just leave their sheep alone; they protect, guide, offer care, and discern need. They are disciplers.

Shepherds can be noticed because, if you look out at a flock of sheep, the shepherd is the one on two feet. That position allows him to see farther than the four-footed beasts. He can see beyond. Do you see beyond? Do you dream of what God may want for your flock (verse 2)?

Besides defending, discipling, and dreaming of what may be ahead for the flock, the shepherd is an example, a demonstrator of what path to follow and how to live (verse 3). While not the core reason to seek expanded ministry, this modeling provides an appropriate motive nonetheless. As leaders and caregivers of the next generation of the church, we are called by God to live lives that demonstrate that we really live according to what we claim holds eternal value (Pollock, 2001).

Our students see our work at school as a job. We may call it ministry, and argue that we could secure much greater pay in another profession, but their perception remains unchanged. But when they see us extend our efforts to reach beyond in ministry, they know we are authentic Christians, people who see the larger kingdom of God.

Meeting Needs

Administrators should consider looking beyond their current ministry because of the pressing need to share expertise within the broader Christian school movement. In Christian schools today, expertise comes from experience in the trenches. Those who have struggled with having too few teachers, balancing budgets with very limited funds, guiding teachers through curriculum development, or developing spiritual formation programs are the very people to help others who have less experience. Teachers in rural settings with multigrade classrooms are much-sought-after consultants in some MK (missionary kid) school settings where, for example, four families have ten children who are in grades ranging from one through six. If God has blessed your current ministry, you can become a resource for others.

You have probably discovered that if you prepare for a presentation, you often learn more than your audience. The same is true when you prepare a workshop at an administrators' conference, serve on an accreditation team, or offer in-service training to other schools. As we prepare for service, we grow professionally, improving the effectiveness of our current ministry.

A biology teacher at one of the schools I served told me, "You're either growing or you're dying." Professionally, that makes sense. Coasting only works in biking. Of course we should concentrate on serving to the best of our abilities in the place we find ourselves now. Like Paul, we need to learn contentment with the position and ministry the Lord has given us. But as we use our skills in our current positions, we should look for ways to grow, to improve, and to become more effective for the glory of God. The goal should never be one of self-promotion or the pursuit of power or self-glory. Rather, as Bruce Wilkinson reminds us in *The Prayer of Jabez*, our goal should be the pursuit of God's glory as we ask Him to put us to His best as we follow His agenda.

Knowing the Options

"And Lord, bless the missionaries all over the world." I can imagine a divine wince when a prayer like that comes from someone's lips. The unspoken reality suggests that the depth of our concern is influenced by how much we know. When we know the issues faced by our brothers and sisters serving in other places, our concerns grow, our prayers deepen, and our hearts are moved. We even reflect on how we may be part of the answer.

We know God leads people in many ways. He has directly revealed to some His will. He has provided to all His Word, through which the Holy Spirit gives us direction and guidance. He has provided us with godly elders and co-laborers in the faith who offer counsel and support. As we maintain a close and constant relationship with our Lord Jesus and these other sources of godly wisdom, we can look for signs that may guide us to expanded ministry. I hope you will pray even now that the Lord will use this chapter to prompt a desire in you to take the next step in expanding your ministry to the glory of God.

Let's consider some of the sources of information and opportunities that can help you expand your ministry:

- Bring the world to your school by completing an I-17 application with the US Immigration and Naturalization Service (INS) so that your school can admit foreign students. The same type of process is available for schools in other countries.
- Lead an administrators' workshop at an ACSI conference.

- Volunteer to serve on an accreditation visiting committee, even one in another country.
- Explore the possibility of a school-to-school partnership with a school in another land. These need to be two- or three-year commitments to be effective.
- Contact the ACSI Office of Urban School Services to find out how your school can partner with an urban school or a school serving disadvantaged students.
- Contact the ACSI Office of Student Ministries to find out how you can take some of your students on a foreign mission trip.
- Budget for your school to provide one-third of a salary each year for any teacher willing to serve overseas for one or two years (sabbatical system).
- Check out <www.finishers.org>, the website of an organization that helps those over forty begin second careers in missions.
- Contact one of the ACSI international regional directors and offer to lead seminars at conferences overseas.
- Come to an ACSI International Christian Educators Recruiting Fair to learn about the hundreds of opportunities to serve in schools for missionaries' children and in other international Christian schools. Some are paid positions, while others require raising financial support through a mission agency.
- Check out <www.acsi.org/intmin> and click on *overseas teaching opportunities* to search a current database by position or country. ACSI's overseas member schools keep this list current.
- Check out these websites to learn even more about missions and short-term or career service:
  - www.wheaton.edu//Moreau/
  - www.mislinks.org/
  - www.strategicnetwork.org/
  - www.globalmission.org/fingertip.htm
  - www.greatcomm.org/
  - www.ccci.org/comission2/challenge.html

Some begin by exploring the outreach activities of their own church missions committee or denominational office. Being part of what your church does in broader ministry is a wonderful way to build on the vision of your household of faith. Many evangelical mission agencies send educators and administrators overseas. Why not ask them where you may be used most effectively?

The Mystery of the Call

What issues should you consider if you sense that the Lord is prompting you to expand your ministry? Isn't awareness that the Lord wants you to undertake some new or expanded ministry sufficient cause to carry you forward, no matter what? Let's not be too quick to attribute to God what may be coming from another source.

Confirming Your Call

Guidance from God will be confirmed in some way: by your spouse, your church, your pastor, or others who know you well. Confirmation, or the lack thereof, may also come from your children. The older your children, the greater the need is to determine whether your transition is appropriate for the entire family.

When IBM transfers a family, a child can blame the company. When God is offered as the reason for the move (which an older child may see as stripping away friends and home and rootedness), God can become the enemy in the child's mind. Because of damage to a sufficient number of families, some mission agencies will no longer give a family with teenagers an overseas assignment. The family should never be seen as being baggage, or as having no voice. If you have a family, you must make sure they have also been called to ministry beyond.

God still calls His people. If you hear Him, listen! Dwight Carlblom tells his story like this: "I experienced a definite call from God. I believed I was called by God to stay on my dad's farm and take it over from him. But in ninth grade God called me into missions with what, to me, was an audible voice—but no one around me heard it. At least no one else jumped as I did when I heard it! He did the same thing when I was a freshman in college, directing me into MK education—again, with an audible voice that no one else heard." Dwight and Lori Carlblom have served with the Christian & Missionary Alliance denomination in MK education at Dalat School in Malaysia since 1981.

Carlblom's time in college prepared him to serve beyond, in support of the Great Commission. Going overseas demonstrated obedience. Even before their marriage, he and Lori made the decision that they would not become rooted in a comfortable North American lifestyle, lest it would make leaving for international service too difficult.

Trusting God for Your Needs

Not all "calls" are as clear as Dwight Carlblom's. Sometimes God calls us through others who challenge us to consider a new path of ministry. Dr. David Brooks, a successful public school administrator in suburban Detroit, attended a church banquet prior to the beginning of a missions conference. "One of the mission leaders asked me what it would take for me to do what I was currently doing overseas for the Lord. After a short pause I answered, 'I guess He would have to make it very clear to me that was what He wanted me to do, and if He did make it clear, that is all it would take for us to serve overseas,'" Brooks reminisced.

That was February of 1982. By August of that year, the Lord had not only made His will very clear, He had shown His provision spiritually, materially, and personally to allow the Brooks family, with their sixteen- and thirteen-year-old sons, to relocate to Taiwan. On August 11 Dr. Brooks got off the plane as high school principal of Morrison Academy and prepared for his first faculty meeting, scheduled for the next day.

Serving since 1994 in Budapest, Hungary, as president of SHARE Educational Services, Brooks marvels at how the Lord provided for his family's needs. "Part of what God gave us when we accepted what He made clear to us was His promise to provide for our needs," he explains. "In that regard, financially and in other ways, He has never failed. He must have really wanted us to go; we had the support we needed in just a little over three months of fund-raising. In nineteen years overseas, our financial needs have always been met."

Some may say that the decision to explore a new ministry was not a major event in their lives but simply a decision to seek new ways of developing the talents God gave them. They view looking beyond as a logical step in their stewardship of the talents they received from God. Most, however, see the loss of economic security as a major hurdle. They must address this loss and other problems as they consider ministry beyond. These challenges often include fears about loss of friends, professional opportunities, and even personal safety.

Coping with Insecurity

Ann Christian was an English lady serving as the head administrator and science teacher of the 230-student Carachipampa Christian School in Cochabamba, Bolivia, with SIM International. She looked at those fears, counted the cost, and stepped out in faith. According to Ms. Christian, "It takes a large step of faith for teachers and school administrators securely employed in their homeland to hand in their resignations and head for an unknown school in some distant land. The questions are many. What about my pension? Is this professional suicide? How will I ever get back into teaching here? Where will the money come from? I recognize these as the very questions I asked when I knew the Lord wanted me to teach overseas and not in the safety of a large state comprehensive school in England."

She continued, "The Lord is *more* than able to provide the support required by missionary teachers, and it is thrilling to see Him at work—often in the least expected way. All I can say is that after almost ten years in Bolivia, I have found God faithful; He has provided, and He has done *exceedingly more than I could ask or even imagine*! God is not looking for perfect Christians, model teachers, or supersaints. All He requires is a willing heart that says, *I don't understand it all, Lord. I feel very scared about leaving my job and my country, but I will trust you—whatever you bring into my life!*"

Called to Lead

I trust that you have received affirmation from colleagues in Christian schools that you have been called to lead, and I hope that this book and other resources serve you well in your ministry, right where you are. Your school needs you to be credible, competent, and consistent. It needs you to bloom right where God has planted you. At the same time, I want you to see that the Lord may use your present situation to prepare you for ministry beyond. That ministry may not be international service, but it may be. It may be in your extended community, in an urban center, or in new kinds of ministries not even envisioned here.

Reflecting on the nature of your calling is a healthy endeavor. God calls us all to faithfulness, to stewardship of all we have and all we are. He calls us to endure the cost of followership, reminding us that the suffering and trials we experience are temporary compared with the everlasting blessings we have in Christ Jesus. A sense of call helps us through the hard times, such as the times when foreign government officials nearly spat at me for being a missionary, when rebellious students spray painted my name with vulgarities on city walls, and when parents questioned my faith as I supported a teacher's choice of a secular textbook.

Both my sense that I was called and my confidence that God was helping me to achieve His purposes provided sources of great strength. The Lord also surrounded me with godly people, including my wife, to support me. God's calling can get us to ministry beyond, and it can help us persevere once we are there.

Do you remember the goals of this chapter? They are meant to challenge you to:

- Reflect on the nature of your call to lead and serve
- Consider the reasons for an expanded vision for ministry
- Be open to God's promptings and respond to needs that match your skills
- Know some of the possibilities for expanded ministry and specific next steps

Of what does your call consist? Write it out as a personal mission statement, making sure you have not limited it more than you should or made it more specific than you should. I pray that you will experience your call as a yearning and see it as an obligation to serve wherever God's Spirit leads. And may that realization prompt you to pursue actively and prayerfully the possibilities of expanded service or, as we have called it here, ministry beyond. It's your call.

Bibliography

Pollock, D. (2001, July). *Teachers and caregivers as shepherds.* Speech presented at the Third Culture Kid Pre-field Orientation, Houghton, NY.

Wilkinson, B. H. (2000). *The prayer of Jabez.* Sisters, OR: Multnomah.

Selected Reading List

Blue, R. (1997). *Master your money*. Nashville: Thomas Nelson.

Brinckerhoff, P. (1997). *Mission based marketing*. New York: John Wiley & Sons.

Carver, J. (1997). *Boards that make a difference: A new design for leadership in nonprofit and public organizations*. San Francisco: Jossey-Bass.

Collins, J. C., & Porras, J. I. (1997). *Built to last*. New York: HarperBusiness.

Decrane, A. C. Jr. (1996). *A constitutional model of leadership*. In F. Hesselbein, M. Goldsmith, & R. Beckhard (Eds.), *The leader of the future*. San Francisco: Jossey-Bass.

Drucker, P. F. (1995). *Managing in a time of great change*. New York: Truman Talley Books/Dutton.

Engstrom, T. W., & Dayton, E. R. (1976). *The art of management for Christian leaders*. Waco, TX: Word Publishing.

Gaebelein, F. E. (1995). *Christian education in a democracy*. Colorado Springs: Association of Christian Schools International.

Gaebelein, F. E. (1996). *The pattern of God's truth: Problems of integration in Christian education*. Colorado Springs: Association of Christian Schools International.

Gangel, K. O. (1997). *Team leadership in Christian ministry*. Chicago: Moody Press.

Gangel, K. O. (2000). *Coaching ministry teams*. Nashville: Word.

Groothuis, D. (2000). *Truth decay*. Downers Grove, IL: InterVarsity Press.

Hendrix, O. (2000). *Three dimensions of leadership*. St. Charles, IL: ChurchSmart Resources.

Hunter, J. D. (2000). *The death of character in an age without good or evil*. New York: Basic Books.

Keenan, D. J. (2001). *Curriculum development for Christian schools*. (Rev. ed.). Colorado Springs: Association of Christian Schools International.

Kienel, P. A. (1998). *A history of Christian school education (Vol. 1)* . Colorado Springs: Association of Christian Schools International.

Lockerbie, D. B. (1994). *A passion for learning: The history of Christian thought on education*. Chicago: Moody Press.

Maxwell, J. C. (2001). *The 17 indisputable laws of teamwork*. Nashville: Thomas Nelson.

Moreland, J. P. (1997). *Love your God with all your mind*. Colorado Springs: NavPress.

Piper, J. (2000). *The pleasures of God*. Sisters, OR: Multnomah Publishers.

Pritchett, P., & Pound, R. (1995). *The stress of organizational change*. Dallas: Pritchett & Associates.

Schultz, G. (1998). *Kingdom education: God's plan for educating future generations*. Nashville: LifeWay Press.

Stott, J. R. W. (1992). *The contemporary Christian*. Downers Grove, IL: InterVarsity Press.

Vincent, M. (1997). *Teaching a Christian view of money: Celebrating God's generosity*. Scottdale, PA: Herald Press.

Willard, D. (1998). *The divine conspiracy*. San Francisco: Harper & Row.